LABOR IN ISRAEL

LABOR IN ISRAEL

Beyond Nationalism and Neoliberalism

Jonathan Preminger

ILR PRESS

AN IMPRINT OF CORNELL UNIVERSITY PRESS   ITHACA AND LONDON

Cornell University Press gratefully acknowledges grants from Ben-Gurion University
and Cardiff Business School, which aided in the publication of this book.

First published 2018 by Cornell University Press

Printed in the United States of America

Library of Congress Cataloging-in-Publication Data

Names: Preminger, Jonathan, 1975– author.
Title: Labor in Israel : beyond nationalism and neoliberalism /
    Jonathan Preminger.
Description: Ithaca : ILR Press, an imprint of Cornell University Press, 2018. |
    Includes bibliographical references and index.
Identifiers: LCCN 2017039998 (print) | LCCN 2017043972 (ebook) |
    ISBN 9781501717130 (pdf) | ISBN 9781501717147 (epub/mobi) |
    ISBN 9781501717123 (cloth : alk. paper)
Subjects: LCSH: Labor movement—Israel. | Labor policy—Israel. |
    Labor unions—Israel. | Labor market—Israel.
Classification: LCC HD8660 (ebook) | LCC HD8660. P74 2018 (print) |
    DDC 331.88095694—dc23
LC record available at https://lccn.loc.gov/2017039998

To Ophir, who will inherit the world we're shaping today

Contents

Preface

In 2008, when I first began thinking about undertaking a broad study of unions in Israel, I had been active with a small general union, the Workers Advice Center (WAC), for some seven years. I had witnessed various workers' struggles from close up and seen how difficult it was to unionize in the current social and political circumstances. My first thought was to investigate alternatives to classic union organizing on the possibly mistaken assumption that unions—though still hanging on—were a thing of the past. The wave of organizing activity that began around that time was therefore very exciting for me, and the focus of my research changed.

Like many industrial relations scholars who are "rather friendly towards labor" (Baccaro 2010, 341), I viewed organized labor as more than merely a sociological concept or structure. Unions, I thought, could be a force for positive change, a framework for participation in shaping society, and a counterweight to powerful entities whose main objectives did not prioritize the welfare of the person in the street. This normative vision shaped the way I approached the wave of organizing and influenced the choice of issues that were to be the focus of my research. This same vision drove me to take a wide view of organized labor: I wanted to understand whether it had anything to offer the citizens of Israel, whether it was an appealing framework for those seeking to have their voices heard and their opinions taken into account. Thus I wanted to go beyond the analysis of individual struggles to look at the wider role and status of organized labor in Israel today, particularly in light of its important historical role in this country.

Of course, this is an almost infinitely broad concern, and in the natural course of writing this book I have had to delimit the field and sharpen my focus. Nonetheless, I trust that what results not only meets the standards of rigorous academic research and contributes to scholarly debate on labor representation but also offers insights to those involved in their own struggles, whether in the workplace or in the street.

Over the years I have become convinced that the cooperative nature of academic work is insufficiently acknowledged. Whether by a casual observation during a chance conversation in the street or through heated debate in more formal academic frameworks, numerous people have contributed to my work, nudged my musings in new directions, provided crucial information, and—no less significant—pointed out errors and discrepancies in my logic and my writing.

Most prominent among them all is Uri Ram, who supervised the entire research process that led to this book. His laconic observations and uncompromising approach kept me on the right path, while his breadth of knowledge and depth of comprehension were a constant inspiration and a reminder of committed academic work at its best. I also thank Guy Mundlak for valuable insights, and Harry Katz and Michael Shalev for excellent comments on a previous draft. In addition, Michael's subsequent generous guidance and support greatly assisted me in shaping the manuscript into a more readable and logical form.

I owe an enormous debt of gratitude to the many people who spoke to me, whether informally or within the formal structure of an interview. I was repeatedly amazed by their willingness to give of their time and knowledge, and many made considerable effort to assist in additional ways, introducing me to other people or obtaining documents they thought would help my understanding. Of these, I would like to mention my friends at WAC, particularly Roni Ben Efrat, Orit Soudry, and Steve Langfur, who also provided inspiration of a different kind. I would also like to mention Yeela Lahav-Raz and Yael Ben David, who assisted on occasions too numerous to list, and Benedikte Zitouni, who has long been my spiritual guide to intellectual, academic, and literary life.

Thanks are due to all at Ben-Gurion University's Department of Sociology and Anthropology and Kreitman School of Advanced Graduate Studies, without whom this book would not have been possible. The department provided an inspiring environment for research, and I was lucky to receive the support and encouragement of faculty members and staff. Similarly, staff members at Ben-Gurion University's Aranne Library and Tel Aviv University's law and social science libraries were invaluable during my search for material and for a peaceful corner to gather my thoughts; I am very grateful for their assistance and kindness.

In the final months of writing, Fran Benson and Meagan Dermody at ILR Press were crucial in shepherding the manuscript to publishable form, and I would particularly like to thank Fran for her enthusiasm and support for the project and for her gratifying conviction that the material presented here was worthy of a wider readership.

Some empirical material in this book as well as certain insights have appeared in some of my previously published work. A small portion of chapters 2, 4, and 5 and the conclusion draws on "Activists Face Bureaucrats: The Failure of the Israeli Social Workers' Campaign," *Industrial Relations Journal* 44 (5–6): 462–478; copyright © 2013 Brian Towers (BRITOW) and John Wiley & Sons Ltd. Some parts of chapters 3 and 4 draw on "The Contradictory Effects of Neoliberalization on Labor Relations: The Health and Social Work Sectors," *Economic and*

Industrial Democracy 37 (4): 644–664; copyright © 2014, reprinted by permission of Sage Publications. Part 2 builds on ideas developed in "Putting Israel's Recent Unionizing Drives in a Broader Social Context," *Israel Studies Review* (forthcoming from Berghahn Journals). Some parts of chapters 13 and 14 draw on material from "Effective Citizenship in the Cracks of Neocorporatism," *Citizenship Studies* 21 (1): 85–99, copyright © 2016 Taylor & Francis, available online. I am grateful to these journals for their permission to use this material.

Finally, but most importantly, my deepest gratitude and love to Eynav, who has weathered the storms with remarkable fortitude, supported me through navigational uncertainties, and rejoiced with me during the sunlit passages.

Acronyms and Abbreviations

Histadrut	New General Federation of Labor (previously named General Organization of Workers in the Land of Israel)
IAA	Israel Antiquities Authority
IBCA	Israel Builders and Contractors Association
ICT	information and communications technology
IEC	Israel Electricity Corporation
IMA	Israel Medical Association
JNF	Jewish National Fund
JO	Journalists Organization
MAI	Manufacturers Association of Israel
MK	member of Knesset (the Israeli parliament)
NII	National Insurance Institute
NLC	National Labor Court
PGFTU	Palestinian General Federation of Trade Unions
PLL	Palestine Labor League
PMO	Prime Minister's Office
SWU	Social Workers Union
WAC	Workers Advice Center

LABOR IN ISRAEL

AN INQUIRY INTO LABOR IN ISRAEL IN THE TWENTY-FIRST CENTURY

In 2013, I found myself sitting in a small office on an upper floor of the historic trade union building at 93 Arlozorov Street in Tel Aviv. The walls of this building, the physical hub of Israel's once-powerful labor movement, heard many acrimonious debates and crucial decisions being made over the years, and the old-fashioned tiles and wooden panels showed signs of wear. Despite the echoes in the grand entrance lobby, an air of weariness hung in the poorly lit stairwell, reflected in the creaking of the old elevator. Even the air conditioning seemed able to do little more than stir up the dust on that warm October day.

In the small office, however, things were very different. The windows were open, and the endless honking of the city's morning traffic poured in together with the sunlight and birdsong. This was the central node of the newly established Organizing Unit of the Histadrut, Israel's hegemonic labor federation, and it was buzzing with energy, enthusiasm, and above all confidence. The two young people in the office, the heads of the unit, were sitting with sleeves rolled up, answering emails, phone calls, and my questions all at once, seemingly intent on putting as much distance as possible between themselves and the remnants of a previous era. Determined to transform the Histadrut's image as a bullying behemoth protecting coteries of privileged workers at the expense of the country's citizens, those in the Organizing Unit have their sights on the unorganized: those in precarious employment, those earning barely enough to get by, those in jobs and sectors that did not even exist when the Histadrut was at its zenith.

This contrast lies at the heart of recent organizing activity. After all, organized labor in Israel has a long and exalted history. From the early days of Jewish settlement in Palestine, through the establishment of the State of Israel in 1948, and up to the 1970s, the labor movement was a powerful social and political force, and the image of the worker has a hallowed place in Israel's state-sanctioned historical narrative. From the late 1970s, however, organized labor in Israel found itself being undermined, and the main labor federation was drastically weakened. It seemed that organized labor, once crucial to the Zionist project and central to the governmental structure, no longer had a significant role in the new, neoliberal Israel.[1]

Then, toward the end of the first decade of the new millennium, organized labor appeared to wake up. In 2007, a new general union known as Koach Laovdim ("power to the workers") was established and rapidly became familiar to the general public. In 2008, a labor dispute in a chain of cafés achieved wide media attention and was taken up as a flagship campaign by the Histadrut. In the following years, workers' committees were established in previously unorganized workplaces, a process that often required determined struggle. Likewise, some unionized sectors experienced major labor disputes that involved peak-level bargaining and the participation of many of the traditional institutions of collective labor relations in various configurations, including the state, employers' organizations, labor organizations, and the labor courts. The resurgence of organizing, then, cast doubt on the widely accepted view that the old labor regime was moribund and that organized labor was no longer a significant political force.

On the one hand, those involved in this resurgence often positioned themselves in opposition to vestigial unionist institutions, which they viewed as corrupt and sclerotic, an integral part of the same despised establishment that became the focus of massive popular protest in 2011. As a social worker activist put it, "The feeling is that it's not the Finance Ministry that screwed us, but the union—the union and the Histadrut, of course" (Farber, interview). It was not just the Histadrut in the crosshairs; other established professional bodies were viewed with mistrust by a new generation of workers seeking a different kind of relationship with representative organizations. A journalist involved in unionizing media professionals said of the old Journalists' Association, "They even made a blacklist of us, people who should not be allowed to reach management positions, all sorts of tricks" (Tarchitzky, interview). In efforts to organize cell-phone employees, the Histadrut was even viewed as a liability: "We tried to reduce the Histadrut presence as much as possible," one activist said (Avitan, interview), even though the Histadrut was supporting their efforts.

On the other hand, workers recognize that despite years of attrition, the Histadrut is still an extremely powerful organization. One of the heads of the Organizing Unit expressed the point perfectly that October day in the small Histadrut office: "We are facing the biggest sons of bitches . . . so we need the biggest son of a bitch with us. To fight big dogs you need a serious dog!" (Dvir, interview). The labor courts too seem to favor the Histadrut as the organization most able to bring stability to labor relations, something not always viewed with satisfaction by workers: "There's a feeling [the courts] undermined our struggle, cooperated with the Histadrut. . . . They didn't stand by our side. . . . [It's] as if we weren't represented [in the courts] at all" (Farber, interview). At the same time, many workers have more ambitious objectives than merely addressing workplace issues. As another social work activist put it, "It isn't a struggle over wages but over the welfare system, the welfare state—a social struggle" (Shlosberg, interview).

This messy, contradictory, and tension-riddled resurgence of organizing in Israel is the focus of this book. Through interviews, court documents, reports from various organizations, and media accounts of labor struggle, it explores the relationships between well-established institutions and grassroots activists, and the new forms of unionizing in new economic sectors among workers in new employment frameworks, among a range of worker groups. While many scholars have addressed the apparent decline of organized labor and debated signs of its revival, this book has two main objectives that have not been addressed by scholars currently investigating Israel's political economy. The first is to investigate the new organizing initiatives and recent workers' struggles, which—perhaps simply due to their novelty—have been subject to few detailed analyses (the cases in Mishori and Maor 2012 are among the few). The second is to understand organized labor's social and political status and role today. In many ways, then, the book addresses the issues and concerns of much research in the Western world into organized labor and its decline. However, given the critical role of organized labor in Israel's history and its central position in the Zionist project, this book has a third objective, much wider in scope: it aims to investigate the importance of organized labor in Israeli society today in relation to the political community and labor's current nationalist political role. Thus the main question this book tries to address is this one: Following the decline of the Israeli (nationalist, Zionist) variant of labor movement, what is the status of organized labor in Israel today, and what is its current role in the representation of workers in the Israeli sociopolitical regime?

The book, then, will be of interest to all those who seek a new perspective on Israeli society and wish to understand the wave of organizing and its connection with other trends in Israel, particularly in light of the country's celebrated labor history. It will also be of interest to scholars of the political economy and industrial relations without any affinity to Israel who seek to understand unions and other labor organizations in a postcorporatist society, the challenges they face, and the new paths to organizing being paved by workplace activists.

The Rise of Organized Jewish Labor

Organized labor in Israel is inextricably linked to the New General Federation of Labor, or under its previous name, the General Organization of Workers in the Land of Israel, commonly known as the Histadrut. Founded in 1920, this organization rapidly gained considerable power in the *yishuv* (the prestate Jewish community in Palestine under the British Mandate) and retained its hegemonic position well into the 1970s, negotiating with employer organizations and the state over a wide range of social and economic policies.

On a rhetorical level, organized labor and even socialism were granted an honored status in the history of Jewish settlement in Palestine and later Israel: this was to be a state of the workers, embodied in the figure of the philosophical pioneer who tilled the fields during the day and discussed the finer points of political theory in the evenings. Indeed, according to some Zionist thinkers such as A. D. Gordon and Dov Ber Borochov, working the soil would also connect the Jewish immigrants to the new land (see Wolkinson 1999, 72–73).

However, the influx of Jewish immigrants to Palestine and later the establishment of the State of Israel can also be seen as a colonial project (Shafir 1989). Waves of immigrants were settled on land obtained in various ways from the local population, resulting in a society that favored one group (the newcomers) above the other, and included the expulsion of hundreds of thousands of the "natives" during and after the war of 1948 (Morris 1987), which Israel calls the War of Independence and the Palestinians call the Nakba ("catastrophe"). Organized labor and its institutions were implicated in this colonialism; indeed, as Shafir (1989) and Shafir and Peled (2002) have argued, labor was organized in keeping with the needs of the Zionist project, which had no army to count on as other colonial enterprises had. In particular, the (Jewish) labor movement was developed along collectivist lines in order to circumvent market principles in two areas crucial to settlement, land and labor, and this labor movement became hegemonic in Jewish settlement efforts. Thus the institutions of the *yishuv*, and later those of the new state, took on a social-democratic, corporatist appearance: these institutions and then the state had a central role in directing industrial development and channeling outside funds (including reparations from Germany).

An economy developed whose collectivist institutions encompassed agriculture, industry, construction, marketing, transportation, and banking, and employers too accepted this collectivist bent (De Vries 2002; Frenkel, Shenhav, and Herzog 2000). The labor movement's economic bodies were owned and administered by the Histadrut's holding company, Chevrat Haovdim. The various firms were protected from outside competition and enjoyed shared resources and an internal market. This central ownership was meant to avoid the danger of (Jewish) employers taking on cheaper (Arab) hired labor, thus ensuring employment for the Jewish immigrants and increasing the numbers of those who stayed in Palestine.

The labor settlement movement had no interest in nationalization (except for land) and was not opposed to private enterprise as long as it employed only "Hebrew labor" (Shafir and Peled 2002, 48–55). In fact the state, after 1948, encouraged the accumulation of private capital just as much as national or Histadrut-owned capital, though it maintained control of the distribution of capital, both from external sources and generated locally (Frenkel, Shenhav, and Herzog 2000; Gozansky 1986; Rosenfeld and Carmi 1976, 135–140; Shalev 2006). The circular flow of capital that made the Histadrut's pension and provident funds available to the government for loans to private and public investors (for investments approved by the government itself) made it hard to discern the boundary between the Histadrut and the government. This flow of capital also led to the development of strong ties between the labor movement's political and economic elites and reduced political conflict between them.

The social rights and welfare associated with the efforts of organized labor were also linked to national aims (Arian and Talmud 1991). Welfare was not universal, and different groups received different levels of support and protection. Social welfare was seen as contrary to the pioneering spirit, and the labor movement supported the concept of welfare as mutual self-help within a union structure. Social rights, however, were necessary to enable workers to fulfill national aims, and while universal welfare provisions were limited, very broad welfare services were provided to Histadrut members according to settlement requirements. Such social citizenship rights effectively protected members from market vagaries, essentially decommodifying their labor. Welfare in Israel, then, did not develop in the context of class struggle or compromise; instead, welfare and nationalism went together, while social rights were not universal but depended on the recipient's involvement in state-building (via the Histadrut) (Rosenhek 2006, 2002a, 2002b; Shalev 2006).

In short, labor was not politicized as a grassroots oppositional movement but organized by a national leadership elite (Shapiro 1984, 1976) for the main national objectives of settlement and immigrant absorption. Labor institutions established by the Jewish settlers largely excluded Arabs, while the epitome of the labor movement—the kibbutz—can be seen as the ultimate closed shop, established on land belonging to the Jewish National Fund that could be leased to Jews alone (Shafir and Peled 2002, 47).[2]

The Histadrut, then, was both an extremely powerful labor organization and an executive arm of Zionist settlement efforts. It was not primarily envisioned as a union but founded by socialist-leaning parties to coordinate certain welfare functions offered by these parties, and its collective bargaining function came later (Haberfeld 1995).[3] At least until the mid-1990s, it was never a union or even a federation of unions; the branches known as unions today started out as administrative units for governing various worker groups, and dues were paid directly to the organization, not the unions. Though it sometimes represented workers vis-à-vis employers, this was not its main function since the interests of both labor and capital were presumed to be the same: national (Jewish settlement) interests. All the main political parties took part in Histadrut elections, not just parties that looked favorably on labor. Indeed, as Ben-Eliezer (1993, 400) has it, the Histadrut was designed to solve the problems of Jewish workers "irrespective of their political leanings."

The link between the Histadrut and the Labor Party (in its various incarnations, from Mapai through the Alliance) was particularly strong (see Shalev 1992, especially chap. 3).[4] While the Histadrut's role as a nation-building institution differentiates it considerably from the typical West European model of trade union or labor federation, its close relationship with what was the dominant political bloc made the Histadrut an exceptionally powerful labor institution. For some forty years, it channeled the demands and interests of workers—and thus, according to the prevailing ideology, the general (Jewish) citizenry—to the state's main decision-making forums. Even after the State of Israel was established, the Histadrut continued to be central to immigrant settlement and absorption efforts, partly because the dominant party, Mapai, needed the Histadrut to retain its political strength and so permitted it to continue in many of the roles it had had during the prestate period. The network of employment bureaus previously run by the Histadrut was taken over by the state in 1959, but the Histadrut held on to its health services, pensions, finance (Bank Hapoalim), industry (Koor), housing and construction (Solel Boneh and Shikun Ovdim), and trade (Hamashbir and Co-op), and maintained extensive control of transport (through the Egged cooperative) and agriculture (Grinberg 1996). In this way the Histadrut continued to receive new members, create jobs for its functionaries, and enjoy huge economic strength. Other state functions were taken on by other quasi-state organizations such as the Jewish Agency while the government and Mapai took certain functions upon themselves. In some places, according to Grinberg (1993, 39), branches of the Histadrut and Mapai were perceived as branches of government. Thus a complex web of interdependencies developed between the government, Mapai, and the Histadrut (explored in Grinberg 1993; see also Harel 2004). This severely limited the state's ability to act autonomously, and particularly hampered the government's attempts to manage the economy and liberate market forces (workers and employers) from institutions such as the

Histadrut. This same mutual reliance, however, gave organized labor enormous power and influence in the political sphere.

The Histadrut's role in the Zionist project is clearly reflected in its relationship with the Arab population (discussed more fully in part 3). Under the British Mandate, the Palestinian Arabs underwent a process of rapid proletarianization; by the 1940s, about half the Arab population were waged workers, which led to an increasing interest in unionization. In the *yishuv*, there were fears that cheap Arab labor would undermine Jewish labor and drive out immigrants, which led Histadrut and *yishuv* leaders to adopt a policy of limited cooperation with Arab workers but separate unions (Bernstein 2000; Lockman 1996). Various mechanisms were put in place for ensuring Jews received preferential treatment, including policies for issuing credit, labor exchanges (Wolkinson 1999), and exclusive welfare services (Rosenhek 2002b). The leaders of the new state adhered to these same principles after 1948 (Haidar 2008). The Histadrut was used as a mechanism for distributing favors, thus ensuring a kind of coerced Arab loyalty to the state and, particularly, the ruling party (Mapai). Israeli Arabs were accepted as union members in 1953 (Landau 1973), as Histadrut members in 1959, and as full members with voting rights only in 1965 (Shalev 1989, 109).[5] As labor needs changed, Israeli Arabs were increasingly incorporated into the economy, particularly the private sector, but in the main strongholds of organized labor in the public sector, Israeli Arabs were (and remain) underrepresented (Wolkinson 1999).

This situation held until the 1970s, when a number of processes combined to undermine the corporatist sociopolitical regime and eject organized labor (the Histadrut) from its dominant position.

The Decline of Organized Labor—and Its Resurgence?

The year 1977 marks a watershed in the history of organized labor in Israel and the start of the labor movement's decline. In that year, the liberal-right Likud Party won the elections and set out to undermine the Histadrut that had been the electoral base of Mapai, Likud's main rival. As Ram (2008, 49) notes, Likud was antiunion "for the pragmatic reason that the union was considered as the bulwark of Mapai's bureaucratic power." In addition, Likud's main constituency was the small business owners who had little sympathy for the socialist posturing of Mapai (Grinberg 2001). Histadrut ties to the Labor Party remained strong, but Chevrat Haovdim required increasing subsidies, becoming increasingly dependent on the state; thus the Histadrut, as owner of Chevrat Haovdim, was no longer an asset to the Labor Party but a liability (Shalev and Grinberg 1989). Moreover, with the Emergency Economic Stabilization Plan of 1985 the state succeeded in enhancing its autonomy as reflected in the Finance Ministry's ability to resist pressure from the Chevrat Haovdim (as well as the industrialists), as Shalev and Grinberg argue (1989, 67).

Liberalization and deregulation soon followed the 1977 Likud election victory, particularly following the Emergency Economic Stabilization Plan. This included the reduction of subsidies for industry, the removal of protective tariffs, and the privatization of state and Histadrut enterprises (Grinberg and Shafir 2000; Shalev 2006; though Katz and Zahori 2002, 124–125, note that privatization began piecemeal some years before). This process was accelerated in 1994, when Haim Ramon was elected Histadrut chair with the aim of stripping it of its assets and turning it into just a union. In 1995, the National Health Insurance Law took the leading HMO Clalit out of the Histadrut's hands, thereby depriving it of one of its main recruitment tools. The following year, two major Histadrut assets, Bank Hapoalim and the industrial conglomerate Koor, were sold off (see Ram 2008, 48–53).

This period saw the state decreasing its direct intervention in the economy, the increased use of the private sector for economic development and the reduction of state responsibility for production and welfare, an increasingly powerful business sector, and capital market reforms (Maman and Rosenhek 2007, 2012; Shalev 2006). Institutional changes included placing control of interest and exchange rates in the Bank of Israel's hands, augmenting its autonomy. Indeed, as part of its own bid for autonomy, the state took a step backward as economic entrepreneur and regulated to facilitate the increased (unmediated) role of capital, including foreign direct investment (see Levi-Faur 2000). Filc (2004) applies the label "post-Fordist" to this phase, characterized by postindustrial development emphasizing information and communications technology (ICT) and rooted in the private sector though administered and strongly supported by the state.

The weakening of the Histadrut was part of an increasing assault on organized labor by governments of both left and right (Maor 2012). This was accompanied by the decline and decentralization of collective bargaining together with growing wage inequality (Kristal and Cohen 2007), the fragmentation of labor representation, and the growth of new organizations, including new unions outside the Histadrut framework and nongovernmental organizations (NGOs) active in the field of workers' rights (Gidron, Bar, and Katz 2004; Mundlak 2007, 1998). Extensions to collective agreements decreased (Kristal, Cohen, and Mundlak 2006), and by 2006 the coverage of collective agreements was down to 56 percent (Mundlak 2009, 768). In 2005, Israel had one of the highest rates of inequality in the Western world, second only to the United States; by that year, labor's share of national income had dropped to 64 percent from some 75 percent before 1974 (Kristal 2013). By 2014, Israel had the fifth highest rate of inequality among Organisation for Economic Cooperation and Development countries, after Chile, Mexico, the United States, and Turkey (Keeley 2015, 23).

Union density also declined, from almost 80 percent in 1981 to some 43 percent in 2000 (Kristal, Cohen, and Mundlak 2006) and about 33 percent in 2006 (Mundlak 2009, 768). This reflected a change in worker characteristics, particularly a decline in the number of blue-collar workers from some 32 percent of the waged labor force in 1967 to about 21 percent in 2005 (Harpaz 2007, 451). In addition, as Harpaz (2007, 452–453) puts it, a new breed of younger, better-educated, and individualistic employees grew up who saw the Histadrut as a dinosaur that hampered their individual efforts to advance; many of these were, and are, golden-collar workers in the fields of law, ICT (the high-tech sector), and other professions, who have little ideological commitment to labor solidarity. Mundlak (2009, 770) notes, "As inequality grows, the stronger groups in the labor market view trade unions as archaic, while low-waged workers perceive trade unions as an unreachable option, and also as part of 'the system' that disadvantages them in the labor market."

At the same time, the state has been retreating from direct management of many areas of public service. Since the 1980s, governments have deliberately transferred services to private firms and nonprofit organizations. This transfer has been shored up by a desire to cut expenditures, lighten the state's administrative load, and circumvent legislative restrictions. Hence the vast majority of third-sector organizations are active in service provision, taking over tasks previously administered by the state and the Histadrut, while many address issues that the government is unwilling to address directly itself. The increase in the number of such organizations, reflected in the legislation of the Nonprofit Associations Law of 1980, is also due to public disillusionment with the political system and a feeling that the public has no power to influence policies and the state via this system (Gidron, Bar, and Katz 2004).

These processes have been reflected and affected by changes in the judicial and legislative sphere, including the decline of the corporatist legal framework, the so-called constitutional revolution marked by the legislation of two Basic Laws, and the liberalization of jurisprudence (Mautner 1993; Mundlak 2007, 1998).[6] As Hirschl (1997, 136) puts it, the constitutional revolution "reflects and promotes the neoliberal, individualist, 'free enterprise' worldview upon which the new economic order now emerging in Israel is based." The rise of this worldview was accompanied by the retrenchment of welfare, though certain structures remained strong as mechanisms for (Jewish) immigrant absorption (Rosenhek 2002b). Social rights were increasingly excluded from the interpretation of Basic

Laws; instead, property rights and universal human rights were emphasized (Gross 2000, 1998; Hirschl 1997; Raday 1994). In the sphere of labor relations, these changes have been manifested as a move from corporatist to pluralist labor law and the growing use of regulation instead of tripartite negotiation between the traditional social partners (labor, capital, and the state): "The previous legal regime sought to a great extent to isolate industrial relations from legal rules and entitlements and to leave the definition of rights and duties to the social partners. The current system is based on stricter, far-reaching, and intrusive legal rules that govern individuals as well as the social partners. Law [has been] transformed from a *facilitative* into a *governing* instrument" (Mundlak 2007, 5). Organized labor as a political force embedded within the structures of government was one casualty of this process: labor law decreasingly upholds the privileged political status of unions (Mundlak 1998).

The changes to Israel's economy, and society in general, have also included the rapid growth of nonstandard employment frameworks and the influx of new worker groups, most notably migrant laborers (*ovdim zarim*—"foreign workers," as they are commonly referred to in Hebrew). Since the 1990s, migrant labor has become the main labor force in certain industries, particularly agriculture and the care industry, undermining local labor and disproportionately affecting Palestinian citizens and Palestinians from the occupied territories who are dependent on employment in Israel (Arnon 2007; Farsakh 2005).[7] Kemp and Raijman (2008) note that in the move toward a neoliberal society, the migrant laborers were a shock absorber that enabled the state to avoid reforms to the labor market and also a way of making employment harder to obtain for much of the population, thus making workers cheaper and dispensable, disciplining the workers, and increasing state autonomy from both workers and employers (see also Rosenhek 2007). If in the 1950s and 1960s the state had worked to wrest power away from prestate institutions, and in the 1970s and 1980s to weaken the Histadrut, it now made efforts to establish its autonomy from the social partners, treating them as mere interest groups (Mundlak et al. 2013, 82).

New forms of employment, most visibly employment via manpower companies, have effectively reduced the price paid by employers for labor by enabling them to circumvent collective agreements and various protective laws (Davidov 2015; Shamir 2016). An increasing number of workers are denied benefits such as pension contributions, sick pay, and vacations, have scant employment or income security, and have no recourse to union assistance, leading to the rise of a "precariat" class (Standing 2011, 2009). As Harpaz (2005) put it, workers are laboring in nineteenth-century conditions (see also Achdut, Sula, and Eisenbach 1998; Knoler 2000; Nadiv 2005; Stessman and Achdut 2000; Tager 2006). This, as Hirschl (1997, 139) noted already twenty years ago, is part of deliberate state-led moves toward the "subordination of social policy to the demands of labor market flexibility, the removal of 'market rigidities,' and structural competitiveness" (see also Maor 2012).

More recently, the middle classes that flourished and expanded during the 1990s (during what Ram 2008, 43–45, calls the "bourgeois revolution"), have felt the effects of these policy changes: disposable income has shrunk as user contributions to the cost of services have increased and the benefits of secure, unionized employment have been undermined. A generation has emerged that can no longer maintain, let alone improve, the standard of living of its parents (Rosenhek and Shalev 2013). This state of affairs was illustrated dramatically in the social protests of 2011, which concentrated on the cost of living, particularly basic commodities (symbolized by the "cottage cheese protest") and housing (see Ram and Filc 2013; Shenhav 2013).

By the new millennium, then, it seemed that organized labor, so central to the Zionist story and so deeply embedded in the structures of government and state, had been shorn of its political power. In 2003, the Finance Ministry announced that its greatest achievement had been the breaking of organized labor (Harpaz 2007, 454). In 2005, a law was passed forbidding a union chairperson to be a member of Knesset (MK) at the same time, cutting yet another institutional link between the Histadrut and the Labor Party and marking the end of the close ties between organized labor and the political elite.

Ofer Eini, who took over the Histadrut leadership from Amir Peretz in 2005, fostered a new kind of connection between the Histadrut and the traditional social partners by nurturing ties with employers' organizations and making himself an important figure in Labor Party internal politics (see Weinblum 2010). His efforts were largely based on personal connections: in 2007, he helped Labor Party candidate Ehud Barak in the party primaries, and in return Barak appointed him to represent Labor in negotiations with the government over the budget. In 2009, Eini mediated between Labor Party members and MKs to enable the passage of Barak's controversial changes to the party constitution. After the elections of that year, Eini led negotiations over economic issues toward the coalition agreement under which Labor joined Prime Minister Benjamin Netanyahu's government. However, Eini's efforts promoted the Histadrut as partner to capital; the result was unstable, temporary, and to a significant extent bipartite (between labor and capital, excluding state representatives). In 2006, the Histadrut and the Employers Organizations Coordinating Bureau reached an agreement to conduct labor relations by discussion, negotiation, and collective agreements, but this agreement was nonbinding ("more like a charter than a binding agreement"; Weinblum 2010, 38) and circumvented state participation. The state was also only minimally involved in negotiations toward the mandatory pension agreement of 2007, though the agreement was later extended by the labor minister to all employees (see also Mundlak 2009). In 2008, the Histadrut and Coordinating Bureau proposed setting up a tripartite social-economic council with the government, but the finance minister at the time, Roni Bar-On, prevented this from happening, calling the idea antidemocratic and a threat to the government's sovereignty. The "Round Table" forum set up in 2009, which followed the same idea, was not anchored in any institutions. Thus, as Weinblum (2010, 39) concedes, the social partnership nurtured by Eini had no institutional framework, was dependent on the figures involved (particularly Eini's close personal ties), and was contingent on narrow political circumstances for its existence—for example, Eini's ability to mediate a unity government was the result of Netanyahu's need for a stable coalition to grant legitimacy to his efforts to cope with the economic crisis (Weinblum 2010, 57).

In short, the hegemonic labor federation, the Histadrut, has lost its dominant position in the Israeli polity: its institutional ties to the political establishment have long gone, while the main channels of influence nurtured by Eini depend to a large extent on personal links. Under certain leaders (such as Shelly Yachimovich, Labor Party leader 2011–13) and certain circumstances, the Labor Party has been sympathetic to the Histadrut's aims, but the Histadrut can no longer rely on the party to support it in promoting a labor-friendly agenda; the party, after all, has been an enthusiastic supporter of the liberalization of the economy (see Ram 2000; Shafir and Peled 2000a; Shalev 2000).

However, in 2008 the labor dispute at the Coffee Bean chain of cafés attracted a lot of attention, and the Histadrut took the employees under its wing, investing a lot in the campaign as a flagship case for what the leadership heralded as a new era of collective industrial relations. Indeed, after a period of rearguard action in organized workplaces under Amir Peretz's leadership, the Histadrut under Ofer Eini seemed to be taking a more active role in unionizing. Moreover, a year earlier, the establishment of a new union had been declared—Koach Laovdim. This union intentionally positioned itself as counterweight to what its founders considered an ineffectual and undemocratic Histadrut, emphasizing its democratic structure and the involvement of its members in decision making. Also in 2008, a small organization known as the Workers Advice Center (WAC) amended its constitution to reflect a new emphasis on unionizing after over a decade of NGO activities assisting workers. In the following years, important economic sectors saw widespread labor unrest, including the railways, the health services, and the media, and nonunionized workplaces organized to set up workers' committees, some quite successfully, including in large firms such as the cell-phone company Pelephone. In 2011, the social protest movement erupted, bringing tens of thousands if not hundreds of thousands onto the streets to protest high costs of living and the deterioration of public services—driven, it appeared, by the same factors that had fueled the organizing drives. In 2012, the National Labor Court gave an important and precedential ruling, defining and delimiting what an employer is permitted to do when workers organize.

These events and others appeared to herald a resurgence of organized labor; and indeed, though reliable union density figures are hard to come by, Harpaz (2007, 448) suggests that since the nadir following the National Health Insurance Law (in effect from 1995), membership figures leapt from some two hundred thousand to about seven hundred thousand in 2007 in the Histadrut alone. Another three hundred thousand were members of the Histadrut's main rival, the National Histadrut. Thus in 2007, about 40 percent of Israel's 2.7 million workers were unionized: 26 percent with the Histadrut, 11 percent in the National Histadrut, and the remaining 3 percent in various independent unions including the Teachers' Organization and the Israel Medical Association (IMA) (Harpaz 2007, 448).[8] In 2010, the Histadrut set up the Workers Organizing Unit to concentrate on unionizing initiatives. In the middle of 2013, *TheMarker* presented data taken from the unions themselves that attested to new unionizing activity: twenty-two new workers' committees had been established in 2011, thirty-nine in 2012, and forty in the first half of 2013 alone. The Young Histadrut had also seen success, with some 7,500 new members in 2012 and 2013 (see S. Peretz 2013; Weissberg, Bior, and Heruti-Sover 2013). By the end of that year, the Histadrut claimed twenty-six thousand had been organized in some one hundred workplaces (Niv 2013e). In addition, a few thousand workers had been organized with Koach Laovdim (according to the organization's website) and a numerically insignificant few hundred with WAC (Ben Efrat, interview). For those who favored a greater role for organized labor in Israeli society, the picture appeared promising.

Current Scholarship into Organized Labor in Israel

Various Israeli scholars, many of whose work has been mentioned above, have addressed diverse aspects of organized labor in Israel. Their research can be divided into three main areas: (1) changing employment frameworks and the weakening of organized labor; (2) the changing nature of the political collective and the implications this has on labor; and (3) the changing nature of statewide corporatist structures. Though of course there are links and overlaps between the areas, and any division is necessarily schematic, the areas can roughly be characterized as (1) a focus on the details of working lives and workplaces; (2) a focus on the links between labor market policies and (national) politics; and (3) a focus on institutions.

In the first research area, scholars are investigating the changing nature of employment, new employment frameworks, the undermining of labor rights, the erosion of corporatist-era protection for workers, and the increase in non-unionized workplaces (e.g., Benjamin, Bernstein, and Motzafi-Haller 2010; Bernstein 1986, 1983; Harpaz 2005; Nisim and Benjamin 2008, 2010; Saporta 1988). Various reports from both NGOs (e.g., Tager 2006) and government bodies (e.g., Handels 2003) have also investigated such problems. Putting these issues in a wider context, whether as cause or result, some scholars (e.g., Cohen et al. 2003; Haberfeld 1995; Kristal 2008, 2013; Kristal, Cohen, and Mundlak 2006) have investigated the decline of unions, the fragmentation of labor, changes to working-class identity and demographic/cultural changes, and the decline in labor's share of the national income. Others (e.g., Helman 2013) have exposed the ideological assumptions that lie behind many of these changes, linking them to some neoliberal individualist, entrepreneurial Zeitgeist that has transformed all aspects of working life.

In the second research area, scholars are investigating the influx of new worker groups and their relation to veteran workers, to the labor market in general, and to the political collective as a whole. Critical scholars unequivocally link the import of migrant labor to deliberate policy choices and to the conflict with the Palestinians; they thus reject the almost deterministic globalization thesis (e.g., Rosenhek 2007, 2003, 2002a, 2002b; Kemp and Raijman 2008). Migrant laborers, they assert, are used to manage the conflict and facilitate the policy of separation from the Palestinians and assist the state in the move toward neoliberal social and economic policies by circumventing and undermining organized labor and welfare. Such scholarship builds on studies of the place of noncitizen Palestinians within the labor market and corporatist structures (e.g., Semyonov and Lewin-Epstein 1987; Portugali 1993) and these structures in relation to Israel's Palestinian citizens (e.g., Lewin-Epstein and Semyonov 1993; Sa'di and Lewin-Epstein 2001).

Guy Mundlak is the most prominent among scholars in the third research area. Though he approaches the subject from a legal perspective, his work is extremely broad, looking at the intricate relationship between the judicial system and a vast range of organizations including unions and NGOs, as well as the place of individuals and various groups not formally recognized as social partners. His work builds on the research of pioneering nonlegal scholars (e.g., Grinberg 1996, 1993; Shalev 1992; Shalev and Grinberg 1989) who have approached Israel's economy from a corporatist point of view but noted its peculiarities. Mundlak's work *Fading Corporatism* (2007) claimed that corporatist structures were in decline but also noted that it was too soon to bewail their ultimate demise. Indeed, just two years later Mundlak (2009) published an article that asked if we are witnessing a corporatist revival. This "second-generation social corporatism," he suggested, was no longer concentrated or centralized as the Histadrut-dominated corporatism had been, does not "huddle under the protection of a labor party," and is no longer separated from the regulatory state (Mundlak 2009, 766). It is corporatist, however, because of the participation of the social partners in peak-level bargaining over policy decisions. In 2013, Mundlak and others suggested we are seeing the hybridization of industrial relations, including a corporatist subsystem that involves peak-level bargaining, whose partners subscribe to the notion of joint governance, and whose broad coverage is not dependent on membership numbers; and a (budding) liberal-pluralist subsystem involving employees in places mostly outside the corporatist system, in which organizing does not always end in collective agreements, and whose representative organizations are mostly concerned with the specific workplace and not with the overall functioning of the corporatist system (Mundlak et al. 2013).

Mundlak has also touched on issues of legitimacy. Low membership in both the Histadrut and employer organizations undermines their legitimacy, which is now dependent on past grandeur, while pluralism in labor representation means a wide range of organizations with very different identities are demanding to be heard (Mundlak 2009, 777–779). Hybridization poses a challenge for legitimacy too: the corporatist subsystem gets legitimacy from the state and must maintain a responsible approach, with a unified and centralized voice (top-down); the liberal-pluralist subsystem draws its legitimacy from the workers (bottom-up) and must be more militant (Mundlak et al. 2013, 97).

The works in these three main research areas clarify important aspects of Israel's industrial relations and labor market, and this book draws heavily on them. However, I take the discussion beyond the boundaries of industrial relations and attempt to understand labor's position broadly and on various levels of analysis, bringing the insights of these scholars together with new empirical material from the recent wave of organizing and the new worker organizations that have received little academic attention as yet. Focusing on labor organizing and representation, I aim to understand how workers perceive themselves in society and how they perceive the role of organized labor, as well as how they are perceived, in light of the changes to Israel's political economy of the last thirty years. In particular, I am interested in the issues of opposition and democracy: the way workers are able, or try, to influence the wider community and society, and the resources they have at their disposal to do so, whether institutional, organizational, or ideational. Put simply, this book strives to complement and update comprehensive and important works such as Shalev's *Labor and the Political Economy in Israel* (1992) and Mundlak's *Fading Corporatism* (2007), taking the recent wave of organizing as the starting point and trying to understand its significance within the broader sweep of Israel's history. Thus, while granting pride of place to worker voice and perceptions on the ground, I aim to analyze this in a national and political context including the historical role of organized labor in Israel and the peculiar character of its corporatism.

Chapter 1 presents the theoretical concerns that the book seeks to address, locating labor struggles in the context of neoliberalization and discussing the possibility of agency. It then outlines the analytical perspective adopted, rooted in neocorporatism and union revitalization scholarship, including concepts of power. This is followed by an explanation of the structure of the book, which is organized according to three broad spheres in which, historically, unions had an important role. A short coda to this chapter explains the research process.

Chapter 2 opens part 1, which corresponds to the first sphere outlined in chapter 1: the relationship between workers and their representative organization. This chapter discusses the groundswell of labor activism, characterized by a desire to participate, and explores the possibility that labor activism may stem from outside the workplace. It also discusses workers' frustration with established institutions, particularly the Histadrut, and the perception that these old organizations are not necessarily on the workers' side. This theme is expanded in chapter 3, which investigates the Histadrut's status among workers in more detail and compares it to Koach Laovdim. Similarly, this chapter also reviews the IMA, another established institution that faced challenges from a new generation of workers seeking a different relationship with their representative organizations. Chapter 4 discusses labor activism as opposition to policies associated with neoliberalism and perceived to jeopardize the status of workers. It also explores workers' efforts to connect with the broader public as an essential part of their struggles, as well as the idea that neoliberal policies do not have a blanket effect on all sectors of the economy: some workers may be in a better position to benefit from such policies than others. However, the continued strength of established institutions cannot be denied. This is the focus of chapter 5, which investigates the Histadrut's power resources and their limitations, as well as its most-favored status in the eyes of the labor courts and the perception among many workers involved in organizing that despite its shortcomings, the Histadrut is still the most valuable organization for labor. The chapter finishes by reviewing recent signs that the Histadrut may be changing and adapting, albeit slowly, to the new demands of members and potential members. Chapter 6 draws together the threads of the previous chapters of part 1.

Part 2 corresponds to the second sphere outlined in chapter 1: the balance of power between labor and capital. This part is organized according to three planes of labor struggle. The first of these, the plane of frontal struggle, is the plane of classic workplace unionist activity, of organizing drives, unionization, and collective action. This is the focus of chapter 7, which discusses a major organizing drive that resulted in a precedential court ruling and fierce opposition to organizing among employers. The second plane is ideological struggle and is the focus of chapter 8, which explores organized labor in the media and the transformation of legal discourse that has significant implications for labor. On this plane, organized labor tries to defend its legitimacy and the legitimacy of collective labor relations among the general public, in society at large. Chapter 9 explores the third plane of institutional struggle. This is the struggle over the institutions and formalized frameworks that enable collective labor relations to take place, and the chapter focuses on the status of the labor courts. Chapter 10 brings part 2 to a close by discussing the shift of the power balance in capital's favor.

Part 3 corresponds to the third sphere outlined in chapter 1: the relationship of labor to the political establishment and wider political community. Chapter 11 begins by discussing new channels of influence for workers, outside union structures—through NGOs—and the nature of representation such organizations offer. Chapter 12 places this in a wider context of the changing nature of politics: individualization, the juridification of legislative process, and the declining status of mass political parties. Further widening the context, chapter 13 overviews the relationship between Israel, its Palestinian Arab citizens, and noncitizen Palestinians in the field of labor. This chapter shows how the workforce has increasingly expanded and discusses structures of political separation and economic inclusion that have been developed over the course of Israel's history. This theme is taken up in chapter 14, which explores the porous nature of the borders of Israel's labor market in contrast to its insular (Jewish) political community and discusses the contemporary position of Palestinian citizens in this labor market. Chapter 15 concludes part 3 with a discussion of some of the themes that arose in the preceding chapters of this part.

The conclusion to the volume takes a broad view of labor organizing and representation in Israel today. It discusses the possibility of organized labor establishing itself as a democratic, participatory force and the likelihood of success in its opposition to policies associated with neoliberalism. It then explores the idea of the workplace as site of resistance, attracting activists who use existing collective frameworks to promote their agenda, and questions whether this new activism can sustain these frameworks. Moreover the weakening of neocorporatist frameworks may have created cracks that facilitate some form of political participation for those who had been economically incorporated but politically excluded. Finally, the chapter discusses the significance of these developments for Israel, in light of the country's singular labor history and the importance of organized labor for the Zionist movement.

NEOLIBERALISM, NEOCORPORATISM, AND WORKER REPRESENTATION

In this chapter I discuss the theoretical concerns that inform the book, which views labor struggles in the context of neoliberalization and emphasizes organized labor's agency. I also explain the analytical perspective adopted and the logic behind the structure of the book, which is organized according to three broad spheres in which unions have been active, or had an important role, under the former labor regime. A short coda to this chapter explains the research process.

Labor Struggles and Agency under a Neoliberalizing Regime

Capital (employers and their organizations) has grown stronger in Israel just as it has elsewhere, reasserting its power over organized labor in labor markets, comparable to such processes in the United States, the United Kingdom, and western Europe (see J. Peters 2012, 2011). The implications have been discussed by prominent researchers in (for example) the volumes edited by Ram and Berkowitz (2006), which investigates the manifestations of inequality in various fields and through various analytical concepts, and by Filc and Ram (2004), which investigates the increase in the power of capital and the effects this has on a range of issues (see also Mautner 2000; Shafir and Peled 2000b). Ram (2008, 138–150) presents the current state of Israel's political economy as a post-Fordist subversion of the Fordist (corporatist) model. The Fordist model was based on a bargained compromise between state, capital, and labor, where each social partner yielded something in exchange for some benefit. This model characterized Israel until the 1980s. In the post-Fordist era, according to Ram, this triangle has been subverted, and new technologies, mechanisms, and frameworks have enabled capital to circumvent the state: "Capital can interact with labor while neutralizing the political factor or bypassing the state's authority. The new technologies . . . release capital from the political limitations that organized labor used to cast upon it and thus disrupt the set of relations that existed within the territorial nation-state and the Fordist regime of accumulation" (Ram 2008, 146). Ram emphasizes the technological aspects that facilitate this new balance of power, but the main point is the depoliticization of labor, which no longer shares a common political framework (the nation-state) with capital.

This transformation of Israeli society can broadly be termed neoliberal as the country's elites increasingly subscribe to what Harvey (2005, 2) calls this "theory of political economic practices that proposes that human well-being can best be advanced by liberating entrepreneurial freedoms and skills within an institutional framework characterized by strong private property rights, free markets, and free trade." Central to this theory is the ideal of individual freedom, which is threatened by "all forms of state intervention that [substitute] collective judgments for those of individuals free to choose" (Harvey 2005, 5). One such collective judgment viewed with great suspicion is of course the peak-level bargaining between worker organizations, employer associations, and the state. However, Harvey also notes the inconsistencies within this theory and the way it has been applied or pursued. The mistrust of state intervention does not align with the need for coercive state action to enforce property rights and entrepreneurial freedoms; therefore we must "pay careful attention . . . to the tension between the theory of neoliberalism and the actual pragmatics of neoliberalisation" (Harvey 2005, 21). Moreover, the process of channeling wealth from subordinate to dominant classes has entailed the dismantling not only of the institutions but also of the narratives that promoted a more egalitarian distribution of resources (Harvey 2007); in other words, the struggle is taking place on an ideological plane as well.

Wacquant (2012, 74) concurs, emphasizing that neoliberalism is not an economic theory but a political project, and as such involves struggle. The state's move rightward is "the structurally conditioned but historically contingent *outcome of material and symbolic struggles* . . . over the responsibilities and modalities of operation of public authority." Thus Wacquant too notes the ideological (symbolic) dimension of the neoliberal project as well as its historical contingency, enjoining us to investigate "actually existing neoliberalism." In keeping with the idea of struggle, Peck and Theodore (2012, 179–183) emphasize that the neoliberal project also has to contend with conflict and opposition that shape neoliberal practices and trajectories; the socioinstitutional hosts of neoliberalism are not passive or merely residual but take an active part in shaping the application and outcomes of neoliberal policies. This is a crucial assertion in light of the tendency to view the transition to neoliberalism in structural terms: Molina and Rhodes (2002, 309), for example, note that most scholars talk of the previous socioeconomic order being eroded from below by technological changes and changes to industrial relations caused by the decline of heavy industry, and eroded from above as the balance of power shifted toward employers and labor markets were loosened, making macropolitical bargaining less useful. Similarly, Offe (1985) emphasizes structural changes to work, the split of labor markets into primary and secondary, and the vertical division among workers. Yet, as Hyman (1992) reminds us, theses of disaggregation and fragmentation of labor are often based on a false idea of past unity and solidarity. The "working class" was never merely an empirical category, but more like a rallying cry and an abstraction. Solidarity between workers was always unlikely, unnatural, and required great effort; working-class life was a range of different experiences, and unions had to cope with both unifying and fragmenting tendencies within the working class. To identify the previous socioeconomic regime "with a stable combination of Keynesianism and Fordism is to underestimate the capacity of actors to seek and sustain its benefits in more difficult times" (Molina and Rhodes 2002, 315).

In this spirit, this book recognizes labor as an active agent, (potentially) able to thwart, influence, and shape the neoliberalization of Israeli society and oppose the demands of capital. It will therefore focus on how organized labor is struggling against the forces and processes that are depoliticizing it and pushing it out of the political arena and what the implications and consequences of this struggle are—however successful they may be deemed to be. These are both material and symbolic struggles; emergent and hegemonic narratives will also be investigated as shaping the role of, and perceptions of the role of, organized labor. It must be emphasized that this book is not concerned about whether Israeli society is an aberration of the sociopolitical regime known as corporatism, in which organized labor (trade unions), organized capital (employers' associations), and the state negotiated over social and economic policies. Neither does it try to discover where corporatism has gone wrong or how we can bring back unions as the main vehicles of worker emancipation. Instead, it attempts to understand the role and status of labor, specifically organized labor, as a sociopolitical entity in Israel's post-Fordist, neoliberal(izing) economy today.

Corporatism: Analytical Concept, Social Structure, and Ideal

In thinking of such labor struggles, the question arises about how we are to make sense of them: What kind of broader conceptual framework can help us get to grips with the issues they raise? Many researchers have suggested Israel has, or had, a variant of corporatism, including a central role for labor organizations and peak-level tripartite bargaining. Corporatism (or neocorporatism, as it came to be known, to distinguish it from its fascist variant) refers to a sociopolitical regime in which labor or workers (through their organizations, mainly unions) and capital (through employers' associations) have a privileged status above all other kinds of interest groups (Berger 1981; Crouch 1983; Martin 1983; Molina and Rhodes 2002; Schmitter 1974). In practice, this meant unions, the state, and employers' organizations negotiated over economic and social policy at various levels, bargaining over wages and employment terms, and in some cases it involved the transfer of certain service provision roles to the union. Given Zionist aspirations to create a state of workers and the centrality of the labor movement in Israel's history, neocorporatism offers an ideal framework for discussing labor's role and status in society.

Corporatism as an analytic concept is intertwined with corporatism as an ideal and as an existing socioeconomic structure. Disentangling the three facets of the term is not always easy, but the strong links between them are in some ways useful to the researcher: the concerns of scholars investigating corporatism as a sociopolitical or socioeconomic structure closely resemble the concerns of those acting within the corporatist structure. Indeed, as Shalev and Grinberg (1989, 2) put it, an important advantage of neocorporatism as a theoretical sociological approach "is the ease with which it translates theoretical concepts into concrete operational definitions. Capital and labor are analyzed in terms of their organizations, political and economic, and their elites. There is no need to employ an intangible concept of the historical or real interests of the working class, as instead different concrete examples of their interests, expressed by trade unions and rank and file workers, are discussed."

The apparent decline of this sociopolitical structure in the region with which it is most strongly associated (western Europe) and elsewhere, and the decline of unions more generally, has led to much research into the ways organized labor is struggling to regain or retain its status and strength (Frege and Kelly 2003; Gumbrell-McCormick and Hyman 2013; Phelan 2007; Schulten, Brandt, and Hermann 2008; Turner 2005). This is the focus of the "union revitalization" literature, a focus that reflects the centrality of unions in the corporatist structure and perhaps also the normative inclinations of many researchers into corporatist industrial relations. As Heery (2003, 278) puts it, "Industrial relations [as a field of research] . . . has never accepted the priority of employer interests or framed its research agenda solely in terms of the needs of managers"; the interests of workers and their organizations are the starting point of this research and the chosen point of view of the researchers. Thus, in addition to tactical and strategic questions of how unions act, much revitalization research contains a normative subtext, as indeed do many of the revitalization efforts of rank-and-file union members: a "vision of expanded democratic representation and social solidarity," of workforce mobilization, democratic voice, the generation of social pressure "that can reform or transform political and economic institutions" (Turner 2005, 387). This is potentially a broader vision of social justice, too.

The study of union revitalization must partly be the study of power and the renewal of the power resources available to workers. Many studies of union power focus on the kinds of activities unions undertake to further their interests (however these may be construed) and the kinds of tangible resources they can muster to ensure these activities take place or are effective (e.g., Freeman and Medoff 1984, 191–206). However, there is a danger that certain union characteristics (such as links with a political party) are perceived as evidence of power in themselves, when they may be leftovers from a previous, more powerful union era or cause researchers to miss other, perhaps more important, sources of power. Thus Sullivan (2010) warns against the "union density bias" that leads to alternative sources of labor power being overlooked, reduces the analysis of a possibly heterogeneous movement (the labor movement) to a single organizational form (the union), and reduces the complex dynamics of union organizing to simple wins and losses of members.

Eric Olin Wright (2000, 1994) offers a conception of power akin to radical theories of power such as that of Steven Lukes (1974), which offers a more critical framework for thinking about labor revitalization. Drawing on Alford and Friedland (1985), Wright defines three "levels of power": (1) situational power is the ability of an actor to get another actor to do as she wants, even in the face of resistance; (2) institutional power (or "negative power") refers to institutional settings that "shape the decision-making agenda in ways which serve the interests of particular groups," and thus excludes certain options from the agenda; (3) systemic power is the most difficult to pin down, the most contentious, and refers to the power to "realize one's interests by virtue of the overall structure of a social system" (E. Wright 1994, 93):

> Systemic power is power embedded in the fundamental nature of the game itself; institutional power is power embodied by the specific rules of the game; and situational power is power deployed in specific moves within a given set of rules. When actors use specific resources strategically to accomplish their goals, they are exercising situational power. The procedural rules which govern how they use these resources reflects [sic] institutional power. And the nature of the social system which determines the range of possible rules and achievable goals reflects systemic power. (E. Wright 1994, 93)

Wright's main concern is class within a capitalist state. He relates situational power to the way actors use resources to maintain class interests, institutional power to the question of how capitalist the state is and how its structures work for capitalist interests, and situational power to how the logic of the social system itself affirms their (capitalists') interests regardless of their conscious strategies or internal organization of political apparatuses (E. Wright 1994, 94–101).

In the later work, Wright (2000, 962) distinguishes between structural and associational power. The former refers to the location of workers within an economic system; thus a tight labor market ("marketplace bargaining power") or the location of workers in a key industrial sector ("workplace bargaining power") would increase workers' structural power (see also Silver 2003, 13). The latter refers to the way workers associate among themselves and create links to other structures or frameworks; thus worker power goes beyond association in a union and encompasses parties, works councils, schemes of worker codetermination, and worker representatives on boards of directors. Dörre (2011, 18–22) elaborates on this distinction by adding "institutional power": this can be conceived as the result of structural and associational negotiation and conflicts, in which institutions "fix and to a certain degree legally codify basic social compromises" (Dörre 2011, 21; this is a more concrete conception than Wright's "institutional power," though of course both conceptions concentrate on the institutions that shape and delimit options for action). Indeed, the tripartite bargaining structures of the corporatist regime are a fine example of organized labor's institutional power. Dörre also notes that institutional power resources can be used when a union's other power resources are declining, at least for a while. Moreover, the development and decline of different types of power clearly influence one another.

An investigation into organized labor's place and role, then, must address those three dimensions or levels of power, going beyond the negotiations between labor and employer organizations to look at the political structure within which such negotiations (or struggles) take place as well as the ideological climate, the political discourses, that affects the legitimacy of structures, groups, and actors in the political and public sphere. Thus this book investigates front-line struggles between specific unions and employers, but also tries to understand how broader structures affect the way the struggle plays out and how various struggles transform broader structures. It also addresses how the "logic" of the social system (in Wright's terms) shapes the struggles and their outcomes—how "systemic power" is manifested and challenged. Indeed, the conceptions of power presented here affirm that it is dynamic, changing over time, and subject to challenge. Structures—the institutions and frameworks of representation and government—are, as Dörre suggests, the concrete results of past struggles and can be strengthened or undermined and delegitimized by new struggles.

Three Spheres of Union Activity

To address these dimensions of power in labor's struggle against neoliberal-ization and the efforts of unions to revitalize, the book views organized labor in Israel through three spheres. As I elaborate below, these spheres reflect the concerns and focus of research into unions and corporatism and draw on the three "levels of analysis" of interest representation as put forward by Claus Offe (1985, 221–258; 1981): the individual (will, consciousness, group identity); the socioeconomic opportunity structure; and the political system that confers status on the organizations. Correspondingly, I have defined these three spheres as (1) union democracy, or the relationship of the workers to the organization that claims to represent them; (2) the balance of power between labor and capital, and the way this potential clash of interests is viewed and played out; and (3) the rela-tionship of labor to the political establishment and wider political community. These spheres can be envisioned as superimposed on the classic neocorporatist triangle of tripartite bargaining between unions, employers, and the state (see figure 1), reflecting this neocorporatist triangular structure but emphasizing the focus on labor and the worker. They can also be imagined as concentric, with the first sphere in the center emphasizing the workers' relationship with the organi-zation that represents them; then the second sphere, emphasizing the immediate struggles of workers and their organizations vis-à-vis capital; and lastly the third, emphasizing the place of labor and its representative organizations within the broader society or polity. These three spheres structure the book, with the first sphere corresponding to part 1, the second to part 2, and the third to part 3.

1. Union Democracy

The centrality of democracy to unions has been lauded ever since Webb and Webb wrote their seminal account of UK unions over a century ago: "When workmen meet together to discuss their grievances—still more, when they form associations of national extent, raise an independent revenue, elect permanent representation committees, and proceed to bargain and agitate as corporate bodies—they are forming . . . a spontaneous democracy of their own" (Webb and Webb 1897, 808).

However, a union's relationship with its members is complex and dynamic (Wood 2004). As a democratic membership organization, a union can emphasize a participatory conception of democracy or a more liberal conception based on a division of labor between leaders (political actors) and the population (mem-bers), in which accountability has an important place (see Parry and Moran 1994, 5). Perhaps due to corporatism's earlier connection with fascism (see Molina and

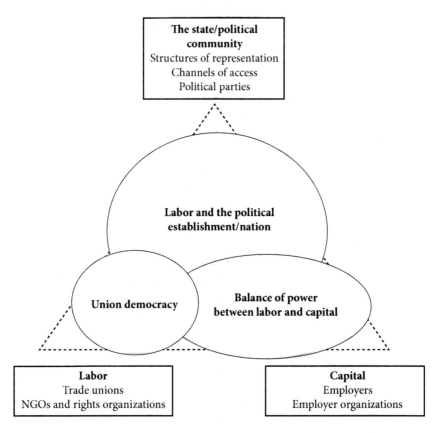

FIGURE 1.   The three spheres overlaid on the standard corporatist triangle

Rhodes 2002), early scholars of corporatism were concerned with the potentially undemocratic nature of organizations controlling or restricting their members and with the possibility that corporatist organizations would undermine parliamentary democracy (see Lehmbruch 1977). Ross Martin (1983), working within the pluralist approach, reviewed the work of prominent "new corporatists" such as Philippe Schmitter, Richard Hyman, Samuel Beer, Leo Panitch, Alan Cawson, and Andrew Shonfield and teased out a continuum ranging from corporatism to pluralism, focusing on groups' access to, and the role they are accorded by, government. This continuum reflected the worry that too much corporatism may be harmful to parliamentary democracy, as it privileged certain interest groups over others, giving them an advantage over sectors of society whose only voice or influence on state and government was via the ballot.

In response, Colin Crouch (1983, 452) noted that Martin had missed a crucial aspect of new corporatism: "interest organizations constrain and discipline their own members for the sake of some presumed 'general' interest as well as (or even instead of) representing them." He proposed an alternative continuum: at one pole, organizations discipline their members in favor of a general interest; at the other, the organization "merely" represents their particular (individual) interests. His continuum thus runs from authoritarian corporatism, in which individuals have little voice or influence; through liberal or "bargained" corporatism, in which organizations exercise discipline to a certain extent; on through pluralism/ bargaining, in which organizations represent members' interests but compromise is still an option; to contestation in which organizations act for the demands of members without compromise at all (Crouch 1983, 456–457). Somewhere between liberal corporatism and pluralism there is a qualitative break, because of organizations' formal role in the sociopolitical structure: "[In liberal corporatism], *in exchange for securing certain ends* (the pluralist or bargained component which differentiates this from authoritarian corporatism), the participating groups accept joint responsibility for the order and progress of the system as a whole and undertake to help guarantee the on-going commitment of their members to cooperation" (Crouch 1983, 457).

Here Crouch touches on the way corporatist organizations are integrated into the sociopolitical structure and granted a formal role in the mechanisms and frameworks of government and administration. Offe (1981, 137) also emphasizes the organizations' formal, legal, recognized status, "as opposed to relations of informal cooperation between political and other segments of the elite, clientelistic relations, and status resulting from ad hoc tactical considerations of various groups or branches of the state apparatus." Lehmbruch goes beyond interest representation to explicitly emphasize the role played by such organizations in shaping political culture and broader political goals:

> Corporatism is . . . an institutionalized pattern of policy-formation in which large interest organizations cooperate with each other and with public authorities not only in the articulation (or even "intermediation") of interests, but—in its developed forms—in the "authoritative allocation of values" [after David Easton] and in the implementation of such policies. It is precisely because of the intimate mutual penetration of state bureaucracies and large interest organizations that the traditional concept of "interest representation" becomes quite inappropriate for a theoretical understanding of corporatism. Rather, we are dealing with an integrated system of "societal guidance." (Lehmbruch 1977, 94)

These views recognize the potential power of such organizations, and it is clear why the concern for fair democratic representation arises. For this reason, the legitimacy of the corporatist organizations also becomes an issue—particularly for labor, whose organizations had a prominent position in the neocorporatist regimes being studied by these scholars and that rapidly came to have a central place in corporatist theorizing.

The ability of members to participate in and influence the union's activities and setting of priority can increase a union's legitimacy, which enhances its ability to impose discipline—most notably, members' acceptance of wage restraint—and the validity of collective agreements. On the other hand, a union must also be legitimate in the eyes of the other social partners (employers' organizations and the state). A militant rank and file can undermine this, making the union appear to be an unreliable negotiating partner. This conundrum has been noted by research on union revitalization that often differentiates between a "partnership approach" based on a union's good relations with the other social partners and an "organizing approach" based on worker activism (see Badigannavar and Kelly 2011; Frege and Kelly 2003; Heery 2002). Legitimacy can also be undermined by low density (doubly so if the negotiating partner, the employers' association, also suffers from low membership numbers; see Mundlak 2009, 777).

Moreover, a union and its members do not exist in a vacuum: other unions may compete for workers' membership by offering better services, more opportunities for participation, more advantageous collective agreements, a more persuasive ideology of solidarity (or, alternatively, of pragmatism), and more established connections with the other social partners. Indeed, as Hyman (2001) notes, the term "social partnership" has not always been used in the same way in different countries in different periods. Sometimes it has implied a harmonious working together toward national economic goals or a temporary cessation of class conflict for short-term gains. Sometimes, on the other hand, it has been criticized as class collaboration or for assuming (or implying) parity of status between the parties in the corporatist compromise. At various times, for various reasons, (potential) members may be drawn by different characteristics and ideologies of a union, or even look beyond unions to other organizations able to represent their interests or permit their participation in campaigns on issues close to their hearts.

In this sphere, then, the book investigates unions as vehicles for democratic action and participation, rivalry between alternative workers' organizations, and worker dissatisfaction with the organizations that are supposed to represent them, particularly in light of the Histadrut's reputation for an autocratic, top-down approach to labor organizing and campaigning. It asks, what new forms of labor organizing and representation are emerging, and what is the nature of these new forms? In what ways are workers themselves active in seeking representation, if at all? The book also explores the potential—and perceived potential—of workers' organizations as channels for voice and influence to reach a wider audience and affect broader social issues. Against what is labor struggling, and toward whom does it direct its demands?

2. The Balance of Power between Labor and Capital

At the most basic level, unions enable workers to face their employer in a labor dispute, supported by other workers and an organization with financial and legal resources. Martin (1983, 89), for example, in his overview of prominent neocorporatist theorists, noted that the centrality of labor and capital (their representative organizations) was among the defining elements of corporatism (though not always stated explicitly). Lehmbruch (1977, 96) noted that "the most important interest groups included in the corporatist pattern are organized labor and business."

Taking a far wider perspective, a union (or labor federation) can represent labor as a class in its struggle against capital as a class. Corporatism provided an institutional structure for settling the clash of interests between labor and capital, based on the class compromise; it therefore acknowledged this clash as an inherent aspect of capitalist labor relations. The struggle between labor and capital, though institutionalized and thus at least partially depoliticized within the corporatist regime (Offe 1981, 146), was never settled once and for all; rather, both labor and capital are waging this struggle constantly, on different levels, with the advantage going sometimes to one side, sometimes to the other.

However, according to Offe (1981), there are important differences between the ways labor and capital are incorporated into the political order. In a paper discussing the reasons for the adoption or development of corporatism, he asserts that the corporatist structure "compensates for the functional deficiencies of democratic institutions by depoliticizing conflict," in other words by institutionalizing the conflict between capital and labor, but it does so asymmetrically. This asymmetry is built into the nature of labor and capital and the possibilities for organizing that are open to each (Offe 1981, 147). First, when capital decides to take action against labor (to withhold employment), it can do so individually, but when labor acts against capital (strikes), it must do so collectively. Furthermore, worker interests are divided within the worker: wages, working conditions, and continuity of employment are all in an individual's interests, but these ends can be mutually conflicting.[1] Only an organization that acts for the collective can calculate the optimal balance between them. Hence a labor organization is a quantitative aggregate of means of power (a collective of workers acting in concert) and also provides a qualitative definition of what that power should seek to gain. This explains the importance of both solidarity and discipline to labor organizations and makes the issue of democracy and legitimacy particularly salient for them.

Capital organizations do not have this problem. They represent interests that already exist, and they pursue ends that are already defined on an individual level. There is rarely any conflict between individual and collective interests.[2] An employers' organization provides services (which a firm would anyway have to provide itself) and acts to "formulate and defend in the political arena those *individual* interests ... that are *common* to all or most member firms" (Offe 1981, 148). Therefore interest organization is more important to labor than to capital, and any restriction on forms of association or the right to organize will be more harmful to labor than to capital.

Finally, unions are expected to control their members, who receive some kind of benefit in return for discipline. Capital organizations, Offe asserts, have no such control over their members, who may do as they please. The only way to control individual firms is for the state to "design policies that are most conducive to profits" (Offe 1981, 150), in the hope of thus influencing their behavior.

The comparison with pluralism made by early scholars of corporatism is still relevant; as Streeck notes, the fear of a few large organized interest groups taking over state branches or defining the "common good" in their own terms has been raised again:

> The hegemonic theory of the day, the dominant public discourse and, increasingly, the practical wisdom of political decision-makers seem to have more or less accepted the neo-liberal equation of interest politics with rent-seeking; of cooperation with collusion; of inclusion of organized interests in the public sphere with exclusion of those *not* represented by established organizations; and of neo-corporatism with social closure and a political-economic conspiracy in favor of a new establishment of job owners, native citizens, old industries and the like. (Streeck 2006, 29)

In investigating this sphere, then, this book tries to determine in which arenas struggle is taking place and what means, tools, and power resources are at the service of the sides involved. It investigates whether and how labor is trying to persuade the public that it represents more than its own narrow interests, and the status of capital in this regard. It asks, how is organized labor maintaining its legitimacy as a political actor, if at all? What connections with the political establishment are being maintained, undermined, reinforced, or created? The book also looks at how structures that once regulated the struggle (including the labor courts) have changed, and what discourses (ideologies) are arising or being shaped and enlisted in the struggle. What are labor rights in today's economy, and how are they perceived?

3. Labor, the Political Establishment, and the Nation

A central pillar of corporatism was labor's privileged access to the political estab-lishment and to decision-making forums. Much of the literature about the cor-poratist regime focuses on what Upchurch, Taylor, and Mathers (2009) call the "dominant party–union nexus." According to this body of literature, and accord-ing to dominant streams of social-democratic thought, the union was to promote (some kind of) socialism by its activities in the sphere of production, while the labor party (or social-democratic party, etc.) was to do the same in the political sphere: thus emerged a division of labor "in which the party pursued the politics of state and the unions conducted the politics of civil society" (Upchurch, Taylor, and Mathers 2009, 2; see also Hyman 2001, 19–20; Tarrow 1994, 139–192). This was in keeping with the fundamental compromise between capital and labor: unions accommodated capitalism in the workplace, while social-democratic par-ties sought reform in the political sphere; thus a social-democratic unionism developed that tried to overcome (settle) the contradiction between (nondemo-cratic) capitalism and democracy. As Piven (1991, 3) notes, despite differences between countries, it can generally be said that in democratic Western states, the "industrial working class, trade union membership and vote totals of labor-based political parties grew in tandem." Labor parties influenced labor politics more widely by helping to shape collectives and cleavages, identify issues of contention, and mobilize people around a common set of programs and symbols. In return, the party could draw on union members' votes and the threat of strikes (Piven 1991, 17).

Close coordination was in the interests of both party and union, and the rela-tions between them were clearly important: the union was in some very concrete ways the voice of the people (see also Fick 2009), and it channeled this voice into the sphere of decision making and policy forming through its representatives in the party. The party, for its part, could count on the union for electoral support, as well as (in some cases) funding. Thus various connections between the party and union developed in countries with a strong social-democratic movement or powerful labor movement, involving various organizational, personal, and struc-tural links (see Upchurch, Taylor, and Mathers 2009).

Unions were inevitably political organizations; regulating the labor market is a political task, and this was unions' main function: labor aimed not merely to influence policies, but to affect the very structure and rules of the game within which policies were formed (Hyman and Gumbrell-McCormick 2010, 316). Rep-resented in democratic institutions, organized labor could also claim for itself (or was granted) various administrative roles such as pension management or wel-fare benefits distribution (the "Ghent system"), thus consolidating its position as an essential part of government and enhancing its influence on the political establishment (Tarrow 1994, 139). To some extent, interdependencies developed between labor organizations and other branches of government and state bodies, which also fostered political norms in favor of labor involvement. This, then, was the basis of the corporatist regime but also of the welfare state even where classic corporatism was weak, such as the United Kingdom (see Upchurch, Taylor, and Mathers 2009).

Now the source of organized labor's mass power has declined as class identities have fragmented, a process accelerated with the influx of new groups of workers; moreover, the power of voters on the state seems less relevant now that international organizations appear more powerful than democratic governments (Piven 1991, 8). Some unions have responded by disentangling "their close relations with political parties and the political system," but this has not done much to increase their strength or make them more attractive to workers (Leijnse 1996, 251). In fact, "unions [have] lost most of what was left of their direct influence on politics" (Leijnse 1996, 251). However, as James (2004, 307–312) notes, the wider political objectives of unions can be pursued through other channels, not just via links with a political party, including lobbying decision makers and parties, publicity campaigns, demonstrations, and campaigns with other interest groups. Other forms of influence include close personal relationships, unionists on party-affiliated councils, and unionists in parliament, as ministers, or on advisory government committees.

Furthermore, as Crouch (2006, 52) asserts, neocorporatism is only relevant if there is a "manageable and definable universe across which organizations can be said to be encompassing"; the theory holds only to the extent "that there is a relatively bounded universe linking fiscal and monetary policy, labor markets and labor market organizations and the scope of firms." With globalization and capital mobility, this may no longer be the case; the position of organized labor as a corporatist partner is thus further undermined, and organized labor's influence perhaps even more dependent on other (nonunion, non–labor party) channels.

In this sphere, then, the book investigates the implications of the unraveling of the link between the labor party and the main labor federation, the ejection of this federation from the sociopolitical regime, and the new paths open to labor for influencing the political sphere. It does this within the context of Israel's globalized economy, in which an increasing number of noncitizen workers take part in the labor market, and explores whether—and to what extent—the "relatively bounded universe" of corporatism has frayed. It asks, what is the connection or relationship between organized labor, the labor market, the economy, and the political community as a whole? Thus it investigates the role of labor and the power of workers' organizations within the framework of the nation, trying to understand the relationship between national identity, citizen, and worker, particularly in light of the labor movement's critical role in the establishment of the State of Israel and the continued—if not increasing—prominence of ethnicity in Israel's national politics and social issues. Do the new labor market structures and organizations provide opportunities for worker representation for those previously excluded from or marginalized by the Zionist, corporatist political regime?

Coda: Some Words on the Research Process

The research that led to this book draws on the tradition of historical sociology and its principal concerns that focus on issues of democracy and the development of capitalism. As Delanty and Isin (2003, 2) note, the rise of historical sociology was a reaction against a historiography that focused on the "birth and 'progress' of nations and the march of liberty," and turned its attention to conflict and struggle. Key areas of concern in this tradition were the relations of capital to the nation-state and the relation of economic forms of social life to political forms, and thus also classes and nations (Fine and Chernilo 2003). Smith (1991) suggests that historical sociology seeks to understand the mechanisms through which societies change and reproduce, or more specifically, the structures that aid or thwart actors in their endeavors. Thus a central focus is the relationship of processes and structures to acts and events, especially as regards the relationship between capitalism and democracy: the "social preconditions and consequences of attempts to implement or impede such values as freedom, equality and justice" (Smith 1991, 1).

I also draw inspiration from Skocpol (1984, 368) who defines historical sociology as a method that "uses concepts to develop meaningful interpretations of broad historical patterns" and explains that "meaningful" means significant for the actors involved, the "culturally embedded intentions of . . . actors in the given historical settings under investigation," and significant for current readers and current issues: "both the topic chosen for historical study and the kinds of arguments developed about it should be culturally or politically 'significant' in the present." This is a method that uses general, broadly applicable concepts to guide the investigation and direct attention to the questions being asked. Similarly, I adopt the focus of comparative historical analysis on processes over time, emphasizing the historically contextualized and wary of the universal; on the other hand, I also accept its enjoiner to tackle big themes that are substantively and normatively significant for many, not just for specialists (see Mahoney and Rueschemeyer 2003).

In practice, for this research, this means concentrating on sites of labor struggle, particularly the struggles of organized labor and the people as they endeavor to make their voices heard and bring their demands to the notice of those with the power to make decisions. I see struggle as an arena in which the balance of forces and changes to that balance become visible to the researcher: in the case of labor struggles, it is here that we see concrete expressions of interests and tangible applications of power, as labor organizations, workers and groups of workers, NGOs, pressure groups, the courts and labor courts, employers and employer organizations, and the state or representatives of various state or governmental bodies face each other over a specific battle line that can have repercussions extending far beyond the specific arena of struggle. Indeed, struggles, specifically workers' struggles, and the issues of common cause, solidarity, identity, and unity they raise, have a long history in sociological thinking and research, from Marx and Marxists such as György Lukács through Antonio Gramsci to Michael Mann, Ernesto Laclau, and Jacques Rancière.

I concentrate on recent labor struggles in Israel that have in some way appeared unusual or have included aspects that could shed light on new developments in the field of organized labor and labor representation. During the period of research that led to this book, I followed many more campaigns than could be analyzed in detail here; this gave me a broader overview of labor organizing in general. In each campaign, my overarching aim was to understand the cause of the struggle, which actors were involved, their aspirations and intentions, the balance of power between them, and the outcome of the struggle.

For general information I turned to the media (mainly though not exclusively the financial papers *TheMarker* and *Globes* and their websites).[3] I also used documents (reports, press releases, updates) and the websites of the organizations involved. Of course, all documents and websites were accessed with the permission of the people involved or else were in the public domain. In some cases I read reports from government bodies and NGOs, and in cases in which the courts were involved I also read court documents, particularly labor court decisions. On top of this, I conducted twenty-nine formal interviews with key figures in worker struggles and labor relations, including heads of workers' committees, union representatives, journalists covering particular sectors, activists, a labor lawyer, a former wages officer at the Finance Ministry, and a former National Labor Court president. (A full list of interviewees can be found before the references.) The interviews were unstructured and lasted between an hour and two hours. The direction of the conversation and the questions raised depended, of course, on the interviewees and their role or position in the organization or campaign that interested me, but in general I asked about the organization, the people involved, the discussions held, the choices made, and any aspects that may not have been picked up by the regular media. I also asked about the past and future intentions of the people or organizations involved, requested clarifications of aspects or events that may have received only partial or vague coverage in the media, and asked about motivations. Interviews were taped with the interviewees' permission and transcribed.[4]

I made it clear to the interviewees that in general I am supportive of organized labor, though I am fully committed to the norms of academic disciplinary fact-gathering and theoretical analysis. Since the interviews were conducted as a conversation, disagreements sometimes arose; it must therefore be emphasized that I bear full responsibility for the interpretation of how and why campaigns were conducted, and that my understanding of these campaigns (and of the status of organized labor in general) does not necessarily tally with that of the interviewees. None of the interviewees requested anonymity, though some requested that certain information be kept off the record, and of course these requests have been respected.

In addition, I conducted many informal conversations with activists and workers involved in campaigns, mostly during my attendance at protests during strikes. None of these conversations has been quoted in what follows, since they were not documented in any formal way, but they did allow me to obtain a feel for the atmosphere and the kinds of issues under debate and often led me to understand who the main figures were in a given campaign.

The empirical research was conducted from the end of 2010 until the middle of 2014. Interviews were conducted from August 2011 to the beginning of 2014 (the date of each interview is noted in the list of interviewees). In analyzing workers' struggles in detail, I limited the research to struggles held during the period of research, but of course background material goes back a number of years (depending on each case or organization concerned), while the broader historical view necessarily refers to many decades of development and change.

Part 1

RENEGOTIATING UNION DEMOCRACY

THE RISE OF LABOR ACTIVISM

From around 2010 onward, a groundswell of activism and a slew of high-profile labor disputes brought organized labor and unionizing into the headlines and raised public awareness of labor issues. For about three years, it seemed that in any given week, one bitter dispute or another was in the headlines, many of them apparently with far-reaching implications for organized labor in general. Some of these disputes led to strikes that left the public without essential services; sometimes the strikers received widespread public support, but at other times the strikes were loudly condemned. Most prominent among these disputes were the strikes by the junior doctors (resident physicians), the social workers, and the railway workers, though there were many other labor campaigns at the time, and in fact the wave of labor activism had begun a few years earlier. These campaigns constitute the springboard for the discussions in part 1.

Participation: Labor Activism as Grassroots Initiative

One of the most salient aspects of many of these cases was the workers' desire to participate. Participation as a value in itself was as important to many activists as improved collective agreements, shored up by the perception that through participation in workplace organizing, they could roll back the policies and processes that were negatively affecting their employment terms. This desire to participate was clearly seen in the social workers' campaign of 2011, which saw an enormous surge of activism and the emergence of various organizations that channeled the organizing energies into existing representational frameworks.

Of the social workers who are organized, most are represented by the Social Workers Union (SWU), which was established in 1937 as a union within the Histadrut and combines the functions of a workers' organization, a professional association, and a lobby. Its 1994 campaign had included a month's strike and had led to an agreement generally perceived as successful. However, during the intervening decades, social work, like all areas of public services, has been affected by increasing liberalization and deregulation, declining support among political elites for welfare services (Filc 2004; Shalev 2006), and declining budget and introduction of means testing (Ajzenstadt and Rosenhek 2002; Rosenhek 2002a). Social workers have seen their professional standing and remuneration decline and their professional field shrink as the government decreased its responsibility for welfare and outsourced provisions of specific services into the private sector, to nongovernmental organizations and for-profit firms (Gidron, Bar, and Katz 2004; Loewenberg 1998). Outsourcing of social services has also led to a decline in SWU membership numbers and a crisis of representative legitimacy. This led activists in 2011 to concentrate on getting social workers, particularly from the private sector, back into the union. They aimed not merely to improve employment terms, but also to end the privatization and retrenchment of welfare services.

In response to muted demands for greater democracy in representation, the SWU had changed its constitution in 2007 to increase workplace representation at the expense of regional representation, and professional cells representing sectors within the field of social work were integrated into the higher institutions of the SWU. However, since the SWU is part of the Histadrut, it had had to have the changes approved, and the Histadrut had added its own stipulations: regional heads, previously elected, were now to be appointed, and SWU general elections were to be held every five years instead of four (Shlosberg 2012). Social workers still felt disconnected from the organization that was supposed to represent them; the union, and the Histadrut, seemed to have no space for their voices.

During the weeks leading up to the strike, social workers made great effort to activate union members throughout the country, and many were very much involved in demonstrations, discussions, updates via social media, and direct action in the framework of new organizations that emerged from 2007 onward, persuading people to sign up to the SWU and explaining the campaign and its aims to the public. Tami Farber, who led the breakaway social workers group Osot Hasharon and later ran in the SWU elections, noted, "We got to the strike very, very much ready for a strike; . . . members saw themselves as very much a part of it, very committed and recruited, and as a result of this I too went, to demonstrations, events, and I was very active on Facebook" (interview).

The emergence of new groups and organizations is a good example of the social workers' desire to participate and take things more directly into their own hands, and some of these groups had emerged from activist initiatives. For example, in June 2007, a petition signed by some three thousand social workers called on the SWU to intervene against privatization and strengthen the SWU as a significant player in social work policies. A group later known as Atidenu coalesced around the initiators of the petition together with members of a group calling itself the Forum for Social Justice. Also in 2007, Atidenu established the Center for the Rights of those Harmed by Privatization of Social Services, in cooperation with the SWU and the Social Work Department of Ben-Gurion University. The center focused on outreach efforts to assist social workers in the private sector and promote the importance of being in the union. According to Inbal Shlosberg (interview), chair of Atidenu from 2007 to 2012, it received some funding from the SWU, but its activities were limited due to lack of resources.

In 2009, Osim Shinui was established. This was a student initiative that aimed to alert social work students to the state of the profession, get the next generation involved, and influence public policy. It cooperated with the SWU but emphasized its independence, though it also fought for students' constitutionally protected right to participate as observers in SWU institutions. In addition to these two principle organizations, other smaller groups of social workers emerged, each with a slightly different orientation and role in the struggle, including the Forum of the Social Workers Struggle, Social Workers for Social Justice, and Social Workers for a Different Histadrut.

The Beersheva demonstration two weeks before the strike is another example of the drive to participate, regardless of the union's position: Atidenu had submitted an activity program to the SWU, aimed at getting social workers around the country involved, but the SWU was reluctant to adopt the program, fearing that a spate of small demonstrations around the country would not look good in the media. Nonetheless, Atidenu went ahead with the Beersheva demonstration: "[The SWU didn't consider] how to keep social workers committed to the struggle. . . . It's important that people don't sit at home as if it's a holiday, that they go out and protest for their wage. . . . And it happened, a demonstration of a thousand people, very impressive. . . . The workers said they felt part of it; in previous strikes they had not participated. . . . That's the power of it, the significance" (Shlosberg, interview).

In many campaigns, this participation was considered necessary in order to extend the issue beyond the specific collective agreement being negotiated, to address broader policy concerns that would affect the future status of labor in each sector. At the railway, for example, the struggle was about more than employment terms right from the beginning.[1] Discontent had begun in 2010,

when certain worker committee members became aware of creeping outsourcing, which was taking place without worker representatives being consulted.
Soon, it had developed into opposition to the planned restructuring of the company. When the outsourcing of carriage maintenance was added to the list of
changes the railway management hoped to push through, the workers claimed
this would undermine organized labor and constituted reform that would affect
employment terms. The labor court too recognized that the carriage maintenance
plans were in effect outsourcing: the contract workers that the company planned
to hire, it said, would work "shoulder to shoulder" with railway workers on the
same premises; it thereby rejected the government's position that outsourcing is
a decision for the sovereign alone and said the government must respond to the
workers' legitimate fears (Request for Appeal 50556-09-11).

The blustery tactics of the transport minister seemed intended to make it clear
that the workers were not entitled to have any influence on company policies or
reform. He noted disapprovingly that the workers' campaign was a struggle for
control over the company and reiterated that he and the government were responsible on the ministerial side while the management controlled the company professionally; the workers were only responsible for workers' rights (Nissan and Niv
2012). He threatened to sign an agreement including outsourcing if the workers
refused to compromise (Nissan and Niv 2012), and on at least two occasions he
made explicit threats to close the railway and reopen it as a new company, thereby
voiding collective agreements (*Globes* 2012b; Nissan, Barkat, and Niv 2012).

Labor Activism from Outside the Workplace

The case of the subcontracted cleaners at Ben-Gurion University is an extreme
example in which labor has been denied any influence at all over employment
terms, but in this case participation took a very different form. The organizing
of the cleaners began as a student and faculty initiative. In 2005, some students
discussed the employment of the cleaners during a course in the Politics and
Government Department, and some of these students then joined an organization known as Tzach (acronym of "social justice" in Hebrew—*tzedeq chevrati*)
and began a campaign to improve the employment terms of the cleaners. Other
organizations joined the campaign, forming the Coalition for Direct Employment, which organized protests and demonstrations and lobbied the university.
Eventually, the general union Koach Laovdim was added to the many organizations involved in the Coalition. Through the collective channels now legally open
to the workers as a result of the union's involvement, negotiations began toward
a collective agreement with the employers.

At that time, some 250 cleaners were employed at the university via two con-tractors. As workers, the cleaners had much in common with precarious workers noted in other studies, especially studies of migrant laborers (e.g., Alberti, Hol-gate, and Tapia 2013; Fine 2005; Gordon 2005; Holgate 2005; Milkman 2000), though in this case the workers had at least formal citizenship. The majority (85 percent) lived in the Negev area (a relatively poor and deprived region), immigrants from the former USSR, Ethiopia, and South America. Most had a low socioeconomic status; some were single mothers and the only breadwinners of the family (Amos and Baharav 2012, 115). Many were employed for just nine months (laid off for the summer, when the university is less active), and this led to the familiar problem of ineligibility for various employee rights and benefits that are linked to seniority. There were also violations of labor law.

The difficulties of organizing such workers have long been recognized (see Shamir 2016), though unions are increasingly attempting to tackle the issue (see Heery 2009). Cleaners are usually physically dispersed among various buildings and tend to work alone; many are new immigrants who do not have full control of the local language and have no language in common with other cleaners; work-ers are often employed on a part-time basis; they often have little knowledge of laws protecting them or channels available to them for redress; and they tend to see problems as one-off issues, not part of a larger struggle (Bernstein 1986, 411). Moreover, union members and contingent workers may often have conflicting interests, though as MacKenzie (2010, 154–155) points out, balancing competing interests of various worker groups has always been a central union role.

As Benjamin, Bernstein, and Motzafi-Haller (2010, 339) note, cleaning work has long been "exclusionary in relation to employment-related entitlements," and increasingly so as more is undertaken via subcontractors. In subcontracted work, profit margins are often slim and the main expense is labor. With high turnover and no tenure, there is no need to invest in a worker's future, no need for pen-sion schemes, sick funds, or sick leave, and the labor process is intensified to the full: "Thus the aspects inherent in capitalist relations, the extraction of labor for the maximization of profits in return for the reproduction of labor power, will be interpreted in the most immediate and narrow sense" (Bernstein 1986, 399).

As cleaning is outsourced, cleaning *work* becomes cleaning *service*, thus commodifying the worker because "it shifts cleaning payment from negotia-tion concerning labor relations to one of the price of a purchased commodity" (Nisim and Benjamin 2010, 221). The worker becomes invisible to the client company (the company ordering the cleaning services from the contractor) and to the client company's employees too, through both physical (work in isolation or during different hours) and social distance. As Nisim and Benja-min (2010) note in their study of the dehumanization of cleaners, this further reduces their access to the forces shaping their working lives, which is reflected in high turnover: the only way workers have of resisting the dehumanizing process is by exiting—absenteeism or simply quitting. They are unable to enter the "negotiated order" (Strauss 1978); they are voiceless. This suggests that lack of unionism among cleaners is not merely related to the power gap between workers and employers, but related to the fact that cleaning employees "are continuously constituted as a non-party in labor relations negotiations" (Nisim and Benjamin 2010, 230).

This exclusion, Maor (2012, 47) suggests, should be seen in the context of attempts to break organized labor, which began in the 1980s under Prime Minister Yitzhak Shamir. One of the first steps was the development of labor contractors instead of employment services to place workers. So it is not merely the objective situation of subcontracted cleaners that makes organizing difficult, but the fact that one of the reasons for their existence is the desire to avoid such organizing.

The organizers in this case faced all these issues. The various cultural and linguistic backgrounds of the cleaners meant the activists had to exercise great sensitivity. For example, according to Orna Amos who was involved in the campaign from the beginning, some from the former USSR were suspicious of the initiative because it seemed like communism to them. Some of those from Ethiopia did not read or write, which meant the usual organizing props such as leaflets and email were completely irrelevant. Some had almost no understanding of their situation as employees and were convinced they were employed directly by the State of Israel. Upon hearing they were to be dismissed, the workers went on strike, but the first steps toward this strike were not driven by any ideas of collective action; rather, they were driven by a much more basic understanding of what it means to be fired: "You screw me, I'll screw you" (Amos, interview).

The knowledge required for organizing was brought in from outside, via the students and staff who got involved initially, in keeping with Nisim and Benjamin's observation: "Under the subcontracting employment system, employees can only become a party in labor relations negotiations under the aegis of solidarity from other social forces (e.g. consumers and/or activists) that provide alternative humanizing sources" (2010, 230). These activists channeled the cleaners' grievances into forms (a workers' committee, for example) of which the workers themselves had had no idea. The same knowledge enabled them to identify the scare tactics used against the workers and the steps taken against a committee member (who had stayed on after other members stepped down), which included increasing his workload, making him work in isolated places to prevent contact with other workers, threats of dismissal, and finally also dismissal.

Moreover, it was the activists' contacts with the organizations in the coalition and support from other committees at the university that led to his reinstatement (Amos and Baharav 2012, 117–118).

Similarly, the strength of the cleaners was based not on traditional threats of strike or disruption but on public pressure applied through the broad coalition of organizations appealing to the young and educated—campus students and staff. The coalition included workers' organizations and representatives of other worker committees, but also rights organizations and student union representatives. At first, the coalition aimed to promote direct employment specifically for cleaners in institutions of higher education, but in 2012 it widened its goal to advance direct employment for all, and many other organizations joined.[2] Pressure was directed toward the university, in a kind of naming-and-shaming campaign; the activists did not address the legal employer (the contractor) at all.[3] Neither did they turn to the courts, believing that public pressure was more effective (Amos, interview).

Indeed, the traditional component of the campaign—the organizing of workers and the collective agreement—was the least successful, even though the activists considered this an important part. Following the strike, the university agreed to some of the cleaners' demands (though it still refused to employ them directly) (Amos and Baharav 2012, 116). From the point of view of many of the workers, the issue was closed. All but one of the committee members stepped down. The main drive for organizing the workers into a more stable committee and representational framework still came from the initial organizers and later from the on-campus lobby that involved various organizations, and not from the cleaners themselves, who were mostly concerned with obtaining direct employment (Amos, interview).

So the case of the university cleaners perhaps indicates the emergence of a more radical conception of labor organizing that, in Israel, has never been seen before. The old style unionism may be on the defensive, but something new is taking shape: a radical labor activism that draws inspiration from a discourse of social rights, rejecting the individualization of social problems and circumventing the apparent unwillingness of the old unionism to act in defense of contingent workers. But it also illustrates the weakness of this style of organizing: the campaign had little structural foundation, instead drawing strength from the moral conscience and social capital of the already privileged, the educated students and faculty of the university, in contrast to the power resources mobilized by traditional unions that were rooted in the social relations of capitalism. Appeals to solidarity were directed beyond the workplace (students and faculty are on campus but do not share their workspace with the cleaners). The Coalition, still very active, risks becoming something akin to top-down assistance, without empowering the workers, and thus perhaps offers only a transient and easily reversible respite from precariousness.

Whose Side Are You On?

The examples discussed so far, as well as other organizing initiatives in the same period, clearly suggest that at least some groups of workers and some of the general public want to participate more fully in labor campaigns and also believe that this participation is necessary for shoring up the union. There is clearly a growing awareness among workers and the general public, reflected in the case of the cleaners in particular, that workers' rights are at risk and that the workplace is a legitimate focus for broader social struggle, even when that workplace has no organized labor. Notably, workers are eager to create new groups to focus their activities, and are even willing to go against the leadership of their union, particularly the Histadrut: the rise of activism is unmistakably coupled to frustration with and lack of trust in established representative organizations.

This was abundantly clear in the case of the cleaners at Ben-Gurion University: before the campaign, the cleaners had paid an agency fee to the Histadrut (they were not members) and said they had turned to the Histadrut for help a number of times, but each time the worker in question had been fired soon after.[4] They were sure the Histadrut and the contractors were colluding. The fear was so great that some cleaners even refused to talk to student volunteers about their employment at first (Amos and Baharav 2012, 117). Later, the students and staff at the university who were still the main leaders of the initiative presented the workers with the option of joining the Histadrut or Koach Laovdim, and the workers chose the latter not because of the supposed benefits but because they had no faith in the Histadrut. Other workers' organizations, too, are seen as undemocratic, fossilized, corrupt, and unresponsive to workers' needs and demands, though the Histadrut is the focus of the most ire.

The Histadrut's "legitimacy gap," Mundlak (2009) suggests, is partly due to its hegemony as a (still) powerful workers' organization affecting the lives of a huge percentage of the population, with a high level of coverage of collective agreements but with low membership density. However, the cases discussed here suggest that this frustration has deeper roots. One problem is the Histadrut's structure with a strict hierarchy and a powerful leadership, which enables the organization to sign collective agreements without the assent of the workers or worker committees. It can also remove worker committees that do not toe the central Histadrut line, though some unions have more autonomy than others and are less subject to the Histadrut leadership's discipline. This centralized structure remained even after the reforms of 1994 (though the reforms, merging the forty-four trade unions into thirty, did grant the trade unions a little more autonomy). The National (General) Convention, the highest elected institution, is still elected according to party or faction (not by workers through trade union branches). These are often identified with national parties, and the number of delegates sent to the convention is proportional to the number of votes received by the party. The convention sets the Histadrut's goals and elects the House of Representatives. The Histadrut Leadership (formerly the Central Committee), responsible for day-to-day operations, is appointed by the Histadrut chairperson and approved by the House of Representatives. The chairperson (formerly the secretary general) is elected every five years in national direct elections of all Histadrut members. Shop-floor representation is through workers' committees that are independently elected in each enterprise and represent the Histadrut, but they are not part of its administration. (Large committees nonetheless wield considerable power due to their ability to paralyze the economy.) Individuals join the Histadrut and are only then assigned a union; membership fees are paid to the Histadrut and distributed among the unions. Thus the power structure remains largely unchanged: the Leadership and the chairperson still have the main power to set and implement policies, and the structure also means the Histadrut is very much identified with the chairperson (see Weinblum 2010, 26–28 for an overview of the 1994 reforms).

The Histadrut is further hampered by its history as an employer and as a national institution. People remember incidents like the seamen's strike in the 1950s and the "night of dogs" at Soltam in the early 1990s when the Histadrut was seen to act brutally against the workers. There remains a feeling that the Histadrut is not interested in worker participation, and indeed the organizing of workers was not the reason behind its establishment and it had no organizing culture (Mundlak 2009, 781). As noted in the introduction, collective bargaining came only after other Histadrut functions had been set up; thus unionizing has historically been a top-down initiative (Haberfeld 1995). Workers joined the Histadrut not so much as an attempt to influence their own lives and workplaces, but as a route to incorporation into the polity in the most extensive sense (for welfare and services including housing, health, and pensions). This is reflected in the fact that members included the self-employed, managers, the unemployed, and homemakers as well as salaried workers. The workers' committees may be a democratic channel (Haberfeld 1995), and have often been more militant than the Histadrut itself, leading to many wildcat strikes; but this reflects the fact that the Histadrut had no mechanism for allowing workers' demands to filter up to the leadership. As Weinblum (2010, 13) notes, most workers' committees were virtually powerless to affect Histadrut policy; moreover, the leadership is formed following elections in which parties with no obvious relation to organized labor or unionist ideology take part (the right-wing parties).

Indeed, Ben-Eliezer (1993, 404) goes further, asserting that the politicization of labor in the framework of the Histadrut should not necessarily be seen as political participation, and membership in the Histadrut should not be seen as a democratic channel: the collective character of the Histadrut served as a "reproductive mechanism" of the dominant culture. The organization's structure did not enable individual workers to express their interests in order to shape the organization's agenda or policies; it was only a path to the expression of the collective, the "common belonging," and was characterized by "noninfluential practices of political participation" (Ben-Eliezer 1993, 408).

Organizational drives following the reforms have been few and of limited success. The Histadrut's history still affects the way it is viewed and causes confusion over its role, status, position within the political structure, and power—some even believing it is a state-supported institution. Rom Dvir, from the Histadrut's relatively new Workers Organizing Unit, said, "The Histadrut is identified as part of the establishment. People say to me, 'what does the Histadrut do for me? I pay all these taxes [and get nothing in return]'" (interview).

The confusion was noticeable in the social workers' campaign, which reflected trust in the Histadrut as a powerful organization but ended in disappointment that stemmed from the Histadrut's suppression of the activists' participation and demands. At first, despite frustration with its behavior and top-down power structure, most social workers believed their best chances of a good collective agreement were with the Histadrut. Indeed, the energies and efforts of the social workers were channeled into the existing representational structures, the SWU within the Histadrut, via the new organizations whose founders had been largely responsible for waking up the social workers. Before the strike, there was a feeling that "everyone" was with the union: "There was a feeling we were going in the right direction, at least until, say, three months before the strike there was a feeling that the union was standing up for itself, that we could accept what it was saying" (Farber, interview).

But trust in the union and the Histadrut was gradually eroded. Social workers sensed a lack of transparency; they were unaware of the Histadrut's role in the negotiations and lacked real understanding of the relationship between the SWU and the Histadrut, and thus too of the extent of the union's autonomy: "It wasn't at all clear what the union was demanding [during negotiations]. . . . Maybe it was clear to the Finance Ministry, but not to us. . . . My impression was that the union [SWU] was handling things, handling negotiations. There was no feeling the Histadrut was a significant actor, though of course in fact it was" (Farber, interview). *Globes* labor relations correspondent Shay Niv called this a "classic example" of the Histadrut's failure to understand what was happening on the ground (interview).

The disconnection between the newly activated social workers and the new organizations, on the one hand, and the Histadrut and the SWU, on the other, grew as the campaign continued. The former pushed for mass participation and a show of strength from the rank and file, while the latter appeared to prefer quiet conversations behind closed doors. This came to a head with the draft agreement, which was brought to the union for approval. The SWU central committee voted against the draft, after huge efforts by activists to make it clear that social workers expected more than the draft offered. The Histadrut, however, threatened it would not support any further struggle, thus effectively forcing through a final agreement even though the social workers were willing to continue the struggle. When details of the draft emerged, Osim Shinui held a demonstration in front of the Histadrut building, which rapidly became "anti-Histadrut" (Shlosberg, interview).

Farber noted the redirection of anger, the feeling that the union had let them down, failed to act in their interests, and silenced their voice: "In the first week of the strike and the weeks that preceded it, there was a feeling the Finance Ministry was the enemy. But this changed, and the union became the enemy. . . . The feeling is that it's not the Finance Ministry that screwed us, but the union—the union and the Histadrut, of course" (interview).

By the end of the campaign, the SWU was understood to be conservative and weak within the Histadrut, despite the amendments to its constitution in 2007. As Tal Goldman put it, "We, the social workers, have a union which is not strong. It acts within the Histadrut. . . . It apparently has all the tools it needs to lead, and its constitution is utopian, it refers to influencing social policy, to shaping welfare policy . . . but in fact [the SWU] takes a very conservative approach to the decline of collective agreements and the privatization of the profession" (interview). Farber noted the feeling that Histadrut chair Ofer Eini was "merely putting on a show," allowing the strike just to let the social workers "blow off some steam."[5] As activists saw it, "the agreement was already prepared [for signing]; . . . it was all too easy, too smooth" (Farber, interview). The Histadrut chair, it was felt, had abused the SWU central committee vote merely to improve his democratic credentials when he himself not only had the authority to sign without any such vote, but was openly dismissive of the chance to achieve a better deal: "Eini said he wouldn't [sign] if we didn't approve it. . . . But it was like he was saying, 'look, try it alone, see how it goes, the Finance Ministry won't even talk with you . . . and in the end everyone will see that what I [Eini] say is what will happen.' . . . [It was as if he was saying] 'I won't go against democracy, I will respect the vote, but you'll see, you can't manage without me'" (Shlosberg, interview).

As a result, the final agreement disappointed most union members who felt it had been imposed upon them undemocratically and was barely an improvement on the draft agreement. This led to further anger and bitterness at the Histadrut and the SWU. Goldman, then joint chair of Osim Shinui, expressed this disappointment: "They talked about wages, including wages in the private sector, and enforcement, but they didn't touch the heart of the matter, the lack of employment horizon, or lack of posts, or an extension order.... The agreement feels like a plaster; ... it deals with side issues, not the root problems" (interview).

The Unacceptable Gap between Worker Aspirations and the Histadrut

As a result of the perception that the Histadrut is thwarting campaign objectives, many workers are beginning to question whether their representative organization is on their side at all. In the social workers' campaign, *Globes* correspondent Shay Niv noted the "unacceptable gap" between the workers' aspirations and the Histadrut during negotiations, and the Histadrut's "take it or leave it" attitude to the draft agreement (interview). An unacceptable gap can be seen in the railway campaign too. During the campaign, relations between the workers' committee and the Histadrut deteriorated, until in July 2012, the Histadrut's disciplinary committee removed the workers' committee and appointed a new committee. But long before this, the committee felt it was being excluded. For example, the committee was not involved in the intensive talks between the Histadrut and the transport minister on the maintenance agreement that had been opposed by the workers and that the transport minister had reached unilaterally. (In fact this was the railway's agreement; the transport minister merely promoted and announced it.) The transport minister also said the Histadrut must remove the committee chairperson, Gila Edra'i, who was perceived as the main source of worker opposition to the agreement, as he himself was unable to fire her for fear of public opposition (*Globes* 2012b). Though in fact he had no authority to fire a committee chair, his rhetoric made it clear that the government's problem was with the committee, and not with the Histadrut.

Yet at first, it seemed the Histadrut supported the workers' committee and encouraged disruption and strikes. Among workers, there was a feeling that "without Eini" nothing much would be achieved, but that the Histadrut chair would not get involved unless things "got hot on the ground." As Edra'i put it, "I would think, why doesn't Eini talk to the [transport] minister, why doesn't he explain things to him? And they said, Eini doesn't get involved at that temperature; ... he waits for the pot to boil over, to bubble ... then the Histadrut chair comes" (interview). The workers' disruption, then, was aimed not only at forcing concessions from the employer, but also at causing the Histadrut's chairperson to get involved—a reflection of the disconnect between rank and file and leadership. The committee's reliance on Eini to make a few telephone calls to sort things out is also a reflection of how the Histadrut's source of power—friends in high places—is perceived.

The Histadrut's initial support for the committee is also evident from the strike of 26 March in which all the Histadrut's transport union workers turned out in solidarity with the railway workers to protest disciplinary action taken by the railway against the committee members. The Histadrut elections may have also influenced relations between it and the committee; until Eini's reelection as Histadrut chair in May 2012, relations were good, and Eini also received the committee's support in his election campaign. "On the day of the election I took a day's holiday [to help in canvassing]. There were those who supported [Labor MK Eitan] Cabel, I said 'no, let's support Ofer [Eini], because he is helping us now with the struggle, loyalty is the name of the game'" (Edra'i, interview).

Relations with the Histadrut began deteriorating when negotiations toward the final agreement were underway, and the committee claimed it was significantly different from the agreement of principles already agreed on with the committee's support.

> Now they come up with an agreement, but the agreement doesn't tally with the agreement of principles. There is no disagreement over the fact that there are large differences. Some paragraphs important to the government have been changed [to the government's advantage]. And [the committee members] say they won't accept it. And they say this loudly. But [the Histadrut] says, "you can't behave like that. This is the best you'll get." And just a few minutes later, the Histadrut issues the letter saying she [Edra'i] is out [removed from her position as committee chair by the Histadrut]. (Cohen, interview)

There was also a split between the Histadrut's transport union, headed by Avi Edri, and the organization's upper echelons—Eini and trade union department chair Avi Nissenkorn. The committee felt it had support from Avi Edri, and regarding the wildcat strike, Avi Edri said explicitly that he understood the workers' plight even though the Histadrut had not encouraged the committee to take such steps (see Bar-Eli and Weissberg 2012). "There was a period in which it seemed Avi Edri was with me," Gila Edra'i said, "But there is a hierarchy [in the Histadrut] . . . and Avi [Edri] has freedom of movement only to a certain extent. Above him is Avi Nissenkorn who is very well coordinated with Eini" (interview).

The labor courts underlined this split, exonerating Eini and the Histadrut from wrongdoing and isolating the committee. The Tel Aviv Labor Court rejected contempt of court claims against the Histadrut and Avi Edri, noting they had done their best to get rail workers to carry out their tasks as required, and the workers alone were to blame (Collective Dispute 20420-05-11). The National Labor Court noted with approval the steps taken by the Histadrut to try negotiating as much as possible and limit the workers' collective steps. In doing so, the court said, the Histadrut was "acting responsibly," as fitting for an organization of its standing; it also reiterated that the workers are expected to act in accordance with the Histadrut and under its leadership (Request for Appeal 50556-09-11, par. 23). The transport minister, too, spoke highly of the Histadrut and blamed the committee for all setbacks in negotiations.

The Histadrut claimed the committee refused to recognize its authority, in particular its orders to respect the court and refrain from wildcat strikes; it emphasized it had the workers' interests in mind and had held talks with Edra'i and the committee throughout the negotiating process (Inter-Organizational Dispute 9685-07-12, par. 10).

Following the removal of the workers' committee, Edra'i tried to join Koach Laovdim and claimed that this union was now the representative union in the railway. However, it was not the removal of the committee alone or even disagreements over the negotiating process that led to the move to Koach Laovdim. The feeling of isolation and the suspicion that the Histadrut was not responding to workers' concerns had begun long before. Rafi Kimhi from Koach Laovdim recalled the gradual increase in contact with the committee:

> Gila [Edra'i] turned to us. She said she couldn't transfer [to Koach Laovdim], but that the Histadrut wasn't giving her the support she needed. I know Gila from childhood. We helped each other. We set up the Forum against the Privatization of the Railway, with academics, professionals, activists. . . . With the committee, but behind the scenes . . . to create a platform of public support. And we began building up a working relationship. . . . At some point, she understood they were going to remove her, and she moved over to Koach Laovdim. It's not something that can be done from outside. We had built enough support [among the workers] . . . for the move. (Kimhi, interview)

The committee headed by Edra'i did indeed have a lot of support, which it earned by deliberately setting itself up in opposition to the previous committee and the corruption associated with it, by its notable success in uniting the forty railway committees that are represented on the national committee, and by confronting the creeping changes (associated with outsourcing and privatization) to employment at the railway:

> [A small group] managed the campaign, and because the workers knew they were representing their interests, they maintained popularity. . . . Gila [Edra'i] changed the norms—the workers knew her interests were not her personal interests. . . . [Edra'i was] very popular, is still very popular, among the workers. (Kimhi, interview)

> There was a destructive degeneration over the years. The previous committee chairs were accused of bribery, and those before them too. . . . There was a problematic way of doing things. A decadent heritage. Corruption and relationships based on power. [Edra'i's] group was in fact made up of younger people, relatively speaking, a new generation that decided it wanted an organization to represent them. (Cohen, interview)

The committee also had workers' support because it had been involved in all details throughout the negotiations toward the agreement of principles, and it was felt that it understood the negotiating process and the operation of the railway better than anyone. Although no membership forms were officially counted, so it is not possible to say whether the committee had a majority support when it transferred to Koach Laovdim, the committee earned the workers' trust, as is clear from the fact that workers were willing to strike as the committee intended even after the Histadrut had called off the strike.

The Histadrut does not need the committee to sign a collective agreement, but it has always tried to sign such agreements in cooperation with the committee for appearances' sake: "Tomorrow they can say, 'the Histadrut is selling out the workers.' . . . If the committee is opposed to signing and the Histadrut signs anyway? That's bad! On the other hand, if the committee and the Histadrut sign together, that's great!" (Edra'i, interview). This is why replacing the uncooperative committee was important for the Histadrut and made easier by widespread public antipathy toward Edra'i: "To remove the committee, they had a kind of public support. That woman, she's crazy. She's disturbed. She's aggressive. She makes decisions," as Edra'i put it ironically, referring to herself (interview).

The same disconnection between the Histadrut and the workers it represents was clear in the Haifa Chemicals North campaign.[6] Here too the workers' committee felt it was being ignored by the representative organization, the Histadrut. For some years the Histadrut, it was felt, had failed to protect the workers. In 1997, following a strike of over three months, the Histadrut and Haifa Chemicals had reached what was then still a relatively novel form of agreement, the two-tier model: existing employees ("generation A") retained a certain level of benefits, but new employees ("generation B") would receive far less. Amir Peretz, then Histadrut chair, said this was the only way of protecting the current workforce. However, since 1997, the Histadrut had not protested the dismissal of some 180 workers or the employment of some 100 via manpower agencies. This meant that by 2011, only about 250 workers remained covered by the collective agreement (down from 500 in 1997), while 100 were on individual contracts and another 100 employed via agencies. The committee also said the Histadrut had not acted when the company violated the terms of the agreement and had even tried to restrain the workers' anger.

In the beginning of 2011, Haifa Chemicals North began negotiations toward a new collective agreement within the Histadrut framework, but frustration rapidly mounted. The workers felt that they were being ignored, that the Histadrut was about to sign over their heads. This increased the frustration already felt due to the deterioration in the strength of organized labor that, they thought, the Histadrut had done nothing to stop and the Histadrut's inaction in the face of violations of the previous agreement. The Histadrut agreed to declare a labor dispute, but the workers felt they were fighting on two fronts—against the employer and against the Histadrut. One of the Histadrut representatives even told the workers, "I'm not working for you" (Vatury and Cohen, interviews). The committee was hardly involved in the negotiating and did not see drafts of the agreement taking shape. In March 2011, the committee decided to transfer to Koach Laovdim, and the new union declared it was inheriting the existing labor dispute. In fact, there had been plans to transfer to another union a year before the campaign, and though nothing came of them, it does reflect the ongoing frustration and the disconnection between the organization and the committee that eventually led the workers to seek representation with Koach Laovdim. In this case, contrary to the railway case, the Histadrut did not challenge the move in court, and together with Koach Laovdim the committee eventually signed a collective agreement.

THE CORRUPT OLD STRUCTURES

As discussed in the previous chapter, some of the recent organizing initiatives and a number of new organizations channeled their energies into existing representational structures, but many workers perceived the Histadrut to be complicit in policies that have undermined organized labor, and they found themselves struggling against the Histadrut's centralized, inflexible bureaucratic structure that they felt did not permit democratic representation. Furthermore, the Histadrut is hampered by its image of corruption; this has made the rival union Koach Laovdim an attractive option, with its highly educated, young, cool activists and emphasis on democratic participation in the organization. It is not just the Histadrut that workers often perceive as fossilized and ineffective: the doctors and particularly the resident physicians revolted against their own very well-established union, to such an extent that their campaign was seen as a potentially catastrophic challenge to accepted industrial relations practices. Though their case illustrates an awakening in organizing terms, it also shows the fragmentation of representation and the collapse of broad solidarity.

The contradictions and dilemmas that arise from this perception of powerful but corrupt institutions on the one hand and clean but perhaps weaker organizations on the other can be seen in the case of the new journalists' union, the Journalists Organization (JO). This organization grew out of a feeling among journalists that their profession was being eroded, and indeed many major news outlets were facing cutbacks and dismissals. After a large and well-publicized meeting of journalists and editors in Tel Aviv's Cinemateque (November 2011), journalists set up workers' committees in various firms and began coordinating between them. Initially they tried to work within the existing Journalists' Association (a professional body that also acts as a union independently of the Histadrut), but the old-timers there saw them as upstarts. JO chair Yair Tarchitzky noted, "It created tension within the organization, suddenly 350 new faces come; . . . it seems like a threat, people coming to change the organization. . . . Suspicions were raised, and the organization's chairperson started acting against us instead of with us. . . . It was dirty business, they even made a blacklist of us, people who should not be allowed to reach management positions, all sorts of tricks" (interview).

Eventually the emergent JO split from the old Journalists' Association and accepted Histadrut patronage, since some kind of existing union framework was required. However, in order that they might express their own interests and push their own agenda, it was important to them to negotiate greater autonomy than the Histadrut has usually given. *Globes* star columnist Dror Feuer, who was a central figure in the now-famous Cinemateque meeting, said: "Our central demand from the Histadrut was that the Histadrut could not sign an agreement 'over our heads.' It's complicated, because it sets a precedent. . . . But we can't on the one hand use the Histadrut's resources and structure, and on the other hand demand complete autonomy; . . . there's a delicate balancing game here" (interview).

Frustration with this "delicate balancing game" is certainly behind the rapidly increasing popularity of the general union Koach Laovdim. Tomer Raznik, an activist in the left-liberal Meretz Party's youth wing and later a central activist in the Forum against the Privatization of the Railway, noted that in contrast to the Histadrut's "poor image," Koach Laovdim is generally perceived as "cool" and receives a lot of positive press coverage (interview).[1] Its activists are young and well connected, and it emphasizes its democratic structure, which attracts workers seeking a new way of organizing and also attracts public support. In fact, Koach Laovdim positioned itself explicitly in contrast to the Histadrut's lack of democracy. Upon its establishment in 2007, its founders, attorney Itai Swirsky from Tel Aviv University's Legal Clinic, Shay Cohen, Dr. Liat Yakir, and Dr. Ami Vatury, insisted on internal democracy. The union's main decision-making forum is the Delegates' Assembly, comprised of delegates from each branch. Branches are defined according to workplace or profession, and unemployed workers are included in the branch relevant to their last place of work or in the general branch. Delegates are elected annually in elections open to all branch members. The Delegates' Assembly elects the Central Committee, which oversees the day-to-day running of the organization and elects the various teams (administration, media, juridical) and regional coordinators. According to the union's constitution, at least a third of Central Committee members must be women. The Delegates' Assembly also elects the central election committee and the members of the internal court and can make decisions on all issues except the termination of a strike, the signing of a collective agreement, and the confirming of a branch budget, all of which must be approved by the branch members concerned—in fact, workers can vote to reject a collective agreement regardless of what the leadership thinks. Through this organizational structure, Koach Laovdim hopes to ensure that all members have an equal ability to influence the organization and prevent corruption by making it difficult for employers to buy off the leadership.

As the southern region coordinator Assaf Bondy put it, the aim is to create a political democratic force, which can best be done via a union.[2] Swirsky, in an interview with *Globes* (Niv 2010; see also Niv 2009), emphasized that they wanted the workers to be aware and involved, to see the advantages of cooperation and the possibility of change. He said it was not a militant organization, but a true representation of the workers' own wishes. He also noted it was unlikely the organization would strive to forge links with any specific party, but did stress that it was "building politics from the ground up." In 2011, then central region coordinator Avi Menkes gave the social workers' strike and the doctors' strike as examples of campaigns in which the issue of legitimacy of representation was foremost: many of the problems that arose during those campaigns stemmed from the fact that the representative organizations were losing their legitimacy. He noted that legitimacy is linked to an organization's internal democracy, which is why Koach Laovdim considered this such an important aspect.[3]

In the railway case, according to Raznik (interview), public support for the workers' committee headed by Edra'i began growing only after Edra'i declared her intention to join Koach Laovdim. Prior to this, the "rough" image of the workers, their association with "corrupt" Histadrut committees such as those in the ports, and their lack of friends in the media had distracted public attention from what the activists considered the main issue:

> [People say] they're all corrupt, that we need to dismantle the railway, the committee, . . . all sorts of statements that clearly serve the interests of privatization. There are lots of Mizrahim [working at the railway], lots of religious workers, lots of Arabs. . . . Most journalists don't have a cousin who works at the railway. They have a cousin who's a teacher so they'll say that work via an agency is terrible; they have a cousin who's a medical resident so they'll say they [the junior doctors] should get more money. . . . They think, why should someone like that, at the railway, earn twelve thousand a month? (Raznik, interview)[4]

By transferring to Koach Laovdim, the railway workers' committee was able to take advantage of this new union's youthful, cool, trendy image and its links with white-collar professionals and students. "Since the Histadrut is so hated by the press, the moment [Edra'i] left and joined Koach Laovdim, which has a certain 'street cred,' the story became more complex. Suddenly the workers are not so corrupt, suddenly [the public] understands that maybe [Edra'i] was victim of some nasty business; after all, she supported Eini in the [Histadrut] elections and then he removed her" (Raznik, interview).

Another sign of the railway campaign's increasing acceptability was the way it was embraced by the social protest movement of 2011. This movement, a cry from the squeezed middle classes (see Rosenhek and Shalev 2013), also rejected the Histadrut's attempts to be associated with the movement. The movement, it has been suggested, expressed the young public's lack of faith in the establishment, in the existing political structures (Ram and Filc 2013). The Histadrut was associated with these structures, especially as its then chair, Eini, was well known for his close ties to politicians and especially his key role in mediating between Labor and Likud toward the government coalition of 2009. Moreover, the Histadrut in its new role as purely union and in its historic role as symbol of Israeli socialism articulated a workers' worldview that jarred with what Rosenhek and Shalev (2013) call the non-class-based articulation of economic issues preferred by the protest leaders. The railway struggle was increasingly mentioned in the movement's demonstrations, and in March 2012, Dafni Leef (a central figurehead in the movement) and social protest activists petitioned the High Court to stop the "wild privatization" of Israel railways (Maanit 2012).

Even where the Histadrut was chosen by the initiators of an organizing drive, there were problems with its image. Itamar Avitan, who was involved in the organizing at the Pelephone cell-phone company in 2012 and was later a member of the workers' committee, noted: "The [image of the] Histadrut hurt us, we tried to reduce the Histadrut presence as much as possible" (interview). This poor image was exploited by the company, which set up an "internal committee" as an alternative to the Histadrut committee (Avitan, Boaron, interviews), thus taking advantage of the instinctive antipathy toward the Histadrut among many of the kind of young people employed in the cell-phone sector.

The most prominent challenge to an existing workers' organization came from the doctors, especially the junior doctors (resident physicians). The doctors' campaign was complex. On the one hand, it appears to illustrate the continued strength of the corporatist labor relations arrangement in the health sector. Despite the intensity of the strikes, severe disruption to services, and tough stance of the negotiators on all sides, the campaign involved the traditional social partners seeking agreement over employment terms as well as negotiating at the higher level of health service policies. On the other hand, however, it also involved the fragmentation of representation and a serious challenge to the union's legitimacy as representative of the infamously disparate worker groups within the health sector: various organizations were established in protest at the union's ostensibly dictatorial leadership, and an alternative, particularist framework was created in the face of adamant opposition from the union, the labor courts, and the state.

The dispute began in 2011, as the Israel Medical Association (IMA), which acts as the doctors' union, negotiated with the government and Clalit (the major HMO) toward a new collective agreement. The IMA is an independent organization, but it soon found itself in a situation similar to that of the Histadrut, with challenges from worker groups seeking independence from what they see as a fossilized, ineffective organization. Part of the problem is the structure of the IMA, which is comprised of two main organizations: the state doctors' organization and the Clalit doctors' organization. It also includes professional unions according to medical specialization, but these are not part of the representational voting structure. The chair of the state doctors' organization is deputy IMA chair and the chair of the Clalit doctors' organization is second deputy IMA chair. Therefore many groups within the union feel they have no representational voice. This structure can be changed by changing the IMA constitution, but under the existing structure effective opposition within the IMA is almost impossible.[5]

Like in the examples discussed above, anger toward the representative organization grew as the collective agreement took shape. Eran Dolev, former chair of the IMA, noted that many felt the union's current chair, Leonid Eidelman, was behaving autocratically (Dolev, interview) and failing to take into account the interests of various sectors the union was supposed to represent. According to Ilan Levine, then wages officer at the Finance Ministry, those sitting opposite the union at the negotiating table also felt that the IMA was not representing all its members, and that the junior doctors in particular were absent (interview).

Of the various formal and informal groups that emerged to challenge the IMA or speak for a specific group within the health sector, one group was particularly prominent: Mirsham. According to Mirsham's chair Yona Weissbuch, this organization began in the early 2000s as informal meetings between resident physicians who wanted to understand the problems they were encountering including inadequate representation from their representative organization (interview). Mirsham also aims to redress a representational anomaly: residents are subordinate to an administrative boss (the hospital director) and a professional boss (the head of the department). The professional boss is responsible for the residents' training and career and is also on the hospital workers' committee. Thus the department head represents the residents within the IMA but is answerable to the hospital director regarding their work.

Resident physicians led the revolt against the IMA, with Mirsham acting quietly behind the scenes. They demanded direct negotiations with the employer, since their own organization had ignored their interests, they said. The revolt took the form of demonstrations against the IMA, then a wildcat strike to protest the agreement being shaped by the IMA, but the resident physicians were ordered back to work by the court because the strike had not been coordinated with their representative organization. The next step was a mass resignation of about one thousand resident physicians; the court annulled this as an illegitimate collective step (General Collective Dispute 722-09-11). About eight hundred then submitted individual letters of resignation, and some senior doctors declared they would not allow work in hospitals to continue normally, in solidarity with the junior doctors. The court annulled the individual resignations, too (General Collective Dispute 2376-10-11), and the resident physicians appealed at the High Court.

During the High Court hearing (HC 7569/11), Judge Hanan Meltzer upheld the resident physicians' right to resign individually but avoided having to rule on whether their move had been a "strike in the guise of resignations," as Judge Nili Arad of the National Labor Court (NLC) had put it (General Collective Dispute 2376-10-11, par. 1), by persuading the sides to talk. Though he did not include it in his final ruling, Meltzer made it known during the debates that he was in favor of reopening the agreement (Collective Agreement No. 267/11) that had been signed by the IMA in the meantime (Niv 2011d). The Finance Ministry and Health Ministry agreed to talk on condition that the IMA agreement would hold, but noted that even talking to the residents was an unprecedented exception to labor relations norms.

During the talks, a new idea emerged: to mark a test point after 4.5 years. If the sides agree to changes to the original IMA agreement, this would be accepted as a new collective agreement. However, if they fail to agree after six months of negotiations, they would begin mediated talks for a limited time, followed by arbitration. Furthermore, if this were to happen, the residents would be granted independent (not IMA) representation in some form (Niv 2011c).

The campaign was charged with an atmosphere of calamity. The public was sure it would be left without medical services, and hospitals made preparations for serious shortages of staff. The trauma of a very long doctors' strike in 1983 (see Ishay 1986; Modan 1985) hung over the health sector. The NLC president expressed this atmosphere: "We stand today before one of the most difficult moments, if not *the* most difficult, in the history of the public health system in Israel," she wrote (General Collective Dispute 2376-10-11, par. 1). This was fear of the collapse not just of the health system, but of the entire edifice of labor relations, a fear expressed by judges, journalists, and various partners to negotiations (Linder-Ganz, interview; Weissbuch, interview). The Finance Ministry wages officer asserted it was the hardest labor dispute in his career, noting the tension between the senior doctors and the junior doctors, and the negative influence this had on negotiations. He also warned that if the prime minister were to intervene to extend the agreement, this would undermine collective labor relations (Linder-Ganz 2011c). During the debate on a petition filed by Mirsham against the nine-year period of the IMA agreement, the Supreme Court president noted the resident physicians were "taking the law into their own hands," which under normal circumstances would be rejected immediately (HC 8382/11). When medical students at three universities held a large protest near the Prime Minister's Residence in Jerusalem, the prime minister emphasized that an agreement that had just been signed could not be opened, while the finance minister added that giving in to the resident physicians' demands would lead to anarchy (Ravid and *Haaretz* 2011).

The IMA was challenged in other ways, too, and organizations were set up to frame discontent. Arbel, the most prominent of such organizations, was established by heads of hospital departments during the IMA's negotiations in response to the rigidity of the IMA's structure. According to Eran Dolev, who later chaired the organization, the idea had originally been to create a group as an internal opposition, but the IMA refused to recognize Arbel in any way (interview; see also Linder-Ganz 2011b). In 2012, an organization called Asli was established to represent interns who are not full members of the IMA but whose professional lives are, of course, affected by IMA decisions. It, too, is seeking representative status and collective negotiations with the Finance Ministry.

At various times during the campaign the IMA's authority was called into question. There were suggestions that the IMA should join the Histadrut to improve coordination between the IMA and the Health Ministry (the suggestion was eventually rejected; Dolev, interview). Workers' committees at four large hospitals submitted a fast-track petition to stop the IMA signing the agreement, claiming it had violated the fair representation clause (the claim was rejected; Labor Dispute 30184-09-11). The Medical Students Union called a strike of studies in solidarity with the junior doctors, threatening it would call an unlimited strike if the Finance Minister refused to talk to the junior doctors (Brenner 2011). Some two hundred interns, in their last year of medical studies, also went on strike for a few hours in solidarity. The Health Ministry said they had no right to do so, but they asserted that as students they are not members of the IMA and can thus do as they like (Even 2011a).

In addition, a group of senior doctors threatened to resign, saying they too were being ignored by their representative organization. One, who was also among the founders of Arbel, noted that the junior doctors were merely the vanguard, that the senior doctors also want to be part of negotiations. It seems one had to resign in order to be granted that privilege, he observed wryly (Niv 2011d). About one hundred senior doctors including department directors from hospitals around the country carried out the threat and submitted their resignations. One hospital threatened to immediately dismiss ten of the thirty-one doctors there who had submitted their resignations (which would otherwise go into effect in a month's time). In response, doctors at the hospital shut down its operations for a few hours one morning and threatened further strikes, rejecting attempts by the Health Ministry director to persuade them to withdraw their resignations.

Nonetheless, unlike in the case of the railway campaign, when the NLC rejected the workers' attempt to join a rival union, in this case the courts were compelled to accept changes to a long-standing labor relations framework in the face of such widespread discontent with the representative organization: the resident physicians achieved a new collective framework without any formal representative status, using unacceptable (from the point of view of accepted industrial relations practice) and sometimes illegal means to force changes to collective bargaining norms despite the apocalyptic rhetoric from the courts, the IMA, and the Finance Ministry.

TAKING THE STRUGGLE BEYOND THE WORKPLACE

The feeling that the Histadrut or other old frameworks are not representing the workers sufficiently was common in many campaigns. While the Histadrut itself may be part of the establishment, the workers themselves are not, and in some cases it is precisely this establishment they oppose. The workers, then, feel they are not part of the "negotiated order" (Strauss 1978), a feeling that led to widespread participation and anger toward the Histadrut's supposedly dictatorial behavior.

However, the campaigns also illustrate the desire to take the struggle beyond the workplace, to influence state policies and involve the public—to "explain" the situation, as the social workers put it—to underline the connection between employment and broader social concerns. The railway workers, for example, sought to influence the management's reform program and linked this to the idea that "they" are privatizing "our" (citizens') railway. Similarly, the social workers tried to limit the privatization of the services they offer and the transformation of their profession. The cleaners, or more accurately the disparate groups involved in the campaign, not only wanted to protect the subcontracted cleaners at the university but tried to halt and reverse the spread of a certain employment framework.

All of these are examples of opposition to a certain neoliberal economic direction that is affecting employment terms, and this opposition goes far deeper than run-of-the-mill negotiation over wage increments. Privatization and its sidekick, outsourcing, are perceived as the policy core of neoliberal trends that directly affect employment; hence this was the target of the campaigns and shorthand way of articulating the issues at stake. It is not by chance that many recent worker campaigns have been in transport, including the bus company Egged, the railway, and the ports, since this economic sector is one of the principal targets of privatization.

Privatization was the main issue for the social workers, who aimed to reunite the private and public sectors by ensuring an extension order that would make privatization of services less appealing to those funding them. Privatization was a relatively new issue. The social workers' strike of 1988 had not addressed it, and the Long Term Care Insurance Law, effective from 1988 and perceived as the start of privatization in the field, was implemented mainly through existing bodies; social workers did not immediately feel the effects on their profession. Tami Farber from Osot Hasharon noted, "These services were provided by nonprofit organizations, some of which already existed . . . in the third sector, and they didn't clash with [state-supplied] social work" (interview). However, today some 40 percent of social workers are employed in the private sector, while some 75 percent of social work students can expect to find employment in the private sector upon completing their studies. Employment in this sector is marked by the now familiar characteristics of high turnover, lack of employment security, low wages, few peripheral benefits, and lack of ongoing training—and a far lower union density rate. In 2009, Atidenu set up a unit known as Amuta, with at least nominal Social Workers Union support, to concentrate specifically on the issues faced by social workers in the private sector.

As Osim Shinui leader Goldman said, "You can imagine a situation where in five years it will be half-half [unionized and nonunionized social workers] and there won't be anything to fight for" (interview). She continued, "As students, we know that three in four [social workers] will work in the private sector, because [public sector] posts are disappearing, so we made the extension order [of the agreement, to include the private sector] our first priority" (interview). The failure to achieve an extension order was therefore a major blow for activists. (It later emerged that negotiators had quietly dropped demands for an extension order even as Atidenu continued to promote this issue in its recruitment efforts in the private sector, which led to further anger against the Histadrut.)

The connection with the broader public was crucial for these campaigns, hence much of Atidenu's and Osim Shinui's work explaining their demands, or the work of the Forum against the Privatization of the Railway. Those leading the social workers' campaign succeeded in attracting very wide public support, with mostly positive media coverage and at least nominal support from many Knesset members: "There was some kind of consensus regarding the struggle . . . mainly Meretz, Labor [considered leftwing parties], even Kadima [centrist], also Shas, even Yisrael Beitenu [rightwing]," Goldman said (interview). For the same reason, Atidenu members were keen to give the campaign a social aspect, emphasizing that this was a struggle over the welfare system, the welfare state (Shlosberg, interview). Those on the other side of the barricade and higher up in the union hierarchies did their best to sever this link between workers and the public. During the social workers' campaign, the union chair emphasized a number of times that it was a struggle over employment terms, not a social struggle, and called on social workers to quit waging "social" battles "on the backs of the workers" (Shlosberg, interview). When the medical students held their protest near the Prime Minister's Residence, the prime minister urged them to "leave patients out of the struggle" (Ravid and *Haaretz* 2011), implying that their campaign was harming people who were not supposed to be involved.

In the railway campaign, since the issues being contested would transform a public company, the workers were involved in a public fight in a very literal sense. Among the first to perceive the struggle in this way were those who later set up the Forum against the Privatization of the Railway, including activists associated with the Histadrut, Koach Laovdim, and Young Meretz (the semiautonomous youth branch of the liberal-left political party Meretz). Forum activist Tomer Raznik claimed that the Histadrut "took a line of accepting the [government's] decisions as long as the workers' committees get good terms" (interview), and that in the railway case the committee went against this trend. "The committee didn't want privatization with good employment terms. This is what they were offered. The railway tried to bribe them at first. They said they didn't want the railway to be privatized. That's why it was important to me that it would be a public campaign. The committee played a public role. Something more than what a committee would normally do" (Raznik, interview).

According to Raznik, the issue of railway privatization was hardly raised before the campaign, even though the Finance Ministry's plans to privatize had been leaked a couple of years before. For some activists in Young Meretz, the campaign seemed like a good opportunity to put the issue on the public agenda. However, this was not easy, because from the beginning of the campaign, public opinion was mostly against the workers' committee, particularly its chair Gila Edra'i who was painted in the media as a typical corrupt, aggressive Histadrut committee member who only knew how to throw her weight about, talk dirty, and protect the committee members' cushy status.

Young Meretz members together with activists from the group Social-Democratic Israel (associated with the Labor Party) contacted the workers' committee and began a campaign that was coordinated on a very general level with the committee but acted independently (Raznik, interview). The campaign included demonstrations, protest vigils, the distribution of material among the general public, and the publication of a campaign newsletter "Hafrata Hayom" ("privatization today"), which was discontinued when the rightwing newspaper *Israel Hayom* (strongly associated with Prime Minister Benjamin Netanyahu) threatened to sue for their use of a similar name. "When [the public] said [the railway workers are] thugs, they're violent, I tried to explain what it means when somebody is fighting for his bread and butter. People really don't understand it. Not to support the committee emotionally, not to say that Gila [Edra'i] is a lovely person—she doesn't need that, she's a strong woman. What's important is to give them legitimacy, to support them publicly. That was our main task" (Raznik, interview).

The connection between the committee and Koach Laovdim, which began nearly two years before the official attempt to transfer, was also based on the realization that the rail workers were fighting a public battle. Union activists came to demonstrations in support of the campaign and were active within the Forum, though as long as the committee remained within the Histadrut they toned down their presence as Koach Laovdim members. Edra'i, the committee chair, recalled, "Since there was already a struggle against privatization, Shay Cohen [from Koach Laovdim] would call once in a while, express support, we are with you, if you need anything we're here" (interview). Shay Cohen confirmed, "Here was a tough struggle of various workers protesting the privatization program . . . and we wanted to show solidarity, but we knew it would be problematic to come as Koach Laovdim, also because of the activities of our activists in political parties, particularly the younger ones. . . . We had to cooperate with members of the Histadrut" (interview).

The struggle was also pushed into the public arena by the Histadrut's claims that the public was calling for the closure of the railway because of the committee's wild behavior and the committee's counterclaim that the public in fact supported the struggle. By leaving the Histadrut, the committee redrew the lines of conflict, positioning the Histadrut on the side of the shady employers and the state with their underhanded, behind-closed-doors tactics. The committee, then, took on the role of fighting in the name of the public for transparency in the management of a public company, as well as for democratic representation within the workers' organization.

The doctors' case, however, is very different. Where other campaigns were opposing neoliberal trends and protesting against the workers' organizations they thought were acquiescing in neoliberal government policies, the doctors stand to benefit from those trends. I suggest that this is why the resident physicians' campaign achieved an unprecedented bargaining framework despite the fragmentation of representation, and explains the doctors' apparent strength as employees—in notable contrast to the social workers.

Where the social workers emphasized the importance of the services they provide for the less privileged populations, and the connection between these services and their employment, the doctors' campaign was conducted in a very different atmosphere. As former Israel Medical Association (IMA) chairperson Eran Dolev put it, "The problem is that you look around, the grass is greener.... You see your lawyer friends making more [money].... Then high-tech calls, says 'you have an MD, come help us in biomedics.' Who wants to be a doctor? Let's make money.... There's no professional pride" (interview). He noted that "reality has changed," that young doctors are no longer willing to apply themselves with the same selfless dedication: "Where we said 'us, ours,' they say 'me, mine'; it's a completely different world" (interview). The Mirsham chairperson and journalists covering the campaign noted this atmosphere as well (Linder-Ganz, interview; Weissbuch, interview).

Unlike the railway workers, whose unpolished speech and behavior undermined public support for their campaign, the doctors are perceived as an elite with friends in the liberal professions and the media. Indeed, the junior and senior doctors hired the services of leading media consultants and public relations firms and won extensive media coverage that was mostly supportive of the resident physicians' bid for their own collective framework. (The main exception was *Israel Hayom*, the widely distributed free newspaper that supports Prime Minister Netanyahu and is critical of worker campaigns in general.) According to a survey carried out for *TheMarker* (Linder-Ganz and Tucker 2011), between 20 August and 8 December, the campaign was mentioned more times in the Israeli media than the Iran nuclear program, which was perceived to be a threat to Israel's very survival at that time.

In his book on the relevance of class analysis, Eric Olin Wright (1997, 462) divides the public sector into the "state service sector," comprised of decommodified services, and the "state political sector," comprised of institutions within which the function of reproducing capitalist social relations is particularly important. For the last couple of decades, the health sector has been moving progressively from the service sector to the political sector, and its importance in the neoliberal regime of capital accumulation is increasing. In a study of the Israeli health sector, Dani Filc (2005) has explained the central role of health care business in the neoliberal/post-Fordist economy and the centrality of health within neoliberal governmentality. According to Filc, the sector is an enormous industry with highly profitable satellite industries such as pharmaceuticals and biotechnologies. As more and more spheres of everyday life are "medicalized" (the "tendency to explain socio-political phenomena as medical pathologies"; Filc 2005, 181), healthcare increasingly becomes a potential field for huge capital accumulation (Filc 2005, 190). From 1979 to 1999, Israel's health industry experienced huge growth relative to the economy as a whole, and relative to other industries, in terms of the number of firms operating, the number of employees, volume of sales, and volume of goods for export (Filc 2005, 185–186). For investors, the sector offers guaranteed spending, since states will ensure their citizens a basic level of health, and citizens will pay for what they can beyond state assistance. On the other hand, according to neoliberal principles, states must reduce public spending, thus health services undergo creeping privatization, opening the way for further profit-making opportunities, and indeed, as Filc (2005, 184) notes, Israel has seen the increasing privatization of financing and ownership of health services; even nonprofit institutions (the four HMOs and public hospitals) have adopted the neoliberal model, offering a range of services for pay.

Relations between the Health Ministry and the Finance Ministry reflect the growing importance of the health sector as the object of neoliberal reforms. The Health Ministry has long been squeezed between the demands of the state and the needs of the health system as perceived by the people working within it, and as the power of the Finance Ministry has increased, individual ministries' independence has declined. At the same time, the position of health minister has become more important, as reflected by the trend to grant this position to major government coalition partners instead of fobbing it off to insignificant parties, as in the past (see Rosen and Samuel 2009, 17).

Moreover, those within the Health Ministry who fail to toe the Finance Ministry's line are not tolerated. In his first speech as Health Ministry director-general (2010), Roni Gamzu attacked the Finance Ministry, asking how much more "streamlining" the health system could take and at whose expense. He later spoke openly to the press against the Finance Ministry and its policies and against the privatization of the health services (Linder-Ganz 2011a). During the doctors' campaign, he took a softer approach compared to the Finance Ministry, delaying the submission of the request for an injunction against the junior doctors, refusing to speak against the directors of certain hospitals, and holding back the submission of contempt of court charges against the junior doctors. In a conversation with them, Gamzu spoke harshly against the Finance Ministry and the prime minister (then acting health minister), especially against the prime minister's threat that he would bring "doctors from India" to replace the strikers (Linder-Ganz 2011a). As a result, though Gamzu was in no way staunchly on the doctors' side, he was later relieved of his role in handling the Health Ministry's response to the doctors' campaign (Even 2011b).

The health sector is being privatized in three main ways: (1) complementary health insurance, offered by the HMOs, which grants various benefits and discounts for services and medication beyond the health basket provided for all by law; (2) increasing patient contributions for consultations with specialists (including the option of a second opinion) and part payment for medication; and (3) the outsourcing of services to private companies or private clinics. The growing industry of medical tourism should be added to this list as well. The doctors, unlike the social workers or the railway workers, are in a position to benefit from the neoliberalization of their professional field. As a highly skilled workforce handling extremely expensive and specialized equipment, doctors are the main conduit for medication and services to patients, able to direct patients to certain treatments or promote certain drugs. This puts them in a strong position of authority and domination in the health system and vis-à-vis the employer (the state) that is seeking to attract companies. Moreover, many doctors in the public sector also have private clinics, which is why they were adamantly opposed to clocking in. Most are in favor of "Sharap"—the provision of private services using public premises and equipment after regular hours.[1] Hospital department heads and hospital directors also tend to be in favor, because it enables doctors to earn more without requiring an additional budget from the state. The IMA was also in favor, though it has tended to keep quiet about this for fear of losing public support.[2]

In the doctors' case, then, opposition to the union and demands for greater representation are not connected to opposition to neoliberal trends. The doctors' highly visible place in the negotiated order (Strauss 1978) was assured and was not threatened by the changes in the sphere of labor relations; on the contrary, those changes augmented their power, which contributed to the success of their campaign, both within the IMA framework and within the new framework demanded by the residents.

This is in stark contrast to the cleaners, who were not visible, not present as workers. Just by way of illustration: the most symbolically significant achievement of the collective agreement of the cleaners' campaign was compelling the university to agree to turn on the air-conditioning when the cleaners come in the morning, rather than waiting until the regular university staff and students arrive, as it had done previously. This is a major step in perceiving them as workers, as humans carrying out a task, and not as a cleaning service. Previously the cleaners were not merely weak at the negotiating table, but not negotiating at all—they were not part of the negotiated order. Their campaign required mediation and initiative from outside, volunteers driven by ideas of social justice willing to put in time and effort, to assist the cleaners in taking part in negotiating the social order. The Histadrut, though perceived to be representing workers, made no effort to draw the cleaners into negotiating the social order at even the lowest level and blocked all workers' demands to negotiate the larger social order. The initiative of the university students and faculty makes the workers visible, while the Histadrut leaves them invisible; the former tries to bring them into the negotiated order, while the latter leaves them dependent on the Histadrut's historical ties and the personal contacts of its leaders. However, despite the frustration with the Histadrut and opposition to the establishment, many workers attempting to organize their workplace decided to remain within the Histadrut, often while fully aware of other, perhaps more democratic, options.

RENEGOTIATING THE ROLE OF THE HISTADRUT

Paradoxically perhaps, the same campaigns that illustrate the opposition to the Histadrut also show its continued dominance, which is why many of those behind recent organizing drives have chosen to remain within the Histadrut framework. Its main power source is its good relations with employers and the ability to restrain workers' demands in one area to gain concessions in another. This was particularly so under Eini's leadership. As *TheMarker* labor relations correspondent Haim Bior put it with just a little hyperbole, "[Eini] improved relations with the industrialists, and with private employers in general, and the state as employer; . . . some of them were close personal friends. He had connections in the Finance Ministry . . . his best friend was [then head of the Manufacturers Association of Israel (MAI)] Shraga Brosh . . . it was a personal friendship, also between their wives; they attended each others' family events" (interview).

The Histadrut's main power has historically been in the public sector; indeed, the private sector was insignificant in the early years of the state. In the 1970s and 1980s, with the growing strength of the private sector, the Histadrut used this sector as a way of restraining wages in the public sector and in its own enterprises (see Shalev and Grinberg 1989), developing close cooperation with the Employers Organizations Coordinating Bureau and the MAI (see Grinberg 1996).

The Histadrut also retains its links with the political system, partly because the Histadrut's political structure leaves it obliged to fulfill its side in deals reached among politicians. Even Eini, famous for being the first chairperson to climb up the ranks of the Histadrut as a unionist, is reliant on political support for his election.[1] Eini's political ties are reflected in the alliance he brokered between the Labor Party and the Likud Party in 2009, and also (in the same year) in his mediating role between Labor members of Knesset (MKs) and party members to enable the passage of controversial amendments to the party constitution. His role in the coalition also enabled Eini to push through the package deal of 2009 that included three paragraphs protecting workers' organizations and facilitating the organization of workers. Indeed, when the doctors were frustrated with their own representative organization's lack of progress in negotiations and suggested the IMA should join the Histadrut (this did not in fact happen), this was tacit recognition of the Histadrut's good relations with the state.

Good relations between the Histadrut and the employer were evident in the railway campaign, when the Histadrut often seemed closer to and more cooperative with the railway leadership than its own workers' committee. Eini was also close to the chair of the railway board, Ori Yogev. In 2009, when the Finance Ministry budgetary officer resigned in protest at the package deal being hammered out with the Histadrut, Eini and Yogev (at the time chair of the National Economic Council Advisory Committee) signed instead, though Yogev was known as being antiunion: "Yogev was . . . very anti-Histadrut, and even today he isn't fond of it, but in dialogue with Eini he was good. Yogev knows how to work with Eini" (Niv, interview).[2] The Histadrut leadership has faced the railway and the government over many issues, repeatedly meeting the same people over the negotiating table, and personal ties are strong.

There are advantages to such friendly terms, not just for the stability of labor relations. For example, at Eini's insistence, the railway's suspension of committee members (over disciplinary violations) was canceled in return for the Histadrut's agreeing to intensive negotiations. But it is precisely such high-level personal partnerships that can work to the detriment of the workers and that they are now challenging. As Edra'i put it, regarding her own suspension, "The Histadrut cooperates with them [the employers]. . . . What does that mean? It means that there is a disciplinary hearing, and the Histadrut representatives sit there and don't say a word. And I need to hire a private lawyer. They cooperate. . . . [The Histadrut leaders say to themselves,] 'when will we finally be rid of that woman?'" (interview). Where the committee sees a fight on principle, it seems to the workers that the Histadrut and its negotiating partners just want to wrap things up. Edra'i also emphasized the way considerations external to the issue at hand can influence top-level deals at the expense of the workers' immediate concerns: "If the [transport] minister says, 'come on, give me that Gila and I'll leave you alone about Alon Hassan,' they make a deal at my expense" (interview).[3]

The case of the subcontracted cleaners underlines the continued relevance of the Histadrut's historical strength and personal ties that lie behind the passage of the two contract labor agreements it reached in 2012. Indeed, this historical strength and resultant legitimacy is reflected in the fact that the Histadrut's role in the negotiations toward these agreements was "unusual and even legally questionable," as Davidov (2015, 13) puts it, considering that it has "no formal status as the legal representative of the various contractors' employees." Thus it has no official bargaining status vis-à-vis the employers but skirted this fundamental unionizing requirement by addressing subcontracting employers "as a whole," thus also avoiding the problem of having to define a bargaining unit (Shamir 2016, 232–234).

However, the Histadrut with its dual role of employer and workers' representative is partly responsible for the rise of this form of employment; this suggests the Histadrut will find it difficult to transform itself into an organization drawing on the collective strength of its members and representing their interests as workers. As Bernstein (1986) notes, the Histadrut did little to oppose the casualization of labor even in the days of the Alignment when it had a direct and strong connection with the government.[4] The casualization of cleaning services in particular affected mainly Arab women to begin with—a population outside the Histadrut's sphere of concerns as a nationalist organization as opposed to a regular workers' union. The Histadrut put up no effective opposition to this trend and did not even stop it in its own enterprises: among Israel's first temping agencies was Mankoor, set up in the 1970s and owned by the Histadrut to employ temporary workers for its Koor Industries conglomerate.[5] The Histadrut's workers' committees, whose main role is shop-floor watchdog, were irrelevant to subcontracted labor of this kind, and those cleaners who were Histadrut members were part of the Service Workers Union, one of the weakest unions (Bernstein 1986, 410–411). In its agreements with the Organization of Cleaning Enterprises and Contractors, the Histadrut accepted the legal minimum wage as the basis for the wage scale, thus not even striving for an improved basic wage for cleaners: the companies agreed to pay the cleaners more or less as required by law and nothing more, but even this was not always effective because enforcement was minimal.

The Histadrut's first decisive step to protect those in manpower agencies and limit the triangular employment relationship was the initiation, together with MKs, of the Employment of Employees by Manpower Contractors Law of 1996, though some saw the law as giving an official seal of approval for such employment (see Raday 2002). An important amendment in the year 2000 limited temporary employment to nine months, after which the temporary employee must be taken on as a regular employee (par. 12a), but the Finance Ministry repeatedly postponed the application of this stipulation by means of the Arrangements Law until 2008. Meanwhile, according to claims in *TheMarker* (Weissberg, Bior, and Dattel 2011), the Histadrut and the National Histadrut had signed agreements with manpower agencies to divide agency fees (fees paid by nonmember workers to the union) between them, even though the workers in the agencies did not know they were paying such fees. Moreover, the Histadrut has not enforced the nine-month stipulation in any case, even though the state is the main violator. Similarly, in the social workers' strike, the Histadrut failed to take the opportunity to prevent the outsourcing of service provision to private companies, which is essentially a form of contract labor like the manpower agencies.

Thus the 2011 strike over contract labor was the first time the Histadrut had taken collective steps against an employment framework. It was an impressive show of strength, with the airport, ports, railways, government ministries, National Insurance Institute, local authorities, the Israel Lands Administration, the courts, public companies, universities, Naamat kindergartens, hospitals, Clalit HMO, and the National Student Union taking part to various extents. Furthermore, the labor court accepted the strike's legitimacy, rejecting government claims that this was a "political" strike (Filut 2011). The court's position broadens the right to strike for the sake of unorganized workers and is thus a significant precedent and augments the Histadrut's strength. The result of the campaign was two separate agreements of principle, one in the public sector and one in the private sector. In the public sector, the state refused to take on more than a minimal number of workers in direct employment, but agency workers were to receive better employment terms, a liaison office was established for handling complaints, and 120 inspectors were to be taken on at the Labor Ministry. In the private sector, the agreement opened the way for greater direct employment, but only for those working at least 90 percent full-time, and only after nine months—a stipulation already provided for in the 1996 law.

The agreements do have the potential to significantly improve the working lives of thousands of agency workers and demonstrate the power the Histadrut is able to wield. This development should not be lightly dismissed: "for the first time the government agreed, under pressure, to sign a collective agreement with the Histadrut that does not concern government employees, but rather the employees of contractors engaged by the government," as Davidov (2015, 13) points out. But it also has some significant holes. First, the Histadrut set out to address the problem of cleaners and security guards above all, yet the security guards were left out of both agreements in the end, on the pretext of the complications of firearms licensing. Since the mid-1990s, this sector has grown rapidly (see Handels 2003), and security guards make up a large percentage of agency workers today. The agreements also left out subcontracted workers in construction (a large proportion of whom are Arab) and employees of foreign high-tech companies (with the dubious claim that their employment terms are determined abroad). Another potential loophole is that the monitoring committee is authorized to approve requests to extend the temporary period from nine months to fifteen.

The main problem with the agreements is that they do not put an end to the triangular employment relationship. Davidov (2015, 12) has even argued that the extension order of 2013 (which ensured the agreements covered all workers) augmented the legitimacy of this kind of employment. Indeed, both the state and private employers expressed willingness to improve employment terms but were reluctant to take on workers in direct employment. The president of the Federation of the Israeli Chambers of Commerce, Uriel Lynn, told Prime Minister Netanyahu that direct employment would mean immeasurable damage to freedom of management in the business sector (Lynn is also the owner of the manpower agency Lynn-Bichler) (Niv 2011a), though MAI head Shraga Brosh was more willing to consider direct employment (Niv 2012b). The state's reluctance is due to the fact that it is one of the main users of contracted labor, in particular within local authorities. According to Dan Ben Haim, labor relations officer at the Union of Local Authorities, some 50 percent of the approximately one hundred thousand local authority employees are employed via agencies and independent firms set up for this purpose (Bar-Eli et al. 2011). The Finance Ministry calculated that taking on agency workers in the public sector would be very expensive (involving wage increases of 30–40 percent), while taking them on in the private sector would not greatly increase wages (Arlosoroff 2012), which explains why Brosh was in favor of taking on a small number while the state preferred to improve employment terms without taking any on in direct employment. Gutwein (2012, 63) goes further, suggesting that the state's reluctance to take on workers shows that its main concern was reducing the power of labor: breaking organized labor makes all labor weaker, even if certain groups of workers (temporarily) enjoy good employment terms, like those in the high-tech sector who were left out of the agreements.

But the most pressing issue with these agreements is that of enforcement. In 2011, another bill was legislated (in force from 2012). This law aimed to enhance labor law enforcement and addressed agency workers specifically, to improve their working conditions though without granting them any additional job security. Among its potentially far-reaching stipulations, it places responsibility for labor law violations and peripheral benefits (such as pension payments or incremental allowances) on the client company as well as the agency and makes it possible to press criminal charges against senior managers in agency companies for certain violations. In addition, a company violating labor rights will not be granted any state contract for three years. This means that agency workers are covered by protective legislation and collective agreements at the highest level. Yet as the Ben-Gurion University cleaners' case shows, without worker involvement, without on-the-ground, ongoing supervision of daily employment practices, even minimal enforcement of basic labor law is difficult. Despite the

Histadrut's assertion that its workers' committees will open their doors to agency workers (Niv 2012d), without direct employment cleaners will not be part of the negotiated order unless they receive the remarkable level of support seen in the Ben-Gurion University case.

Thus the most prominent issue is the lack of participation among the workers themselves: the Histadrut's campaign for agency workers was conducted essentially with no worker input; it was an agreement based on Eini's personal ties with Brosh and the political establishment and on the strike, which involved a top-down directive from the Histadrut's leadership—Eini—to the various worker committees. This highlights the Histadrut's top-heavy power structure and its reliance on the personal connections of its chair. Indeed, shortly after the agreement of principles was reached, Brosh stepped down as chair of the Coordinating Bureau and the problems came to light. In the spring of 2013, the Bureau under its new head, Zvika Oren, began negotiations toward an agreement with the Histadrut, according to which taking on contract laborers in direct employment would be just one option for private-sector employers (see Niv 2013j). In short, just a year after the agreements signed by Eini, the leading actors on each side of the table stood down, and the viability of the agreements was in doubt.

The Histadrut's Most-Favored Status

In addition to the Histadrut's central role in the state-building project, it has been favored by the courts and legal system as the main workers' representative organization, which has further shored up its hegemony (see Mundlak 2007, 1998; Shaked 2002). One reason for this is the Histadrut's status as a primary organization, not a federation of unions: workers' committees have no power to negotiate collectively, sign collective agreements, or declare a strike, and the courts have refused to adjudicate in cases brought by Histadrut organs against the Histadrut itself (Mundlak 2007, 97–98), thereby underlining the Histadrut's central authority. The courts have generally accepted that bargaining units are plant-based, which trivializes the heterogeneity of interests within what are often very large firms and makes it hard for smaller groups to set up a workers' organization (Mundlak 1997, 232).[6] Extension orders make collective agreements valid for all in the bargaining unit, even if they are not members in the representative organization, and can be extended by executive order to include all workers in the sector or entire economy. This strengthens the Histadrut's hegemonic status as *the* workers' organization, since it means that agreements reached by the dominant union are likely to cover many workers outside the workplace or sector, making the possible advantages of rival unions appear less attractive or less pressing (Mundlak 1997, 232). Furthermore, the courts forbid "double and conflicting membership" in a union, which, prior to the National Health Insurance Law of 1995, made it difficult to leave the Histadrut: most were reliant on the Histadrut's services and were thus compelled to remain within the Histadrut, but were forbidden from setting up a rival organization while still members of the Histadrut.

Though the status of the Histadrut is being undermined in many ways, as Mundlak (2007; Mundlak et al. 2013) has argued, the cases analyzed here suggest that the structures favoring the Histadrut are still in place, and the courts still regard the Histadrut as the main workers' organization and shore up its power. In the social workers' campaign, the courts emphasized the Social Workers Union (SWU)'s subordinate position by insisting it accede to the Histadrut's draft. Although the regional labor court rejected the Finance Ministry's request for an injunction, the National Labor Court (NLC) pushed the sides to continue talking and reach agreement within the budgetary framework of the draft agreement. The court's apparent support of the Histadrut's position angered social workers, especially its presumption that the Histadrut represented the social workers: "There's a feeling [the courts] undermined our struggle, cooperated with the Histadrut. . . . They didn't stand up for our rights, didn't stand by our side, didn't understand the complexity of the issue, as if we weren't represented [in the courts] at all" (Farber, interview).

In the railway case, the workers' committee declared it had joined Koach Laovdim, which then asked the court to declare that it was the representative workers' organization. The regional labor court referred the case to the NLC (Collective Dispute 13381-07-12), which ruled that the Histadrut is the representative organization at the railway. It noted that another organization cannot challenge a representative organization during authentic, intensive negotiations and also added a period of immunity of twelve months from the signing of the agreement (Inter-Organizational Dispute 9685-07-12). In December of that year, in response to Koach Laovdim's appeal, the High Court backed the NLC's ruling by refraining from intervening, noting that the NLC was the correct forum for ruling on the issue (HCJ 6076/12). The courts upheld the workers' right to disrupt services and recognized outsourcing as a labor issue, bearing on employment terms, but favored stability over workers' voice, their right to choose representation or participation; the courts have the workers' interests in mind but believe the Histadrut is the only organization with the strength to protect the workers. As former NLC president Steve Adler noted, "The main union organization can only come through the big unions, a union like the Histadrut which has the resources. Unionization takes resources, it takes organization, it's no longer the little union just going out to a store or something: you need Facebook, you need people, you need to be able to sometimes support the people who are out on strike. . . . If you take an industry, the number of companies which have to be organized, it's got to be done on a big level by a big organization" (interview).

In the railway dispute, the railway's position was that transfer to another workers' organization would undermine negotiations, even though Koach Laovdim had declared its intention to work within the framework of the agreement of principles, and even though the workers' committee under Edra'i was the main partner in hammering out the agreement and thus knew it better than anyone. Orna Lin, who represented the Histadrut at the NLC, presented the case as one of stability versus anarchy, warning that if the court were to grant Koach Laovdim representative status, this would create anarchy in industrial relations because any committee that does not accept the Histadrut's instructions would seek a different representative organization (Bior and Shmil 2012). The court followed this line of thought: it did not even address the issue of which organization had representative status based on the Collective Agreements Law of 1957 but weighed the possible effects of a change of organization. In particular, it addressed three principles: fairness, certainty, and stability (Inter-Organizational Dispute 9685-07-12, par. 23–26).

In discussing fairness, the court weighed an individual's right to choose representation against the collective interest in achieving the aims of the negotiations. The idea that an effective way to ensure at least a measure of authenticity of collective interest is through the democratic election of a committee was not addressed by the court at all. In the railway case, the collective interest was deemed to be reaching an agreement rapidly and without further disruption to train services. This, de facto, strengthened the status of the Histadrut as the organization best able to bring the negotiations rapidly to a close regardless of the workers' point of view. It also has another implication: it pits workers against the public, whose interest is deemed to be regular train services, as opposed to uniting workers and public against the employer.

In discussing the principles of certainty and stability, NLC president Nili Arad quoted Judge Sigal Davidov-Motola in the Sprint Motors case (Inter-Organizational Dispute 50718-07-10), saying an organization in the middle of negotiations needs immunity (from challenge by another organization) in order to "enable a group of workers an actual and effective opportunity to hold collective labor relations with the employer," otherwise the employer is liable to wait for the organization to fail and thus avoid an agreement, or workers may refuse to cooperate, suspecting employer intervention in the committee elections. She also quoted Judge Steve Adler in the Open University case (Inter-Organizational Dispute 32690-10-10), noting that this immunity holds during all stages of negotiations, if the period of negotiations is reasonable. Thus the court connected "certainty" to the idea that the representative organization has authority and that a challenge to the representative organization undermines its authority; in other words, the organization's authority is not dependent on the workers' support. (The court also noted that workers may still transfer to another organization and receive services from this organization, thus their democratic rights are assured.)

The court used the agreement of principles to illustrate that the Histadrut was negotiating in good faith, and noted that fairness, certainty, and stability are present in the Histadrut's relations with the railway and that therefore the Histadrut should be permitted to continue to negotiate. This, of course, ignores the workers' wishes entirely: for example, the representative organization may be buying stability and certainty by cooperating with the employer's plans—as indeed the workers' committee and the Forum both claimed as regards the Histadrut.

In addressing the removal of the workers' committee, the NLC noted that no law determines the relationship between an organization and a workers' committee and that the organization's own constitution must guide the court's decision. According to the Histadrut's constitution, the committee is not a party to the collective agreement and not authorized to sign independently: "The committee is not and was never the representative organization. Including the committee in discussions toward the agreement of principles, and in negotiations, and the Histadrut's original intention to include it as a signatory to the agreement, when the time comes—all this does not grant the committee status as a party to the collective agreement" (Inter-Organizational Dispute 9685-07-12, par. 35). The court noted that it is customary for a committee to sign together with the representative organization, to show its commitment to the agreement. But appointing another, more compliant, committee undermines this idea of partnership between the workers and their representative organization. The court did not address the question of whether the committee was the main partner in reaching the agreement of principles and was supported by the workers, as Koach Laovdim claimed.

The High Court, responding to Koach Laovdim's appeal against the NLC ruling, declined to intervene. It said the case was the "core business" of the NLC, but also noted that the NLC is well aware of the "new winds" blowing in the sphere of labor relations, meaning new organizations and organizing drives, and that the NLC is proceeding cautiously, so as "not to sink veteran ships" (the Histadrut) yet "allow new ships a channel" (HCJ 6076/12, par. 13).

It is clear that the labor courts have the workers' welfare in mind but are less attentive to the issue of workers' voice or democratic participation. The strength of the Histadrut is used to protect workers, but according to the courts' perception, this strength is not connected to participation or voice. The former wages officer at the Finance Ministry noted, "The Histadrut is seen as a responsible body, stable, able to understand the consequences of irresponsible behavior." He added that the new unions will have to change, too, if they want to gain more influence—meaning that they had to tone down their radical stance and increase their control of the workers they represent (Levine, interview).

"To Fight Big Dogs You Need a Serious Dog!"

Workers involved in the campaigns are aware of the Histadrut's strength, and in many cases this has led them to choose the Histadrut despite its corruption-tarnished image, its links with the sometimes loathed establishment, and the lack of internal democracy or channels for expressing workers' voice. Rom Dvir, from the Histadrut's new Workers Organizing Unit, put it this way:

> There's a sentence I hear in the [new] journalists' union, it makes me crazy but it reflects [what's going on]—they say, why are we in the Histadrut? "We are facing the biggest sons of bitches, meaning the media owners, the capitalists, so we need the biggest son of a bitch with us. To fight big dogs you need a serious dog!" Or sometimes I hear, "I can't stand Ofer Eini, but if I need someone to fight on my side. . . ." It's strange, that the Histadrut is seen in this negative light, but they also need it. It will take a long time to change [this attitude]. (Interview)

Dror Feuer, from the *Globes* workers' committee, said,

> We chose the Histadrut because it's the strongest organization. . . . You have to see who we have to confront—Tshuva, Dankner in *Maariv*, Fischman, Lauder in Channel 10 [referring to the powerful business-men who own Israel's media]. . . . And it's good we went with the Histadrut; . . . what we're doing in Channel 10, *Maariv*, we couldn't have done without the support of the Histadrut. . . . The Histadrut helps first of all on the logistics—if there's a demonstration in Jeru-salem, the Histadrut brings buses, assists with getting a hall. . . . It has resources, these are things that WAC or Koach Laovdim can't offer. If we had gone with Koach Laovdim, we would have had to pay member-ship fees right from the start, more or less, thirty or forty shekels. . . . But it's more an issue of power. Channel 10 for example: for more than a year there was this crisis and the Finance Minister refused to meet with the management, absolutely refused. Then they got the workers' committee set up, and Eini made a few phone calls, and a meeting was held. (Feuer, interview)

Yair Tarchitzky, head of the Journalists Organization (JO), confirmed this approach: "I understood the forces we would have to contend with . . . Noni Moses, Sheldon [prominent businessmen]. . . . Or, at Channel 10, the top echelons of the Finance Ministry, the finance minister, the prime minister, and with all due respect to these organizations [Koach Laovdim], with their principles and independence . . . this isn't their league, they don't have the political strength or resources that the Histadrut has and has invested in us since the JO was set up" (interview).

The social workers also recognized the Histadrut's strength. One loose and informal group of social workers from the Sharon region, Osot Hasharon, contacted the Workers Advice Center (WAC, a small independent general union discussed in part 3) after the campaign for advice and support, feeling that the Histadrut had failed them, but they did not officially join WAC. According to Tami Farber (interview), who was involved in the group, there was a sense that social workers were reluctant to leave the "safety" of the Histadrut and afraid of striking out alone. Farber also said that one activist had tried to form a pressure group to leave the Histadrut, but this attempt received very little support from other social workers and was short lived.

Both Atidenu and Osim Shinui consciously chose to remain within the SWU (and thus Histadrut) framework, and even after the campaign and the frustration it engendered, they expressed their support for the existing channels. At first, Osim Shinui cultivated a wild-child image, free to act outside accepted frameworks, but this attitude was moderated especially after it began exercising its right to participate in the SWU as observers: "We do work in partnership. . . . [SWU chairperson Yitzhak] Perry has become a big enemy of the social workers but we don't want to make this personal. . . . One of Osim Shinui's aims is to strengthen the union's institutions, and not to set up an opposition. We see the union as a representative organization, active for its social workers, without alternatives" (Goldman, interview).

Atidenu's former chair, Inbal Shlosberg, said "I want people to be members of the union, that's my ideal, that's where strength comes from" (interview). Explaining why it was best for the social workers to remain within the Histadrut, Goldman said: "Ideologically, if we go back forty years, the Histadrut reflects my values" (interview).

The chair of the Pelephone workers' committee also noted the Histadrut's strength and size as important factors in the campaign's success: "The Histadrut is the biggest organization; it even has a strike fund. . . . No other organization can offer a strike fund, [the Pelephone strike] cost two or three million shekels. . . . For such a huge step, you need the biggest organization, and the Histadrut is the biggest." He noted that when the employer confiscated the workers' vehicles in retaliation, the Histadrut brought them vehicles: "A truck came, they unloaded the cars, and for every committee member there was a vehicle. Some of the activists ... not necessarily committee members, got a car too" (Avitan, interview). An activist at Pelephone put it more colorfully: "It's unbelievable, the organization. During that month I ate more sandwiches [from the Histadrut] than I've ever done in my life" (Boaron, interview). In their 2012 campaign, technicians from the cable TV company HOT also clung to the Histadrut after previous organizing attempts had failed: "We needed support, a big workers' organization. . . . We needed strength behind us, because it's not the first time [we've tried to organize], and in the first time, they very quickly managed to stop the organizing effort" (Berezovsky, interview).

One notable aspect of the Haifa Chemicals campaign in which the committee succeeded in leaving the Histadrut was the committee's relative independence: generally, each Histadrut committee negotiates the extent of its autonomy or the character of its relations with the organization, and most committees do not receive any membership fees directly. They receive funding only through the Histadrut, which passes on a certain amount of funding it receives in the form of membership and agency fees. At Haifa Chemicals, the committee had independent sources of funding. First, it had agreed with the Histadrut that some of the fees would go directly to its own coffers, so it had some funds to support the strikers regardless of the Histadrut's position. In addition, there was a cooperative store at the plant whose profits went to the committee. Furthermore, because the plant has stores of dangerous chemicals, some employees are obliged by law to continue working throughout a strike, and the committee was able to take advantage of this to keep as many people in work as possible while still ostensibly "on strike" (Kimhi, interview).

Moreover, the Haifa campaign was waged against a private employer, where public support for workers' struggles is less important than it is in the public sector. Here, the committee had support from families, other committees, activists, and the workers themselves with whom the committee was in continuous contact. Thus the Haifa workers were able to continue their struggle regardless of outside opinion, as long as they had funds, while the railway or social workers, for example, were dependent on Histadrut funds and public support.

The difficulties of the struggle did not deter the Haifa Chemicals workers, but according to Koach Laovdim, the case did frighten other committees who had thought of leaving the Histadrut. "There were committees who told us, well done for the effort, but we don't want to go through the same [tough] experience" (Vatury, interview). A committee at Sunfrost (a Tnuva subsidiary) also wanted to transfer to Koach Laovdim, but a ruling for the Sonol case, which granted the representative organization a year's immunity from the time an agreement was signed, stopped the process. The Sunfrost lawyer wrote two mocking sentences to Koach Laovdim: "There is a ruling at Sonol. It's not easy to leave the Histadrut" (Vatury, interview). Following the railway ruling, Koach Laovdim was forced to say to some committees that it was simply not possible or else pointless for them to transfer from the Histadrut.

Signs of Change in the Histadrut

So for historical and strategic reasons and also due to the chairperson's personal history and preferences, the Histadrut retains its hegemonic position in Israeli industrial relations as well as its good connections with employers. The labor courts have tended to support its position, safeguarding the stability of labor relations even at the expense of dampening workers' voice or being perceived to do so. This has been the cause of much anger and frustration among Histadrut members. But the pressures and demands from frustrated and increasingly activist workers are having some effect within the Histadrut, and there are signs that the Histadrut is changing. Demands for workers' participation and increased democracy within the organization are affecting its priorities and activities, as are attempts to undermine organized labor in general. Aware of such developments, the leadership has made some efforts to revitalize (see also Weinblum 2010), taking a more active part in organizing workers and taking the initiative in seeking high-level agreements.

Regarding high-level agreements, the first major initiative came following the Second Lebanon War in 2006, when the Histadrut reached an agreement with employers to push the government to grant compensation (as vacation pay) to those in the north affected by war. The pension agreement in 2007 came next, followed by the public-sector agreement for wage supplements in 2008 after a long period in which no such agreement had been reached. Regarding workers' organizing, that year also saw the campaign at the Coffee Bean chain of cafés, which the Histadrut took under its wing and in which it invested a lot of its activists' time and its own resources (though this ended in a collective arrangement, which is less binding than a full collective agreement and has no legal standing). This was the first of various campaigns that were taken up by the Histadrut as flagship campaigns, including those at the credit card companies Visa and Isracard, the fuel company Sonol, and the transport company Egged. Then in 2009, Eini succeeded in getting the package deal through the Knesset, whose most significant clause compels employers to talk to workers' committees and prevents employers from stopping union representatives from entering company premises—paving the way for the Histadrut's increased organizing activity. The campaign for subcontracted workers is also a sign of the Histadrut's renewal. Though its strength stems from the Histadrut's historical status and the personal contacts of its chair, it also involved cooperation with Koach Laovdim and the social protest movement leaders.

According to Rom Dvir from the Histadrut's Organizing Unit, there was a feeling within the Histadrut that the organizing drives of the early 2000s had failed partly due to the lack of organizing experience within the organization: "[There was an] understanding within the Histadrut that some kind of revitalization was needed. This was real; it's not just a question of rebranding. It's something that they [in the Histadrut] began to understand" (Dvir, interview). The new structure of firms in the economy was also making it hard for the Histadrut's region-based branches or profession-based unions to meet the needs of workers: new nationwide chains with various offices, depots, and customer-service centers scattered around the country mean that workers ostensibly within one company are in fact geographically dispersed and carrying out a huge range of very different tasks. This led to the establishment of the Organizing Unit in 2010.

Though not officially acknowledged, the rise of Koach Laovdim also influenced the Histadrut's decision to start actively organizing, as noted by many interviewees (including Feuer, Matar, Basha, Dvir, and Bior). *Globes*'s Shay Niv claimed there are minutes from Histadrut meetings in which competition from Koach Laovdim is specifically mentioned, and Histadrut leaders admit the organization knows nothing about reaching people on the ground (Niv, interview). In addition, the Organizing Unit was an opportunity to polish the Histadrut's image. As Niv put it, "The people in the new Organizing Unit are young and hip; they could easily be in Koach Laovdim" (interview). Dvir noted the importance of bringing younger people into the unit along with their new ideas: "To make such a dramatic change both within the Histadrut and in the Israeli economy, you need ideational power. I mean it wasn't just a technical issue; it's a question of worldview" (interview).

There are also signs the Histadrut is more willing to negotiate increased union independence, as it did with the SWU in 2007, thus attracting new organizing initiatives drawn to the Histadrut's power but wary of its dictatorial reputation: "The Histadrut is the only place where you can set up a branch union, within [the Histadrut] but separate, with a constitution that gives it a certain independence. . . . So it's a combination of an organization that gives support: you don't have to pay membership fees to begin with, the Organizing Unit gives full support for free, legal, media [support], everything; and on the other hand you can achieve a certain separation" (Matar, interview).

The social protests of 2011 were a shock to the Histadrut leadership, which found itself pushed out of the social protest movement even though it had supported the leadership actively, even putting its offices on Tel Aviv's Arlosorov Street at their disposal for meetings (Dvir, interview). The energy of the protest movement galvanized both the Histadrut and many workers who grasped the opportunity to bring social justice into the workplace, particularly later when it seemed that the protests had fizzled out ineffectively. As the Pelephone committee chair said, "I think the committees, and the organizing drives, will create social justice. . . . This is social justice. Within the companies, if in each company a committee were to be established, the committee were to make its demands, you'd see, the middle class would rise up, and there'd be social justice" (Avitan, interview). Dvir noted the awakening that had begun before the social protests broke out and had influenced the Histadrut too, what he called the "new organizing": "People in the city squares felt powerless facing reality and wanted to influence the place closest them, their workplace. They created a lot of energy. The [new] journalists' union is a great example of this. It's not by chance that Dror Feuer [who was prominent in setting up the JO] was an important figure in the social protest movement" (Dvir, interview).

One further cause for change in the Histadrut may be the waning of its old sources of power, based on its position in the corporatist structure and its institutional ties—"institutional power" in Dörre's terms (2011, 18–22). This waning meant it was compelled to agree to various employment frameworks such as the triangular employment relationship and two-tiered agreements. The power of the social partners is no longer guaranteed by the state (Mundlak 2009), yet the decline of one source of power was not compensated by a rise in "associational power" (collective power based on organizing; E. Wright 2000, 962), creating a representational vacuum. Koach Laovdim was set up to fill this vacuum, at least partially, and now we see the Histadrut making the first tentative efforts to do the same—to draw at least some of its strength from organizing and rely less on leftover structures and personal ties. In this sense, the Histadrut is in a process of revitalization, as Weinblum (2010) suggests.

However, the literature on union revitalization also suggests the Histadrut may struggle to draw on associational power unless it is willing to yield far more of its institutional power. Revitalization literature concentrates on union attempts to regain their strength following the decline of the corporatist regime and reposition themselves as important actors in shaping social and economic policies (see Badigannavar and Kelly 2011; Frege and Kelly 2003; Heery 2002; Phelan 2007; Turner 2005; Voss and Sherman 2000). There is some confusion about what constitutes revitalization—which union activities are to be considered the aim of revitalization efforts and which are the means (see Hickey, Kuruvilla, and Lakhani 2010 for an account of circular argumentation in revitalization studies). Nonetheless, various activities that result in more effective organized labor as measured in terms of bargaining power can be seen as direct or indirect revitalization activities. These include expanding membership, activating members, restructuring the union to reflect a change of priorities, enhancing services to members, creating broader alliances with other organizations, and redirecting resources to new goals. Revitalization can include a normative vision, too, of democratic representation and social solidarity able to affect political and economic institutions, leading to social justice (Turner 2005, 387).

Revitalization literature has categorized the many strategies and tactics that unions may adopt into two broad approaches: the social partnership approach and the organizing approach (Phelan 2007; Turner 2005). According to the social partnership approach, a union may develop its links with the traditional social partners, building on historic structures and seeking common ground for mutual benefit. This approach, I suggest, corresponds to seeking strength in institutional power sources. According to the organizing approach, a union may concentrate on recruiting new members and activating existing members, thus enhancing its membership-based power through participatory, more radical grassroots activism. This approach, I suggest, clearly corresponds to associational power. Partnership and organizing, of course, are imprecise terms, more like ideal types: "these competing positions do not map neatly onto established factional divisions within the labor movement" (Heery 2002, 31). However, as Heery (2002) has suggested, they are distinguishable by their different view of capitalism and hence of worker interests: the organizing approach tends to be more adversarial and uncompromising, a fight for social justice, which does not always sit well with the idea of cooperation based on mutual interests. A union may use different approaches at different times or in different struggles concurrently, but since unions are ideological organizations, it is hard for a union to promote both approaches at the same time in the same place (see also Badigannavar and Kelly 2011).

Despite the decline in the Histadrut's institutional power, Eini's strategy has been to nurture partnership based on historical ties, at least until the recent wave of organizing. Weinblum (2010, 38–39) sees the Histadrut unequivocally adopting the social partnership approach in three major social pacts achieved under Eini's leadership. (1) In 2006, the Histadrut reached a nonbinding agreement with the Coordinating Bureau, which expressed the intentions of both sides to regulate industrial relations through dialogue and collective bargaining. This agreement marked a change of approach from Eini's predecessor Amir Peretz, noted for his adversarial attitude to employers. (2) In 2007, the same organizations reached a mandatory pension agreement, which was later extended to all employees in the economy by the minister of labor. (3) Also in 2007, during hearings at the NLC on a case regarding privacy at work, the Histadrut and the

Coordinating Bureau asked the court to allow the case to be decided through negotiation, and a collective agreement was rapidly drafted (see Mundlak 2012). The agreement deals with an issue outside the scope of traditional union activities and establishes a grievance procedure "strongly grounded in the tradition of collective bargaining, intentionally to marginalize judicial intervention in labor relations" (Weinblum 2010, 39). The Round Table agreement in 2009, which was intended to ensure that the Histadrut would be consulted on all socioeconomic issues, can be seen as another example (see Weinblum 2010, 45), though this initiative was less than successful.

If the two revitalization approaches are indeed incompatible, the Histadrut's efforts in organizing and recruitment may undermine its status based on social partnership.[7] The social workers' campaign suggests that this is indeed the case: here, the intense participatory energies of the newly awakened social workers were channeled into the existing union frameworks. These frameworks, the union bureaucracies and hierarchal structures (encompassing the Histadrut and the SWU, with the new organizations within it), thwarted their radical approach to participation and neutralized the social workers' voice for the sake of industrial quiet. The Histadrut made no effort to recruit new members, to activate existing members for the sake of creating a stronger front, or to form alliances with other organizations. It gave up on the most important demand of putting a halt to the privatization of services. It also ignored the energy and activism on the ground and tried to limit the campaign to the issue of wages. This was reflected in the SWU leader's demand that the social workers quit waging "social" battles "on the backs of the workers" (Shlosberg, interview).

In demanding solidarity with the private-sector social workers, as well as with the social justice movement and the various groups involved in the demonstrations, the social workers challenged the Histadrut's position of cooperation with employers' organizations. In demanding a welfare state for all, they challenged the Histadrut's acquiescence in the dismantling and privatization of welfare. And the sheer scale of involvement and democratic participation threatened to subvert the Histadrut's hegemony and centralized power. Because the social workers refused to accept the compromises required for the kind of partnership approach favored by the Histadrut, it was unable to fight for the demands they were willing to fight for, and instead of supporting the union in its campaign, the Histadrut suppressed its aspirations and those of its members (see also Preminger 2013).

The railway case is less clear-cut, but similar. The Histadrut failed to use the energy of activists and workers on the ground to strengthen the case for far-reaching demands: it did not use the Forum against the Privatization of the Railway, many of whom were Histadrut activists (Raznik, interview), or the links the Forum had among activist groups such as Social-Democratic Israel (*Hug*

Yesod); this group, which explicitly aims to bring back social democracy, was established when the Labor Party abandoned (according to the group's founders) its social-democratic roots and participated in privatizing and budget-cutting governments, becoming a pale shadow of the neoliberal right. The group supports organizing workers and is against privatization of public services. Associated with the Labor Party, it could have been a natural ally. The Histadrut also failed to work with Koach Laovdim as part of a more general struggle against privatization and outsourcing in the public sector, though Koach Laovdim activists were present at demonstrations and involved in the Forum. Instead, it struggled to maintain control of the committee and discipline the workers, in order to maintain its ties with public-sector employers.

Compared to the social workers' case, in this case it was easier for the Histadrut to rid itself of the workers' challenge to its authority: partly because Edra'i and the committee were found to be in contempt of court and had taken very radical steps in disrupting services, including abandoning one train, complete with passengers, in the middle of the track; and partly because of the poor image of the rail workers, Edra'i above all, in popular opinion. Most significantly, the attempt to transfer to Koach Laovdim transformed the issue from one of voice and participation within a union to one of rivalry between two legitimate unions.

The lack of democracy and workers' participation in the Histadrut, then, may well be not just a historical anomaly, but also a structural problem. If the Histadrut's institutional power continues to decline, it may find organizing to be an increasingly useful source of power. However, if employers, the state, and the courts prefer to maintain a hegemonic Histadrut for the sake of stability and efficiency (see also E. Wright 2000 for an analysis of employer interests in a strong union), the Histadrut may find its organizing drives detrimental to its other sources of power, or at least fear that this may be so. In this case, workers are likely to find their democratic aspirations suppressed.

CONCLUDING REMARKS TO PART 1

The cases investigated in part 1 have left us with a rather confused picture: workers are consolidating their unions, yet breaking away into new unions and organizations; workers are fighting the Histadrut, yet clinging to it as the strongest dog in the pack; workers are struggling against the privatization of services, yet also benefiting from privatization; workers are forming particularist groups and insisting on their own group interests, yet expending great energy and resources on assisting those apparently unable to voice their own concerns, such as the cleaners. What they have in common is the desire to act, to make their voices heard and influence their representation and workplace—and possibly beyond their workplace, too. It is not by chance that there is talk of a wave of organizing, after almost two decades in which the strength of labor has declined.

If we view this wave in revitalization terms, we see that the Histadrut still bears the baggage of its singular historical role, and its status as a well-connected, top-heavy hegemonic workers' organization may compel it to oppose greater democratic participation. Similarly, in the case of the doctors as well as the social workers, we see that revitalization initiatives may come from outside the union, and the union may oppose them it if feels greater democratic representation or active participation are undermining existing structures of power and interest representation. This supports Bellin's (2000) note of warning in an article entitled "Contingent Democrats": unions will not necessarily support greater democracy; their support depends on whether democracy advances their material interests, and this depends on historical circumstances. Labor's support for democratization, she suggests, depends mainly on the extent to which organized labor is dependent on state cooperation and on how economically privileged organized labor is compared to unorganized labor. We should note, then, that while revitalization studies generally concentrate on the union, revitalization efforts may come from the rank and file, with little support or assistance from established union institutions. Likewise, while revitalization efforts generally pit the union against employers or the state, unions may also oppose their own workers if activists adopt strategies perceived as threatening union strategies. The state—and the courts—may also oppose greater worker participation if it perceives this to threaten the stability of industrial relations and hence of the economy.

Moreover, as the doctors' case shows, the same neoliberal processes that undermine collective labor representation in general may strengthen certain groups of workers; this may be particularly significant if it opens opportunities for workers who did not benefit from the previous collective structure. This is likely to become increasingly common as representation is fragmented, solidarity breaks down, and workers no longer share—or believe they no longer share—the same overall interests. But this fragmentation due to the individualistic reconfiguration of demands—activists of disparate groups making their voices heard—may also weaken the union and undermine its ability to balance conflicting demands while showing employers a united front. Thus we should be attentive to the internal dynamics and clashes of interest in a workers' organization as it strives to revitalize, especially in large, hegemonic unions.

But looking at the Israeli case in revitalization terms misses what is new in these campaigns. This is not merely a "corporatist revival" (Mundlak 2009); nor is it just the development of a pluralist, fragmented subsystem mostly in the private sector alongside the corporatist subsystem that continues to survive in the public sector (Mundlak et al. 2013). I propose that we see this as the renegotiation of union democracy and the emergence of a kind of activism among workers that had never existed in the context of a Histadrut-dominated corporatism. This is a small but growing movement based on the understanding that the old structures—including the Histadrut and the welfare state—have crumbled, that the old order cannot be relied upon to protect the people, not even those who were once at the heart of the corporatist regime. Those involved are seeking new ideas for active participation, not merely voting, and a different conception of representation, not necessarily related to formal democratic voting structures.

In a number of cases, the trigger for the organizing initiative was the threat of dismissals and the transformation of the profession to the detriment of those working within it, such as the social workers and the railway. At Pelephone, there were threats of dismissal due to a possible merger with Bezeq, and employees began getting concerned almost a year before any collective steps were taken

(Boaron, interview). The Journalists Organization followed fears of the collapse of journalism as a profession and continued threats of dismissal especially in the local news, which led to the now famous conference at Tel Aviv's Cinemateque in November 2011 where Dror Feuer, the popular and well-known star columnist from *Globes*, called on those present to unionize. But job security and improved employment terms were just one side of the coin; the demand for participation and voice was no less important, the result of frustration with the existing formal structures that apparently failed to represent the workers' interests as they saw them and were out of touch with their concerns. This was reflected in the popularity of Koach Laovdim among certain groups and among the general public, in the high levels of involvement in many new organizations, and also in the representational legitimacy granted these new organizations despite their lack of a formal representational structure. Atidenu and Osim Shinui, for example, had an internal democratic voting structure but cannot be said to formally represent the populations in whose name they speak. However, as Saward (2005) notes, legitimacy of representation can be achieved if leaders are embedded in the populations they claim to represent, especially in nonformal hierarchies where authentic representation is difficult to determine because the group being represented is itself coming into being as part of the process of representation. Osim Shinui and Atidenu leaders were embedded: as social workers, they were clearly part of group they represented. Moreover, they drew part of their legitimacy from the strong normative vision of democratic participation they promoted.

This kind of participation and representational structure has the advantage of linking representatives' interests directly with those of the represented: talk of a cushy job in the union makes no sense in the case of Atidenu and Osim Shinui. Likewise, legitimacy of representation is reliant on participation: the direct involvement of the social workers was an expression of support for the campaign. Though it is impossible to determine the numbers of people involved, and leaders are left to feel the atmosphere, clearly this kind of participation is more persuasive as a measure of support than mere membership figures that can, of course, be relatively easily ascertained (see Sullivan 2010). This may be particularly important when those explicitly excluded from the formal representational structures are nonetheless affected by the campaign. Again the social workers' campaign offers an example: the Social Workers Union had no right to strike on behalf of social workers in the private sector; legally and conceptually, it is not clear how the public-sector social workers could be said to represent those in the private sector in any way, nor was it clear who could declare a labor dispute on their behalf. Yet the democratic participation and expressions of support for the campaign made possible by Atidenu and Osim Shinui enabled nonunionized social workers in the private sector to make their voice heard. The demand for participation and voice, then, was prominent in all these cases, accompanied by a growing awareness that formal voting structures do not guarantee democratic representation: many initiators of the campaigns understood that union democracy is not just about how the union represents the workers, but also how workers are represented within the union.

This is also a struggle for recognition, whether explicitly as organized labor in a hostile environment, when employers refuse to recognize a workers' committee like at Pelephone; or building a separate identity as workers, as the resident physicians strived to do, transforming themselves from general dogsbodies in the hospital hierarchy into an identifiable worker group with its own interests and demands; or recognition as human beings behind the provision of a sterile service, as in the university cleaners' case.

However, the concept of "worker" as the holder of a specific class position in the production process is also fluid. It is not merely that different worker groups have different levels of power to promote their interests, but that waged workers may identify their interests as being closer to those of employers or capital than to other workers; indeed, self-identification as workers may be temporary or only a (small) part of a person's sense of self. Furthermore, self-conception as worker as (possibly) belonging to a broad class or even as part of a small group of other workers is extremely varied: the activists in the university cleaners' case conceived of the cleaners as part of a broad class of wage earners, though most of the cleaners themselves would not have identified with such a class. Similarly, the social workers made great efforts to emphasize a broad, vaguely class struggle (though not necessarily in the Marxist sense of class). The rail workers spoke in terms of state-building and traditional Histadrut values even as they rejected the Histadrut's role in the railway struggle; Edra'i noted her own family links to the Histadrut and the establishment of Haifa Port, emphasizing her family's part in the Zionist project (interview). Yet they failed to gain the support of the media, even though at that time many journalists were involved in a struggle as workers themselves: the railway workers' image was too closely associated with classic industrial workers and the corruption linked to established workers' committees.

At the other end of the scale, many physicians did their best to shake off the Israel Medical Association, perceived to be overly connected to an old unionist approach of solidarity across the sector. This situation is captured in the concept "contradictory class location," which E. Wright (1997) developed to give the middle classes the conceptual and empirical attention he felt they deserve, in light of their strength and size, in class analysis. This concept extends class identity beyond the boundaries of occupation (job) to family ties, personal history, or future aspirations and expectations, as well as ownership of shares and authority in the production process. Thus class is not only a preexisting space in the production process to be filled by human beings and defined according to their relationship to exploitation (E. Wright 1997, 523). This implies that class location may change over time, and the different components of an individual's class identity may be at odds with one another. Structural location remains important; but as an explanation for action, self-identification is no less significant. Moreover, the balance between the various components at a given time will affect an individual's consciousness, intentions, and perception of what is possible. The doctors, then, are in a position of authority and domination within the health system, and able to benefit from the creeping privatization of their field, while the privatization of social work, on the other hand, mostly entails the outsourcing of service provision and the resultant deterioration of employment terms. Thus the social workers were opposed to the neoliberalization of the economy, while the doctors were in favor—at least of the tangible results of this neoliberalization that includes the growth of private practices and private (high-tech) satellite industries.

A further notable aspect of this wave of organizing is the use of classic union concepts. In their efforts to act collectively, workers have drawn on appeals to solidarity, social justice, labor as a class vis-à-vis capital, influence over our working lives, workers' committees, shop-floor democracy, and of course unions in a way that is new to Israel, where organizing nonunionized workers was rare under the corporatist regime. These are not Beck's "zombie categories" lumbering on with a huge incompatibility between concept and content (Beck and Beck-Gernsheim 2002, 202), but very tangible concepts that have been taken up anew by workers as ways of understanding their insecure position in the workplace and as tools to enable action and opposition. Many of these workers are being guided by a highly educated activist population, familiar with labor law and industrial relations norms in Israel and abroad, and with broad theoretical knowledge of labor–capital relations, the changes to the economy, and Israel's singular labor history (see the introduction). This they bring to bear in strategy decisions and public relations efforts, as clearly seen in Koach Laovdim's staff and activists and the activists involved in the cleaners' campaign—emulated, apparently, in the Histadrut's Organizing Unit.

At the same time, the content of these categories is being reconstrued, and activists are explaining them to the public no less than to their fellow workers, educating and raising awareness in their attempts to counter the image of corruption and fossilized bureaucracy that dogs the institutions of the former corporatist regime. The need for explanation underscores the dichotomy between workers and public, which has affected the activities of the new organizations such as Atidenu. These activities have led to broader alliances and new tactics aspiring to engender public pressure, such as the lobbying, naming-and-shaming work of the Coalition for Direct Employment and the work of the Forum against the Privatization of the Railway. Some, such as the social workers, identify themselves with traditional broad categories of workers, though even they had to appeal to a differentiated public, but in general the idea of a working class with solidarity across the labor market has little traction. A more useful concept for most activists, one that was adopted from the social protest movements around the world and arose in various interviews, is the idea of the 99 percent ("us") against the 1 percent (the "tycoons"), which includes the media barons and the foreign holding companies together with their political allies in the Knesset. As Rosenhek and Shalev (2013) note in their analysis of the Israeli protest movement, this was a non-class-based articulation of economic divisions. It rearticulates the social division, enabling senior physicians to be grouped together with subcontracted cleaners, even if in objective terms of social status or life chances it seems absurd to situate them on the same side of the barricade.

In short, after three decades during which organized labor has been undermined and the economy redirected to the detriment of a growing swathe of the population, there is a conviction that workers' direct, participative influence in their place of work and in their representative organization—union democracy—is necessary to mitigate the effects of neoliberalism on employment terms and affect broader socioeconomic policies. Having seen the growth of nonstandard work arrangements and two-tiered agreements, many workers no longer believe that the Histadrut will fend for them and are demanding greater voice. This is not a corporatist revival, particularly as Israeli corporatism included so little worker participation. Instead, in renegotiating their position, workers are drawing on various resources, including what remains of the old structures, taking advantage of the Histadrut's institutional power as well as adopting new strategies, setting up new organizations, and building alliances outside the workplace. In Streeck's (2006, 24) words, "What is now observed may be better conceived as a collection of fragments, structural and functional, of the old corporatist construction—fragments that continue to be used, like the ruins of ancient monuments, by being converted to new, less grandiose purposes." I have called this a renegotiation of union democracy—a renegotiation of the relationship between workers and the organizations that claim to represent them—and, in a break with most of Israel's labor history, it has grown from the bottom up.

Part 2
RENEGOTIATING THE LABOR–CAPITAL BALANCE OF POWER

THE FRONTAL STRUGGLE

Recognition in the Workplace

In 2012 and 2013, the Israeli press was full of stories of "trapped profits." Large companies, including the Intel Corporation, Teva Pharmaceutical Industries, and Check-Point Software Technologies, had benefited from the Encouragement of Capital Investment Law of 1959, amassing tens of billions of shekels in profits; however, they were forbidden from taking them out of the country as dividends unless they paid corporate tax of up to 25 percent and dividend tax of 15 percent. An amendment in 2005 to the 1959 law relaxed this rule, but it did not affect profits from before 2005, which came to be seen as "trapped."

The companies entered into negotiations with the state, and some cases reached the courts, in their attempts to free the money without paying the taxes. For its part, the state sought a way to solve the problem without setting a precedent for other companies yet also without scaring off potential investors. There was a wide range of opinions and positions within state institutions and the government. The then finance minister Yuval Steinitz and the Tax Authority wanted to issue a temporary order to enable billions to be taken out untaxed, suggesting that companies manage to get around tax regulations anyway, so it would be better to give them some tax breaks in order to get at least a portion of the tax, rather than insisting on it all and losing it all (Filut and Levy-Weinrib 2012). The finance minister defended the compromise idea by saying that if they did not pay at least that portion of tax, the state would have to tax citizens to make up the state's budgetary deficit (Filut 2012). Tax Authority director Doron Arbeli also said he wanted to "reduce friction" with foreign firms, but Accountant General Michal Abadi Boiangiu opposed the idea, noting this would "reward" tax evasion

(Filut and Levy-Weinrib 2012). The controversy goes back to the beginning of 2010, when a committee was appointed, headed by then Finance Ministry director Haim Shani, to check incentives for investment. Shani held that aggressive taxation would frighten off companies, but State Revenues Supervisor Freida Israeli disagreed, and former Tax Authority director Yehuda Naserdishi said there were already enough legal incentives for investment.

At the end of 2012, the so-called trapped profits law was passed by the Knesset, enabling companies to pay just 6–10 percent tax, as opposed to the 25 percent corporate tax and 15 percent dividends tax mentioned above. (It also enables companies to invest profits abroad without these profits being considered dividends, so they can avoid the 15 percent dividends tax.)[1] The taxes were lowered on the condition that at least 50 percent of the profits be reinvested in Israel within five years in plants, equipment, and salaries for new employees (not managers), but not real estate.

The operations of Intel in Israel illustrate the complex relationship between large international companies and the state. In June 2012, *TheMarker* presented figures on Intel's operations in Israel, noting the benefits that were supposed to accrue to the country and the firm (O. Koren 2012): Intel first came to Israel in 1974, but its main investment began in 1999 when it opened a huge facility in Kiryat Gat, which then had high unemployment because of off-shoring in the textile industry on which the town had relied. The plant cost some $1.7 billion, of which $600 million were received from the state in return for a commitment to employ 4,500 workers. Another grant was requested in 2004 to update technologies. Assuming that high-tech would be the "locomotive pulling Israel's economy" and that Intel's presence would draw other international companies, the government granted another $525 million in 2005, on condition that Intel employ an additional 2,500 workers. In 2009, Intel requested another grant, threatening to curtail its operations in Israel if its request was rejected; the state provided $200 million in return for a commitment to employ 3,300 workers. In 2011, however, Intel rejected terms offered by Israel for building a new facility and decided to build the facility in Ireland.

The grants Intel received from Israel totaled $1.3 billion. In return, the government thought, Israel benefited from technologies and management skills of the highest level that trickle into the economy, as well as taxes and employment. Moreover, Intel's presence contributed to Israel's image as a high-tech giant, the company bought up Israeli products and knowledge, and it invested (via Intel Capital, its venture capital fund) in Israeli start-ups. The point is not whether Intel had been treated fairly or been given an unfair advantage, but that the company, along with others, is perceived to have the muscle to negotiate favorable terms with the state—terms that ordinary citizens cannot hope to achieve.

But it is not only the multinational corporations that appear to benefit from Israel's taxation arrangements; local companies seem to enjoy easy profits too. As noted in a report from the Adva Center (Swirsky 2013), the 2005 amendment to the Encouragement of Capital Investments Law of 1959 essentially defined just one main tax benefit, comprised of a lower corporate tax rate for enterprises exporting at least 25 percent of their turnover. Certain other conditions defined benefits according to "strategic areas" for investment and certain benefits for "approved" large companies with revenues of over NIS 20 billion. Crucially, where previously companies had been obliged to invest in order to qualify for tax benefits, now, following the amendment, all companies meeting the export criteria could claim benefits. For this reason, the Adva Center report argues that the amendment essentially removed the "investments" aspect of the 1959 law and transformed it into "a law for the encouragement of capital" (Swirsky 2013, 13). The same report notes that the result of these benefits, following the changes to the 1959 law and the trapped profits law, is a regressive corporate tax that favors the generally stronger export companies and the powerful multinational corporations (Swirsky 2013, 13).

The trapped profits saga highlights the way these large companies are seen to negotiate excellent terms for their operations in Israel ("too big to pay taxes," as one columnist put it; Korin-Liber 2012b), despite widespread public outrage (see Zarhia and Coren 2012) and the opposition of senior government figures. The apparent power of these firms was reflected in a dispute over municipal tax. In 2006, the Kiryat Gat municipality claimed Intel owed NIS 60 million. Though the court ruled against the company, the municipality was powerless to enforce the ruling and eventually a "compromise" was reached—Intel paid sixteen million (Schechter 2012). Teva was in the spotlight in particular: after enjoying tax benefits for years and being one of the largest companies involved in the trapped profits case (see Maanit and Levy-Weinrib 2013; Tsipori 2013; Tzipori 2013a), it then began a wave of dismissals. The immediate official cause was fears that the patent on its main drug (Copaxone) was coming to an end, but board member and son of company founder Chaim Hurvitz also suggested the dismissals were due to efforts to "force" Teva to pay tax (Tzipori 2013b).

A similar recent case of companies being perceived as sufficiently large and powerful to negotiate terms that would be denied ordinary people is the wave of debt write-offs enjoyed by tycoons—or the companies they control—including Nochi Dankner with IDB Holdings Corp. Ltd., Idan Ofer with Zim Integrated Shipping Services, and Motti Zisser with Elbit Imaging Ltd. (the so-called "haircuts," as the Hebrew has it; see, for example, Appelberg and Rochwerger 2013; Avriel 2013; E. Peretz 2014). These are, of course, the same tycoons who found themselves in the crosshairs during the social protest movement of 2011 (see Ram and Filc 2013).

The perception that capital is growing stronger is supported by data: labor's share of the national income fell from some 71 percent in the mid-1980s to 64 percent in 2005 (Kristal 2013, 104; see also Kristal 2008). Inequality also increased: in the early 1970s, the Gini coefficient for Israel was 0.2, but by 2010 it had risen to 0.34 (Kristal 2013, 101–102) and 0.365 by 2014.[2] The middle-class protesters of 2011 really were struggling to make ends meet (see Rosenhek and Shalev 2013). Kristal links this to the neoliberal processes that transformed the economy in this period (late 1970s onward) and shows that labor's share of national income is connected in particular to the "structure of economic and political institutions and the policies they advance" (2013, 107), which are in turn influenced, in part, by workers' economic and political organization—the structures of organized labor. In simple terms, labor's share is determined by "class struggle and class compromise that partly shape the strategies of states" (Kristal 2013, 107; see also Kristal, Cohen, and Mundlak 2006; Kristal and Cohen 2007).

Part 2, then, explores this class struggle. It does so by looking at three conceptual planes or arenas in which the balance of power between labor and capital is being determined. These three planes draw on Hyman's (1996, 61) view of union power that goes beyond the debate on strategies and tactics and acknowledges the importance of the institutional and political-cultural setting. He defines the three dimensions of union power, roughly corresponding with E. Wright's (1994) situational, institutional, and systemic power, as (1) a union's ability to achieve its agenda in the face of resistance; (2) its ability to shape legal or institutional frameworks that increase its chances of success; and (3) its capacity to influence culture and attitudes to create an ideological climate favorable to organized labor. Expanding and making concrete Hyman's conception of union power, I define the three planes of struggle thus.

1. The plane of frontal struggle: this is the plane of classic workplace unionist activity, of organizing drives, unionization, and collective action, corresponding to Hyman's first dimension, a union's ability to achieve its agenda in the face of resistance.
2. The plane of ideological struggle: here, organized labor tries to defend its legitimacy and the legitimacy of collective labor relations among the general public, in society at large, corresponding to Hyman's third dimension, a union's capacity to influence culture and attitudes to create a favorable ideological climate.
3. The plane of institutional struggle: this is the struggle over the institutions and formalized frameworks that enable collective labor relations to take place, corresponding to Hyman's second dimension, a union's ability to favorably shape legal or institutional frameworks.

This chapter explores the first of the planes of struggle—the frontal struggle in the workplace. It begins by presenting the 2012 organizing drive in the cell-phone company Pelephone as the starting point for the discussion. This drive is considered an exceptional case due to the employer's intensive efforts to resist it and the National Labor Court (NLC) decision that laid down the rules regarding what an employer may and may not do in opposition to an organizing drive in the workplace. The results of the decision were immediately felt in other organizing drives, yet employers' ability to (in some cases) ignore the spirit of the ruling—another sign of capital's power—are also noted.

Pelephone: A Hit-and-Miss Method of Union Busting

In the summer of 2012, workers at Pelephone began organizing with the Histadrut. The trigger for the initiative was the rumored merger with Bezeq, Israel's leading telecommunications group, of which Pelephone is a subsidiary.[3] The workers' committee at Bezeq was considered strong, so any dismissals due to the merger, it was thought, would fall disproportionally on Pelephone employees (Boaron, interview). Furthermore, according to Pelephone workers' committee member Itamar Avitan (interview), there was a feeling that those promoting the reforms to increase competition in the cell-phone sector had not taken into account how this would affect employees; this contributed to their uncertainty about their jobs.

The company refused to recognize the unionizing initiative and began a series of steps to prevent it. In November, in accordance with the temporary committee's wishes, the Histadrut declared a labor dispute. A year earlier, there had been attempts to organize at Orange (Partner Communications Company Ltd.), which had been quashed; thus from the beginning, the Histadrut seemed willing to invest considerable effort in the Pelephone campaign, including large sums. This was the first time the Histadrut had agreed to pay wages of striking workers who did not yet pay membership fees to the organization; moreover, the Histadrut committed to paying full wages (usually, the strike fund provides 80–85 percent of wages) (see *Globes* 2012a). This may also have been due to criticism that it had not sufficiently supported the Clal Insurance organizing attempt,[4] which was still ongoing when Pelephone began (see Niv 2012e).

Pelephone's attempts to stop the organizing began moderately but soon included more heavy-handed tactics. In September, the human resources deputy director sent an email to all department, unit, and branch managers that included a membership cancelation form, so they could persuade workers to rescind their

Histadrut membership (Collective Dispute Appeal 25476-09-12, par. 7). During a meeting with employees, the deputy vice president called the Histadrut a "political cancer" that will cause the company to become weak, leading to dismissals (par. 8). The company also cast doubt on the reliability of the Histadrut's claim that one third of employees had signed and warned that an organized workforce would weaken the company's competitiveness, noting that clients did not want to do business with a company whose workers were organized with the Histadrut. In its petition to the court against Pelephone's alleged violations of the court order to refrain from speaking against or in favor of organization, the Histadrut claimed Pelephone had said that workers are afraid of Histadrut activists and that clients are leaving the company because they fear strikes and company paralysis (Niv 2012g; G. Peretz 2012).

Later, workers were given unexpected gifts and perks, including unlimited use of phones (Boaron, Avitan, interviews; Nissan 2012): "[Previously,] anyone who wanted a Smartphone had to pay, but as soon as the organizing initiative started, it became possible to get a [new handset] for free. . . . Suddenly on Rosh Hashanah we got three hundred shekels holiday gift. I've been here thirteen years and there's never been anything like that. Throughout the process, Pelephone tried to buy the employees" (Boaron, interview).

Pelephone CEO Gil Sharon warned workers against harming the company, telling them that it had lost its focus and calling on them to get back to work to correct the damage done by weeks of struggle (G. Peretz 2012; Collective Dispute Appeal 25476-09-12, par. 9). He also emphasized that the best path to real cooperation was the "round table" he set up for hearing workers' grievances, and not any union (Boaron, interview). During the strike, an "internal committee" was established to counter the Histadrut committee and a website set up to support this committee (Avitan, Boaron, interviews). Though Pelephone denied its connection to the internal committee and the website, the site was apparently set up by the same public relations firm used by Pelephone (Niv 2012c). "People would ask me, which committee are you with, the internal committee or the Histadrut? They didn't understand that there's no such thing as an internal committee. It's a fiction they try to sell you. But you see it works" (Avitan, interview).

> One day we went down, and there was a really good gathering [of workers protesting], we were there five to ten minutes till a security guard came and told us, "enough, go have lunch." We really behaved nicely. As soon as they said "enough," we went to eat. Suddenly, with no warning, we heard music and noise, and people appeared [wearing] white T-shirts with the slogan "I'm blue in spirit."[5] . . . Pelephone employees. It was ridiculous. Arrogantly taking advantage of employees, mainly

customer service [employees] who are trained to feel complete loyalty to the company. They tell them, they [the strikers] want to destroy the company, and dress them in those shirts. (Boaron, interview)

Pelephone prevented reporters from entering the premises (Niv 2012f), released pictures of employees happily at work to "prove" that the strike was ineffective, and insisted that the strikers were a small group of irrelevant trouble-makers (Niv 2012h). "In many cases police came [to demonstrations]. At Wolfson parking lot, when we would decide where to go [to demonstrate] that day, a Pelephone security vehicle would wait for us and follow us wherever we went" (Boaron, interview).

When Pelephone confiscated company vehicles in December, both workers and other employers in the cell-phone sector who had been warily watching the campaign felt that a red line had been crossed. One day, Pelephone said all those intending to strike must return their vehicles, but the Histadrut ordered them to ignore the message. The following day, strikers found their cars had been towed away, sometimes together with various personal belongings (the cars are intended for private use, and employees pay a monthly fee for this) (Sadeh 2012). "The moment we went on strike, they took away all our benefits—they didn't allow us into the building—whoever wanted to enter had to be accompanied by security people; I think they even canceled our employee cards. They disconnected some people's cell phones, [took away] their vehicles. The firm made life seriously difficult" (Boaron, interview).

The struggle at Pelephone is recognized as an important case because it highlights employer efforts to prevent organizing, which is a worker's right according to Israeli law (Collective Agreements Law, 1957) and Israeli labor relations norms (as noted in the landmark ruling, Collective Dispute Appeal 25476-09-12, par. 54–55). There have been many other unsuccessful attempts to organize, but Pelephone was notable for the intensity of the conflict and the NLC ruling. The court's decision effectively forbids employers from interfering in or expressing any opinion about an organization initiative. Responding to the suit filed by the Histadrut against Pelephone, the panel of judges headed by NLC president Nili Arad stated the employer must not suggest it is illegal to organize or include any paragraph in an employee's contract that forbids the employee from joining a union. The employer is also forbidden from setting up his own workers' committee (such as the "internal committee" at Pelephone) or taking any position on a struggle between two representative organizations within the workplace. He must not compile any list of workers who join a union, or pressure workers or try to frighten them, or dismiss or threaten to dismiss them on the basis of their involvement in organizing. Moreover, the employer must not discriminate between employees on the basis of membership in a workers' organization (Collective Dispute Appeal 25476-09-12, par. 81–82).

Even before the ruling, Pelephone's tactics were viewed with concern by employers who feared a backlash and suspected that the company's heavy-handedness would undermine chances of preventing organizing in more subtle ways. Indeed, Hadas Boaron, active in the Pelephone committee, noted: "The more opposition there was—at the level of email discourse, and emails were being sent all the time, and at the level of sending us company employees to confront us—all this opposition made us more certain of the justice of our path. When you see one side so adamantly opposed, it gives you the drive to continue" (interview).

Employers said Pelephone made every possible mistake, drawing fire and causing Histadrut chair Eini to intervene personally. They noted that plenty of unionization attempts had been successfully thwarted by the management's careful action, and some, such as the Federation of the Israeli Chambers of Commerce chair Uriel Lynn and the Manufacturers Association of Israel chair Zvika Oren, blamed Pelephone for "causing" the ruling and thus limiting employers' freedom of action (see Niv 2013m).

Former NLC president Steve Adler said the Pelephone decision is even more important than the 2009 package deal. Keeping the employer away from any organizing initiative, he said, is "perfectly sound, it's perfectly right, it's been shown, proven to be right." Referring to employer attempts to prevent organizing at Migdal,[6] Adler continued, "The employers just can't keep away. Any time the employer's going to get involved in anything, communicating with the workers during an organization campaign, they'll do something wrong, so you just have to keep them away. This [the Pelephone ruling] is a very important decision" (interview).[7]

Moreover, the Pelephone ruling appeared to spur a number of organizing initiatives. In the cell-phone industry, Partner (Orange) and Cellcom employees set up a workers' committee. In the insurance branch, Pelephone appeared to influence events at Clal. Organizing attempts here had begun a long time before Pelephone, but the committee was finally recognized by the employer only after the Pelephone ruling (and achieved a collective agreement two weeks after the Pelephone committee achieved its agreement). Rom Dvir from the Histadrut's Organizing Unit was very certain that the Pelephone ruling had had a galvanizing effect on a number of ongoing struggles: "After Pelephone, after a year of struggle, they recognized the Clal committee, it took a year! The same at Makhsanei Hashmal [electric goods firm]; it was almost dead there, and we managed to get it going again. And LeumiCard [credit card firm]. We've been trying to organize them for a year and a half; finally we've managed to create something there" (Dvir, interview).

Fierce Opposition to Unionizing in Previously Unionized Sectors

The insurance company Clal offers another example of heavy-handed attempts to prevent organizing. Until 1995, the insurance sector was organized. Then Migdal, one of the leading insurance companies, moved to individual contracts, the workers' committee was eventually broken, and the Histadrut was gradually pushed out of the sector. The trigger for the organizing attempt at Clal was fears that the company would be sold due to recommendations from the Interministerial Committee on Capital Concentration and that this would lead to dismissals. CEO Shai Talmon promptly sent a letter to all workers explaining that he was against organizing efforts and reminding them of Hassneh Insurance that, he claimed, collapsed because of unionized workers.[8] He also made an effort to smear the Histadrut (see Niv 2012i).

The temporary committee chair, Roni Raz, who had been in the company for twenty years, was prevented from entering various company buildings and removed from projects on the pretext that he was unable to do them because he was no longer free to move around (Raz, interview). He was also prevented from entering departmental meetings, asked to leave coffee areas, and followed around by a photographer sent by the company. Other employees were supportive, he said, but afraid, especially middle management. Soon after 1,000 had signed Histadrut membership forms, some 250 canceled their membership. According to Raz, they were called by their managers, who asked them to sign the cancellation forms "for me." Managers appealed to personal connections and good relations, claiming the organizing "made things difficult" for them, and mentioned bonuses (Raz, interview; see also Niv 2012a).

There is no denying the significance of the Pelephone ruling,[9] but employers' efforts to prevent unionizing cannot be stopped by court order alone. Following Pelephone and Clal, employees at Migdal began organizing toward the end of 2013 and made rapid progress. Owner Shlomo Eliahu, ignoring the stipulations in the Pelephone precedent, published an open letter to employees in leading newspapers (*Yedioth Aharonoth*, *Globes*, *Calcalist*, and *Haaretz*) on 9 January 2014, in which he declared he does not believe in organizing, that there is no need for it in a company like Migdal, and cast doubt on the "authenticity" of the organizing initiative. Later, he also "suggested" the workers hold elections on the question of whether to organize, despite the fact that at this stage over a third of employees had already joined the Histadrut (Collective Dispute 13125-12-13; see also Niv 2014b, 2014c). The court, which had already issued a number of orders to prevent management interference, ruled that both Migdal (as a company) and Eliahu had violated court orders "without good faith, intentionally and consciously" and expressed its concern that a company considered it worthwhile to pay the fines and continue to try to prevent the organizing (see Collective Dispute 13125-12-13, par. 13 and 30). As Dvir noted,

> There is also an approach in favor of breaking the law. . . . What does it mean for Electra [a large electromechanical systems firm], for example, to get a fine of 180,000 shekels? It's nothing. It's worth doing it. It's even worth investing millions. But for middle-sized businesses, 180,000 shekels is no joke. So there are some for whom it's worth breaking the law, to be hated by the media for a short while, and get kicked a bit, but at the end there won't be any organizing and it's worthwhile for them. (Interview)

At HOT too, attempts to prevent organizing continued after the Pelephone ruling.[10] Attempts to organize in HOT began in 2009, with the National Histadrut. The temporary committee chair, Yoni Mendel, was fired, effectively undermining the attempt. (The court reinstated him, but the damage had been done; see Labor Dispute Appeal 24/10.) Another attempt was made by HOT technicians in 2012 with the Histadrut, and again the chair, this time Jacob Berezovsky, was targeted and summoned repeatedly to disciplinary hearings despite an excellent employee record (Berezovsky, interview). The management also threatened the workers: "As soon as we got organized and submitted the [Histadrut membership] forms, the management told all the managers . . . one by one: 'X number of workers under you have signed,' 'such and such who works under you has signed,' and they knew exactly who of course because we had submitted the forms" (Berezovsky, interview). This organizing attempt was eventually stopped when the labor court ruled the HOT technicians could not be considered a separate bargaining unit (Collective Dispute 15391-12-11; Request for Appeal 18551-12-12). Finally in 2013 HOT employees organized with Koach Laovdim, but still had to cope with aggressive attempts to prevent the initiative, including the removal of personal vehicles (Niv 2013k), which many considered had been the red line crossed by Pelephone.

The Pelephone decision, then, is certainly important and apparently spurred workers to organize in previously unorganized sectors. However, events in Migdal and HOT also show that a court ruling is not sufficient when organizing is perceived to be illegitimate—or easily made to seem so. According to the judges in the Pelephone decision (par. 71 and 80 of the ruling), in the period after being recognized as a committee but before a collective agreement is signed, the organizing initiative is less fragile and an employer is free to speak his mind. This, apparently, was being exploited by Migdal, where in 2015 the employer was still making efforts to delegitimize organized labor by, among other things, painting a worrying picture of deteriorating labor relations, with committee members screaming at managers and Facebook posts against senior management figures (Niv 2014a). The frontal struggle, then, is easily undermined if it has no support within the general polity—general public support on the level of ideology.

THE IDEOLOGICAL STRUGGLE
The Delegitimization of Organized Labor

Employers' attempts to prevent an organizing initiative are relatively new to Israel because unionizing itself is new. (Though there was a wave of organizing following the National Health Insurance Law of 1995, employers' adamant opposition is mostly characteristic of the most recent wave.) Before the weakening of the Histadrut, unionizing unorganized workers was unnecessary: the vast majority of waged workers were already Histadrut members, or members in the National Histadrut or one of the few independent trade unions. According to the head of the new Journalists Organization (JO) noted in part 1, when the idea of organizing journalists was first raised in 2008, many people in the media did not even know that their Journalists' Association (the older, independent body) was also a workers' organization (Tarchitzky, interview), since membership was almost automatic. Organizing—the extensive drives in the large white-collar companies such as Visa as well as the transport industry—began in earnest only at the beginning of the new millennium, following a decade of defensive action by the Histadrut associated with its then head, Amir Peretz (chair from 1995 to 2006). The campaign at the Coffee Bean chain of cafés in 2008, noted in previous chapters, is often cited as the moment the Histadrut woke up to the potential of organizing.

According to Rom Dvir from the Histadrut's Organizing Unit, just as unions and workers were having to learn how to unionize, employers too were learning how to prevent unionization. This was a gradual process, as Dvir notes: "In fact the employers at the beginning weren't so bad. . . . In the Histadrut's first organizing drives, Isracard and Visa-CAL [credit card companies], let's say, they recognized the organizing initiative, started negotiating . . . there weren't big dramas. . . . I think something happened among the employers who suddenly realized they had to put a stop to it [organizing]" (interview).

The organizing drive at *Globes* illustrates the novelty of organizing in Israel. This drive, part of the JO and thus part of the Histadrut, encountered fierce opposition from the employer. One notable hurdle was the employer's refusal to deduct Histadrut membership fees from employees' wages, as had been the norm, citing the employees' individual freedoms. Although in theory a technicality that could be solved by amending the Histadrut's constitution, it also highlights the Histadrut's dependence on employer cooperation, which had never been an issue in the past. Other JO campaigns ran up against employers' adamant resistance to even acknowledge the organizing initiative, too, in particular *Maariv*, *Ynet*, and Channel 10 (Matar, Feuer, Tarchitzky, interviews).

Dvir also claimed that Israeli lawyers were looking to the United States to learn how to prevent unionizing and that union busting has developed as a profession, leading large firms to hire the services of leading consultants: "In Cellcom we were running a campaign against Rani Rahav, *the* PR man of Israel. And Nochi Dankner. [These are] heavy [sic] people, they have the tools to do it [prevent organizing] in a sophisticated manner. If it's middle-sized businesses, it's not certain they have the means to deal with you on that level; they tend more to revert to violence, and it's not certain we can protect the workers" (Dvir, interview).

A central aspect of these attempts to prevent organizing is the delegitimization of organized labor as a concept—persuading both the public and potential union members (at the workplace) that unions are part of an era whose time has gone, a corrupt era of cronyism. As noted in part 1, the Histadrut's image remains a serious obstacle. Though it is easy for the public to support the generally younger, hip, urban employees of telecommunications companies, the Histadrut and its most (in)famous committees are easily tarred as the cause of the economy's inefficiencies and a company's inability to retain competitiveness. And indeed, the public has an ambivalent attitude toward organized labor: according to a 2013 survey for the Central Bureau of Statistics, 59 percent of nonunionized employees are not interested in having a workers' committee at the workplace, though 67 percent of respondents also said they believed employment terms were better at organized workplaces (Niv 2013a).[1]

Leaders of organizing drives have to cope with this ambivalence, and employers use this ambivalence in their attempts to stop the organizing. At Pelephone, according to the workers' committee chair, "the management told the workers, do you want to be like that? And they took the worst [sic] companies [as examples]—do you want to be like the railways? The ports? Phoenicia [at the time in serious financial straits]? They didn't say, do you want to be like Bezeq, Teva, Isracard, Osem, Strauss . . . companies [generally considered successful] that people didn't even know had committees. I didn't even know; I didn't know there was a committee in Strauss" (Avitan, interview).

As noted, Avitan felt he had to downplay the presence of the Histadrut in his efforts to persuade people to join. He also said there was a lot of incitement against workers' committees in the media and that this image of corruption had taken root in the popular imagination:

> They [only] see the corruption. Yesterday someone said, did you see how such and such got his brother into the port [i.e., got him a job]? And I said, where do all Bibi's friends work? Katz's friends?[2] Even in our firm—if someone wants to get into Pelephone, who does he know [i.e., who can help him get a foot in the door]? Those who get good positions, where do they come from? That's how it is everywhere—those with contacts get in. So you can say, wow, Haifa committee . . . but it's here in your own home. And in private companies it's even worse. Those with connections in the management get everything. In other words, the incitement [against worker committees] is huge, people don't understand it. The media does it. . . . You won't read that the Haifa port management wanted to get revenge on a worker with fifteen years' seniority and tried to fire him, and the port [workers' committee] protected him—won in court and protected the worker and his family. (Avitan, interview)

Edra'i, from the railway committee, had a similar view: "I was disgusted by the press, which is so superficial, doesn't go deeply into anything, talks about nepotism, looks for some cousin. . . . And doesn't see that all the guys from the army bring all their friends [into good jobs]. That doesn't interest them" (interview).

The legitimacy of the committees with real power is indeed under continuous attack, led by the *Haaretz*-owned financial newspaper *TheMarker*—chief among them the ports and the Israel Electricity Corporation (IEC), two state-owned semimonopolies whose industries are being gradually privatized. In Alon Hassan, chair of the Mechanical Equipment Workers' Committee at Ashdod Port, the press and public found a suitable monster to embody the corruption and cronyism ostensibly rife in the strong committees, and his operations and private businesses have repeatedly been under investigation, including by the state comptroller (see, for example, Shporer 2013 and Bior 2013a).[3]

Most media coverage of the port committees (*Globes*'s Shay Niv is an exception) gives the impression that the country is being held hostage by a bunch of thugs who are the cause of all its woes, from socioeconomic disparities and soaring housing costs to poor economic performance and the high price of cottage cheese.[4] "The damage from defective port operations – 5 billion shekels a year," a headline from *TheMarker* notes (Bar-Eli 2013a). An article that emphasizes the committee's destructive behavior opens with the sentence, "Israel is losing control over what's going on in its sea ports" (Bar-Eli 2012). Another article is titled, "The government doesn't have the power to deal with the port committees. They get whatever they demand" (Bar-Eli and Shmil 2013), obliquely referring to the government's success in "dealing with" (breaking) strong committees elsewhere, such as the Open Skies deal that was reached despite opposition from the El Al workers' committees.[5]

The chair of the board at Ashdod Port makes the point clearly: the workers' committee is the real boss at the port (in an article titled, "Ashdod Port is operated under terror of threats," Bar-Eli 2013b). The same article notes that wages there rose between 2009 and 2011, even though profits fell during that period. As another *TheMarker* columnist put it, the "switch" must be put back in the hands of the public (Arlosoroff 2013a). This article claimed the struggle at the ports was not about workers' rights, but about maintaining the Histadrut's strength—thus directly connecting arguments about efficiency and competitiveness to issues of labor power. The columnist proposed compulsory arbitration as a way of preventing the Histadrut from "castrating" the government. In arbitration, she said, wages would be decided by a "professional, objective" party according to workers' "contribution" and not according to workers' power to compel the government to pay more.

Economics Minister Naftali Bennett built his election campaign around the idea of fighting those with contacts, including the strong workers' committees. On a "humorous" Facebook posting, he compared the port workers to insects that must be exterminated and blamed them for the high cost of living in Israel (though cargo tariffs are set by the government) (Niv 2013d).[6]

The state is also under pressure from importers and exporters to take control of the ports. Controlling a key position in the movement of goods, the port committees are blamed for causing "huge losses" during labor disputes. This means that traders who are not directly party to the conflict are nonetheless involved in such disputes. In February 2012, for example, the Manufacturers Association of Israel (MAI) submitted a request for an injunction against the strike at the two ports, even though the immediate cause of the strike was deadlock in talks toward a new collective agreement (the previous one had come to an end in December 2011). The Federation of the Israeli Chambers of Commerce also criticized the port workers and the Histadrut. Federation chair Uriel Lynn said the strikes were undermining the Israeli economy's stability and reputation, which would cause enormous damages. He said the strikes were nothing but "demagoguery" and that the only thing the strikers wanted was better employment terms (Filut, Azulay, and Barkat 2012), though in fact there were a number of unresolved issues, including the workers' demand that pension payments be made to an external company, so the money does not remain in the port companies' hands, and disagreement over the functioning of the joint management-workers production councils.[7] Chair of the Shippers' Council in the MAI Zvi Plada noted the strike caused great damage, particularly in light of the global economic slowdown (Filut, Barkat, and Azulay 2012). Following the transport minister's success in reforming the airlines industry (the Open Skies reform), a *TheMarker* columnist expressed her hope that he would now succeed in reforming the ports, calling them a "naval blockade" on Israel (Arlosoroff 2013b).

Delegitimization of the port committees in recent years has taken the form of attacks on monopolies. The need for increasing competition in the economy has become a common trope, widely accepted and rarely questioned; this was the theme running through the Open Skies deal and the reforms in the cell-phone sector, for example. It is claimed that capital is too "concentrated"—a theme habitually aired in Guy Rolnik's weekly column in *MarkerWeek*, which regularly categorizes the "big committees" along with monopolistic companies, claiming that they prevent real competition and increase inequality. This same premise led to the establishment in 2004 of the Interministerial Committee on Capital Concentration.

Reform at the ports, too, is intended to increase competition. In May 2013, the Anti-Trust Authority declared the ports a cartel, which means that the planned new wharfs must be operated by new competitors (Bar-Eli 2013c). A headline from July quotes Netanyahu: "The age of monopolies is over, nobody can prevent us from opening the ports to competition" (Shmil and Bar-Eli 2013). The article quotes the prime minister noting the first stage of increasing competition was the reforms of 2005, when Netanyahu as finance minister split up the Ports Authority and established the Ashdod Port Company Ltd. and Haifa Port Company Ltd., as well as the Israel Ports Development and Assets Company Ltd. to handle and manage the ports themselves. The second stage, he said, was the privatization of Eilat Port in 2011. Now, he said, was the third stage.

During the transport minister's efforts to push through the Open Skies reform, El Al workers were subject to similar hostile media coverage. According to the cover article of *MarkerWeek* (Gavizon 2013), the workers' committee is the company's "real controlling shareholder." "El Al pilots are grounding the chance of saving it [the company]," the headline screamed. In this same article, Shaldor Strategy Consulting, which was commissioned to do a study of the firm's employment structure, is quoted as blaming the pilots (in other words their employment terms) and "overly restrictive" regulation for the company's financial difficulties.

In fact, the ports are not a complete monopoly: if one port is on strike, vessels can dock at the other. Strikes at both at the same time have been unusual; the cooperation between the workers' committees at the two ports against the establishment of private terminals at the end of 2011 and beginning of 2012 was exceptional. Furthermore, according to Shay Niv, wages at the ports are not as high as headlines would have us believe: in 2013, the average wage for "generation A" port workers (those in the top tier of the two-tier agreement) was NIS 27,000 before tax, but Niv also notes that over 60 percent of port workers are "generation B" (in the bottom tier), receiving an average wage of NIS 16,000. Furthermore, those organized in the "strong committees" make up just 3–4 percent of waged workers, and most of these do not make the high wages frequently reported (Niv 2013l).

Liberalization and the Balance of Rights

However, the challenges to organized labor must also be considered in the context of changes to the judicial system that have influenced the legal context of union activity, reflecting a profound change in the discursive context. These changes have been characterized as "liberalization" and linked to what has come to be called the "constitutional revolution" (Mautner 2000, 1993). This constitutional revolution takes as its watershed event the legislation of two Basic Laws in 1992—Freedom of Occupation, amended 1994, and Human Dignity and Liberty—and led to a reconceptualization of rights in the courts and rulings and the rise of a civil rights discourse. This reconceptualization, Hirschl (1997, 136) asserts, "reflects and promotes the neo-liberal, individualist, 'free enterprise' worldview upon which the new economic order" in Israel is based (see also Hirschl 2000).

Similarly, Gross (1998, 81) argues that the constitutional revolution resulted in the "entry of economic rights into Israeli constitutional rights discourse in a way that protects the current regime of holdings, i.e., the economic *status quo*." By taking advantage of the limitation clauses of the Basic Laws,[8] the courts could still uphold what Gross calls "social legislation" even if it is deemed to violate economic rights. However, he suggests, this would have a detrimental influence on social rights: first, there is the symbolic effect of having progressive legislation considered an infringement of basic human rights; and second, it would create an illusion that the "constitution" protects rights when in fact important human rights are neglected and only liberal "negative" rights are protected (he also notes other detrimental effects; see Gross 1998, 97–98).

Regarding the influence of liberalization on labor relations, Hirschl (1997, 143) notes that the Basic Law: Freedom of Occupation has generally been interpreted to favor the autonomy of the economic sphere and the rights of employers (such as the right to hire and dismiss workers), and not the right to be employed;

the Basic Law's interpretation by the courts "does not include a complementary constitutional obligation of employers (or the state) to create economic, geographic, or social conditions for full employment."

Two aspects of liberalization have particular implications for labor relations: the "relative rights doctrine" and the connected issue of the rights of third parties. Hirschl (1997, 140–141) lists the relative rights doctrine as one of the legal mechanisms that weakened the collective bargaining power of labor. A relative right is weaker than an absolute right, so where labor rights were once paramount as protecting workers from more powerful interest groups, the principle of balancing contradictory rights undermines labor's collective strength. Raday (1994) notes that the roots of "human rights" lie in the need to protect individuals from the power of the regime and traces their entry into private law as promoted by Justice Aharon Barak (who is credited with coining the term "constitutional revolution"):[9] if human rights prevent the abuse of power such as state power, then nonstate bodies such as unions and corporations should also be bound by the need to observe human rights. However, she notes that thinkers such as Barak give no indication of how the application of human rights in the private sphere will necessarily protect the weaker of the parties. He and others talk only of "balancing rights" and note that rights are not absolute. Mundlak, for example, notes that the entrance of human rights discourse into labor relations has improved protection for workers on some issues traditionally outside the scope of unions, such as privacy at work and sexual harassment, but that "given that the right of property is explicitly protected by the Basic Law: Human Dignity and Liberty and the freedom of contract is derived from the explicit right to dignity, ... employers enjoy constitutional protection just as much as employees" (2007, 182).

The second aspect with implications for labor relations is the consideration of a third party (not the workers) whose interests the labor courts nonetheless want to protect (R. Ben-Israel 1993, 436). In a strike, the public is also hurt. This growing consideration of third-party interests undermines the principle of workers' collective action. While a strike may be illegal in the sense of being illegitimate, under collective labor law an illegitimate strike "is not illegal in the criminal sense, nor does it deny the striking workers their immunities" (Mundlak and Harpaz 2002, 755). However, punitive damage claims have already been made against strikers (see Raday 1995).[10] Since the 1980s, claims for damages following strikes "have been submitted to courts based on civil wrongs, such as misappropriation of personal property, negligence, or trespassing" (Hirschl 2000, 197). According to R. Ben-Israel (1993, 438), in disputes between workers and employers, labor law recognizes labor as the weaker party and hence in need of protection, but when labor's rights are balanced with a third party's rights, labor is perceived as the stronger party. The legislature, she continues, is silent on the issue, leaving the labor courts to rule on a sensitive issue, which means they are perceived as political and trust in them is undermined. Third-party interests can also be conceived as rights, as Raday (1994, 42–44) asserts—thus the "right" of the public to get passports (related to its right to freedom of movement), to use her example, can override the right of the Interior Ministry workers to strike.

This emphasis on individual rights is also reflected in the increase in legislation to compensate for the decline of collective agreements and their inability to determine labor rights. A paradigmatic example, Mundlak suggests, is the Minimum Wage Law, first proposed in 1978 but enacted only in 1987, which marks the turn toward legislation for issues previously determined by negotiation among the social partners (2007, 112–113). A further example is the Law for Increasing Labor Law Enforcement of 2012, which reflects the fact that shop-floor workers' committees are no longer able to ensure labor law and collective agreements be upheld. Cases of labor law violation brought before the court are discussed in terms of the infringement of individual rights and undermine the collective management of the workplace with its implied values of equality and solidarity.

These issues were prominent in the National Labor Court (NLC)'s ruling in the landmark Pelephone case. The judges dedicated some thirty pages of the ninety-eight-page ruling to discussing the clash between the workers' right to organize and the employer's freedom of speech and property rights (Collective Dispute Appeal 25476-09-12, par. 49–78). Employer organizations also used the language of rights: in its position paper, the Coordinating Bureau asserted that the employer's property rights and freedom of speech should be paramount throughout the organizing process (par. 35). A much bolder position was taken by the Federation of the Israeli Chambers of Commerce, which claimed that limiting freedom of speech (of the employer) could even undermine democracy, because it would lead workers to make decisions based on incomplete information, which was also liable to harm the property rights of the employer. One cannot let the right to organize push all other rights aside, the Federation asserted (par. 45).

The court agreed (par. 50) that freedom of speech was indeed a fundamental element of the spirit of democracy. It linked this freedom to an individual's autonomy, right to self-determination, and ability to develop and nurture her character and dignity. Moreover, the court said that Israel's Basic Law: Human Dignity and Liberty grants freedom of speech the status of a basic constitutional right and noted that it encourages the maintenance of a "free marketplace of ideas." The court asserted (par. 52) that the employer's freedom of speech also stems from his property rights and management prerogative and includes the freedom to express the company's vision, policy, development, and profitability. The workers' freedom of speech, the court said, is connected to their right to express opinions (individually and collectively) about employment terms and their promotion, their right to criticize the sides involved in labor relations, and their right to organize labor relations along collective lines. Indeed, the court said a worker's right to organize is constitutional, one of the human freedoms stemming from human dignity. The right to organize, then, reflects the autonomy of the workers and their freedom of speech (par. 53–54).

Having neatly conflated freedom of speech with the right to organize via the basic right to human dignity, the court then explained why the workers' right to organize takes precedence (at the initial, fetal stage of organizing) over the employer's freedom of speech. The right to organize, it asserted, reflects the structural imbalance of power between worker and employer and facilitates the achievement of the aims of collective labor relations as well as promoting greater equality between workers (par. 54–55). Regarding this fetal stage, the court noted that Pelephone and the Coordinating Bureau had ignored the individual worker and only addressed the issue of a strong union (par. 58). However, the court implicitly accepted the argument that following this initial stage, when a representative organization has been recognized and the workers are conducting collective negotiations, the union is a fair counterbalance to the strength of the employer. This initial organizing, the court asserted, changes the balance of forces and in practice marks the transition from individual to collective labor relations. At this "advanced pre-collective" stage (par. 60), the employer regains his freedom of speech.

Pitting the Workers against the Public

The second aspect of balancing rights with implications for labor relations, as noted by R. Ben-Israel (1993) and Raday (1994), is the increasing need to consider third-party interests in disputes between labor and capital. This aspect of balancing rights pits the workers against the public (see also R. Ben-Israel 1994). Indeed, the distinction between "the workers" and "the public" is part of the general discourse on labor struggles and is not limited to the labor courts. For example, in order to undermine the legitimacy of the big committees, media accounts of workplace disputes emphasize the line between the ostensibly aggressive, corrupt workers and the regular citizens of Israel. Thus the port workers in the examples above are accused of holding the public to ransom and causing the high cost of living. The headlines assert that the workers' committee is the de facto owner of the ports, while the legal owners—the public, via state institutions—are denied control of their own assets. This claim conveniently sidesteps the issue of the privatization of these public assets that has often been a central concern in workers' struggles, as we have seen.

The difference between the public and private sector is also clear. In the private sector, companies are perceived as operating in a competitive market. When times are good, it is thought, employees should enjoy the fruits of their labor, too. When they are seen as being unable to do so, the company owners are easily categorized as tycoons—symbolic enemy of the 2011 social protest movement—and public support for the struggles in Pelephone, Migdal, and HOT, for example, is easy to come by though less involved than such support in the public sector. The public is affected, if at all, as consumers who have other options. Campaigns in the public sector, on the other hand, affect the public both as consumers (of state-supplied public services) and as (ostensible) owners. The need to balance between the public's right to services and the workers' right to participate in collective action for better employment terms (or retain existing terms) is acknowledged not only by the courts but also by campaigners.[11]

The courts discussed this balance in the railway campaign, for example when deciding on the legitimacy of the strike that aimed to protest a decision by the "sovereign"—the owner, the public—and thus deciding on whether it was a "political" strike (forbidden) or "quasi-political," which has been permitted by the courts (see IDI 2004, 25–26): "A political strike is a means of pressuring the sovereign against a legislative process, changes to legislation, a sovereign decision and everything that results from this" (Collective Dispute 20420-05-11, ruling summary). The court decided in this case that it was indeed "quasi-political"—a protest against a decision of the sovereign but one that threatens to affect employment terms—and that as such the strike must be a "short protest strike only and subject to limitations." For such cases, the courts use the concept of "proportionality." The NLC noted that sometimes the right to strike must be limited not just in essential services but also in key services like the railway, when a strike would cause "serious harm" to the entire population (Request for Appeal 50556-09-11, par. 22; see also Niv 2011b).

Mundlak asserts that the conceptual distinction between "the workers" and "the public" also alters perceptions of democracy: strikes are construed as illegitimate interest-group action undermining the workings of normal democracy. In the Bezeq case Mundlak discusses, it was argued that "the workers' ability to exert economic constraints on employers and, more important, on consumers and the users of services gives them an unfair advantage over the rest of the citizenry, which has access to the ballot box only every few years" (2007, 167). However, Mundlak also points out the fallacy in this comparison between a "surreal description of democracy" and a "concrete description of what striking workers do," a comparison that ignores the role of lobbyists hired by companies with huge resources, for example.[12] This conceptual distinction engenders the perception that collective organizing by labor is inherently political while collective action by capital is a "natural component of capitalist society that resonates with the democratic ideal" (Mundlak 2007, 167). Indeed, the strike is the main weapon wielded by workers—as threat or in practice—and hence a logical target of delegitimization. In 1995, the Supreme Court declared that the right to strike is not constitutionally protected and that the right to freedom of association in a union is an individual not a collective right, thus further undermining the collective bargaining power of labor (Hirschl 2000, 197).

Activists' awareness of this distinction between workers and the public was reflected in efforts to explain the link between employment and wider social issues. In 2011, for example, the social workers did "a lot of explaining, both to [those receiving social services] and also to the public, that [the strike] is good for them too, that a social worker with such poor working conditions cannot give proper services" (Goldman, interview). Goldman noted the difficulty of making this complex claim understood, when the public "has to go three weeks without getting social services *because* there is a policy that doesn't allow proper social services to be provided" (interview). Similarly, Shlosberg said social worker activists wanted "to give the struggle a social aspect, so it isn't a struggle over wages but over the welfare system, the welfare state—a social struggle" (interview), to emphasize the benefits of the struggle to society in general. Raznik, a central figure in the Forum against the Privatization of the Railway, also noted activists' efforts to explain the link: "We needed to do a lot of explanation work, because the public also reads the regular press, and its basic opinion of Gila [Edra'i] and the railway was not positive. The general spirit of things was not to the committee's advantage" (interview).

The employer—the railway management and the state—made counterefforts to drive a wedge between the public and the workers, noting that the committee was endangering the public, causing inconvenience instead of negotiating, and that passengers were merely hostages in the committee's struggle to prevent progress in Israel Railways (see *Globes* and Weissman 2012; Shmil 2012). The minister of transport noted the committee was "holding the public to ransom," ignoring the public's right to transport, and hindering the development and proper functioning of the company (Nissan and Niv 2012). MK Carmel Shama-Hacohen, who was chair of the Economic Committee during a committee meeting on the railway, noted the strike had made the railway a symbol of contempt for passengers, for law, and for the economy, and MK Ophir Akunis declared that the railway was the property of the public, not the committee or the management (Zarhia 2012).

An opinion piece in *Globes* in February that year reflects the issue well. The columnist notes that the rail strike is not a strike over workers' rights or employment terms, or over organized labor, or for social democracy or an enlightened society. The issue, she says, is millions of (other) workers who pay taxes that fund a state company—the public is the owner, and the public cannot really be termed an exploitative capitalist. She thus underlines the distinction noted above between the public sector and the private, where workers found it easier to garner public sympathy in their struggle against the tycoons. She goes on to note that public interests come before those of the railway workers, or those of workers in other companies commonly perceived to suffer from aggressive workers' committees, including the IEC, the ports and airports, and the national water company Mekorot. She also raised the idea that workers are lazy or aggressive or incompetent, hired only because they are friends of committee members (Korin-Liber 2012a).

The transport minister also referred to the need to return control of the railway to "the public" (Bar-Eli, Shmil, and Zarhia 2012), and later that year blamed the committee and workers' collective action for the delay in opening the new Beer Sheva–Tel Aviv line (Bior 2012a). Referring to industrial conflict at El Al the same year, a senior *TheMarker* columnist asserted that workers there, whom he compared to those in the IEC and the banks, are enjoying security and great wages but consumers are paying the price of the workers' "free lunch" (S. Peretz 2012).

Limiting the right to strike would be an effective way to protect the public from the caprices of the big committees, and various proposals have been mooted though none—as yet—has been adopted. The two most common proposals are to broaden the category of "essential services" and to impose compulsory arbitration.[13] In the 2011 dispute, for example, the Tel Aviv Labor Court ruled that the railway is an essential service and that rail workers' right to strike should be greatly restricted (Collective Dispute 20420-05-11), though the ruling was reversed by the NLC (Request for Appeal 50556-09-11). In 2013, the Prime Minister's Office (PMO) said compulsory arbitration would be imposed in what he was now calling "essential" services such as the ports and airports, and that the Arrangements Law would be used to limit the right to strike in these services (Z. Klein 2013). That same year, the PMO, Finance Ministry, Justice Ministry, and Economics Ministry were trying to promote legislation that would limit the right to strike in "large state monopolies" and "give back to the public its right to its own property" (Bior 2013c). According to the proposed legislation, a new arbitration body with judicial authority and "objectivity" would be established, the implication being that the labor courts are biased in favor of the workers. It asserts that reforms are an issue for the government to decide; the arbitration body will have the authority to discuss the effects of reforms on workers but will be unable to take any position regarding the reforms themselves. A "senior source" in one of the ministries is quoted as noting that in these companies, monopolistic dividends that in the case of private firms would "ordinarily" go to the owners are pocketed by the workers in the form of high wages and good employment terms (Arlosoroff 2013c).

In calling for restricting the right to strike and demanding compulsory arbitration, the government and capital are going beyond discursive delegitimization of organized labor to undermine the frameworks and institutions that shore up collective industrial relations. Such activities are therefore moving away from the ideological struggle toward a more concrete institutional struggle, the third of the three planes of struggle in which the labor–capital balance of power is being renegotiated.

THE INSTITUTIONAL STRUGGLE
Undermining the Labor Courts

As discussed in the previous chapter, the big committees are under fire in the media as a leftover from the heyday of Israeli corporatism, benefiting from a slew of ostensibly anachronistic privileges and overly restrictive labor legislation that thwart the implementation of supposedly necessary reforms. The institutional and legislative frameworks that enable the big committees to maintain their power include the labor courts. The popularity of the labor courts among employers and unions waxes and wanes according to who benefits (or is perceived as benefiting) from recent rulings, as illustrated by the Zamir Committee case, noted below (Committee Investigating the Labor Courts 2006). However, as a central institution in Israeli labor relations that has been instrumental in maintaining the hegemonic status of the now much-maligned Histadrut, the labor courts are generally perceived to be on the workers' side. The labor courts were once again the focus of delegitimization efforts following the Pelephone ruling, but this ruling should be seen in a historical context of ongoing shifts in the status and strength of organized labor.

In the years following the establishment of the State of Israel, the remarkable power of the Histadrut as a labor federation meant that organized labor had the potential to cause great disruption. However, the Histadrut was also an employer and national institution, as wary of powerful organized labor as any other employer, and indeed, the Histadrut as an employer was facing wildcat strikes and tough labor disputes in the 1950s and 1960s. In 1969, the Histadrut joined employer organizations to set up the labor courts, which should be understood as a first step in the creation of a balance of forces between labor and capital—a balance at the heart of the neocorporatist labor relations regime. Therefore the establishment of the labor courts can be seen as an important step in the taming of the powerful workers' committees by channeling the activities of organized labor through legally sanctioned and judiciable frameworks. The Histadrut supported the move also in its role as a national institution that had to bear some of the responsibility for the young state's economy (see IDI 2004, 42–46). The move was effective: immediately after being set up, the labor courts began issuing injunctions against strikes (Mundlak 2007, 165).

In 1977 the Agreed Arbitration Institute was set up. This can be seen as a second step in delimiting the role of organized labor: though arbitration takes decision-making power away from both workers and their employer, and thus does not weaken organized labor vis-à-vis capital in any single given dispute, it does undermine the collective and participatory logic of neocorporatist labor relations.[1] In this sense it undermines organized labor's position in the socioeconomic structure. The Histadrut was involved in this move, too, for the same reason: concern about the power of the workers' committees, a concern shared by the government that was under pressure from the Knesset and the public to legislate against strikes (Finkelstein 2003; Goldberg 1994).

At first, then, the labor courts were conceived as a crucial mediating factor between two legitimate partners in the neocorporatist labor relations regime. However, as this regime was undermined, the labor courts began to be perceived as too prolabor. In 2004, then justice minister Yosef (Tommy) Lapid, responding to employers' pressure, set up the so-called Zamir Committee to investigate the possibility of incorporating the labor courts into the main judicial system (see Ram 2008, 52).[2] However, before the committee began hearings, a wave of strikes threatened to paralyze the ports, which caused great anxiety among manufacturers and industry. Former president of the National Labor Court (NLC) Steve Adler recalled the case as he saw it as presiding judge: "Two weeks is what the government figured the Histadrut could go; they were going to fight it out for two weeks. . . . The employers went out of their minds; they said, 'What's going to happen to us? For years we've been building up clients; we have a big industry here; people are going to leave us'" (interview).

The dispute was between the port workers (through the Histadrut) and the government. According to Adler (interview), the Histadrut did not want the strike, fearing bad publicity at a time when its image was already tarnished; it also feared the strike would harm other workers in the economy. The government, for its part, did not want the labor court involved, as it was determined to push forward its privatization program. It was the industrialists who turned to the courts as a third party, though they were not directly involved. The court's success in

limiting the strikes and bringing the sides to an agreement led to increased political support for the labor courts, and even the employers' organizations withdrew
their criticism (Adler, interview). As a result, the Zamir Committee ended up by
recommending the courts remain more or less as they were, as well as noting the
courts' contribution to maintaining stability in industrial relations (see the Committee Investigating the Labor Courts 2006).

After Pelephone, there were once again calls for canceling the labor courts.
According to reports from January 2013, a bill to limit the NLC's authority was
being formulated with the involvement of Uriel Lynn, head of the Federation of
the Israeli Chambers of Commerce (Niv 2013i). This bill, which would be channeled through the Knesset and government as the bodies able to enact legislation, was no doubt spurred by supportive voices in government, including the
economics minister and the finance minister. The main thrust of the proposed
bill was to limit the NLC's ability to set precedents that were liable to impose
additional burdens on employers or limit what employers were able to do. It
also aimed to curtail the labor courts' authority in handling collective labor disputes and strikes. The chair of the Coordinating Bureau, Zvi Oren, declared that
labor court judges were overstepping their authority because of their "ideology"
(Bior 2013d). Leading labor lawyer Nahum Feinberg (known for representing
employers) implied that the labor courts were to blame for attracting criticism by
being too prolabor. Using the language of soccer, he said that such criticism was
a "yellow card" for judges who had given rulings that hurt employers and cited
the Pelephone case as one example. He said the Pelephone ruling was not "legal"
but "ideological" and was given by a court that wants the labor laws of a "socialist state" (Bior 2013d; Niv 2013m). Later in the year, Lynn responded to further
labor unrest at the ports by suggesting the use of paragraph 160 of the 1977
penal code that enables the government to declare an emergency if it believes a
labor dispute will disrupt imports and exports. In a letter to the prime minister,
Lynn proposed that this stipulation be extended to "Italian" strikes and suggested
that worker action against government decisions should be considered a criminal
offence in "essential" services, punishable by up to two years behind bars, even if
such decisions affect their workplace (Niv 2013h).

The labor courts are also having to learn how to handle issues of organizing,
including the new legal problems associated with employer opposition (as
reflected in former NLC president Adler's recent change of heart) and the new
"pluralism" in labor representation (see Mundlak 2009), and having to lay
down case law in light of the lack of direction from the legislature. According to
Mundlak (1998), labor law reflects social values as well as influencing them. The
courts are now receiving conflicting signals from society and are unsure how to
respond (those in labor law are also human, susceptible to the same pressures and

ideologies that all are subject to). The new labor law, he suggests, is struggling to find a path among liberal values while maintaining some aspects of the old labor regime, as can be seen in the fact that rulings sometimes go one way, sometimes another, with the higher courts overruling the lower courts. This was clear in the Pelephone ruling, but also in the railway ruling discussed in chapter 5 that laid out the ground rules for competition between unions (Inter-Organizational Dispute 9685-07-12) and in the El-Batuf case between the Histadrut and the National Histadrut that codified them (Inter-Organizational Dispute 31575-02-13). Many of these issues had not been raised even in the recent past, as evidenced by the relatively smooth organizing initiatives in Visa-CAL in 2011 and Isracard in 2010, for example.

Moreover, the labor courts are on the defensive as being too biased toward the workers, too activist, and not sufficiently judicial. As reflected in employers' responses to the Pelephone ruling, the courts are expected to avoid any rulings that may harm employers or the economy, and they are painted as ideological—in contrast to the supposedly objective expertise of Finance Ministry economists who know how to run the economy. The main criticism against the labor court as a semiautonomous judicial system is necessarily against its mediating role, because it could do its judicial work as part of the general judicial system as a magistrate court specializing in employment issues; therefore criticism against the court is de facto against the collective labor relations regime, or against industrial relations based on agreement between capital and labor (IDI 2004, 45–46). Thus despite the court's attempts to couch the right to organize in liberal terms, it still states its commitment to collective labor relations—without them, as clearly understood by the Federation of the Israeli Chambers of Commerce and the Coordinating Bureau, the labor court will find it hard to justify its role as a semi-autonomous institution even though collective disputes make up just a small part of the labor courts' work (see IDI 2004, 43).

The idea of somehow appending the labor court system to the general judicial system while maintaining labor as a separate legal sphere is therefore misleading. Beyond their role in issuing rulings on legal questions, the labor courts aspire to a democratic, participatory settlement of disputes, reflected in the presence of public representatives.[3] This aspect of the labor courts' role was particularly emphasized by Adler during his term as NLC president. As he noted:

> They'd come to the court, the judge would sit with the sides, try to get them to agree, try to get them to go back [to talking] ... but my predecessor didn't spend as much time sitting with the parties [as I did]. ... I would sit with them for hours, sometimes twenty-four hours even, 'til they reached an agreement ... worked out all the details, which was

quite a feat.... When this first happened, the government was ferocious, they didn't want to get the court, they didn't think the court should have anything to do with it ... [privatization] was none of the court's business.... Even though case law says, the government has all the right to pass the law but if it affects the workers, it should be negotiated. (Interview)

Indeed, in response to the increased popularity of the courts following the successful settlement of a major dispute (as noted by the Zamir Committee), the government mooted the idea of simply canceling the role of the public representatives (workers and employers).

The labor courts, then, are an essential institution in collective labor relations and reflect the overall neocorporatist structure in which worker, employer, and state come together to manage economic and social policy. Attempts to limit their authority undermine de facto the democratic management of industrial relations—the granting of economic voice to capital alone. In light of opposition to these attempts to delimit the power of organized labor, it may be that nondemocratic means may be required. And indeed, the Prime Minister's Office proposed using the Arrangements Law to limit the right to strike: this law is arguably one of Israel's least democratic legal instruments that enables the government to push through reforms or delay the application of social legislation using budgetary constraints as a pretext (see Shenhav 2013, 136, for a discussion of the undemocratic aspects of this law, which he calls "an archive of corpses of social legislation"; see also IDI 2004, 19–31; Maor and Bar Nir 2008). Navot and Peled go further and connect the discourse of human rights (the "rights revolution" of the 1980s) and the constitutional revolution not only to the rise of a (neo)liberal perspective, but also to the weakening of elective, democratic institutions:

> Not only did this economic transformation [from a corporatist to a neoliberal economy] require a new emphasis on the individual, as opposed to the collectivity, but these "revolutions" also shifted power from the elective, majoritarian institutions to professional, non-elective ones, primarily the Supreme Court. This move could be crucial for the success of the economic transformation, in case the opposition to liberalization (coming from bodies such as the Histadrut) succeeded in mobilizing masses of voters to its cause. (2009, 430)[4]

These developments potentially position the labor courts in opposition to the rest of the judicial system and suggest why the NLC made efforts to couch its Pelephone ruling in the language of individual rights.

The proposal to limit the right to strike is aimed at the public sector because this is a significant stronghold of organized labor and because the big committees are thwarting government programs to reform and privatize the large public-sector industries. In providing legal protection for the committees, the labor courts are implicated in harming the economy and maintaining Israel's high cost of living. This was the way they were portrayed in the recent Israel Electricity Corporation (IEC) case concerning the introduction of competition to the electricity market by, among other things, the building and operation of private power stations. Here the Haifa Labor Court ordered the state to desist from any action that might change the current situation for the IEC until an agreement had been reached between the government (the Yogev Committee charged with recommending reforms) and the management. The court thus stopped the Electricity Authority from granting an operating license to a private station (Dorad) that was due to begin generating. In this case the High Court intervened against the labor court decision by permitting a license to be issued (see Bar-Eli 2014a; Barkat 2014).[5]

Reducing the strength of the labor courts is thus directly linked to undermining the big committees as a necessary step in the dismantling of public companies—privatization. The position of the Histadrut should be noted here. While some of the strong workers' committees have acted against privatization programs, such as the railway, others, including the head of the Histadrut transport union, Avi Edri (Niv 2013b), have spoken out in favor as long as the interests of the organized workers are not harmed. Furthermore, the Histadrut itself has done little to oppose privatization, and agreed to privatization in the railway and in the ports (see Niv 2013g). Where a committee sees privatization as going against its interests, as in the railway, it is likely to oppose the Histadrut. Here the courts indirectly supported the railway reform program by upholding the Histadrut's status at the railway. The labor courts, then, are not simply in favor of or against privatization, but are seen to be protective of workers' committees that are able to restrict the state's ability to apply reforms if it wishes.

This is not to say that everyone is against labor courts—many public and government figures spoke out in favor, noting their important role in settling disputes, often arguing that they are not (contrary to common opinion) necessarily on the side of the workers. For example, a former wages officer at the Finance Ministry, Yuval Rachlevsky, spoke up in defense of the labor courts, noting that they do a good job balancing interests. He said reforms are a legitimate aim, but it is not legitimate to attack the labor courts as a way of gaining a better position in collective bargaining, thus implying that the attacks may be intended to force the Histadrut to compromise on public-sector wage issues. Another former wages officer, Ilan Levine, agreed (Niv 2013c).

Former Manufacturers Association of Israel head Shraga Brosh also defended the courts, noting that they had always been attentive to employers and pointing to various benefits to employers due to the partnership nurtured by the courts (Niv 2013f). However, Brosh is part of an older school that believed in social partnership; he also maintained a close personal relationship with the head of the Histadrut. His successor, Zvika Oren, has been far less willing to countenance Histadrut partnership in managing social and economic policy. Oren is the owner of the railway industries firm MTR where workers are not organized. He invited the Histadrut chair to discuss the rules of organizing, but his idea of partnership does not include the idea that workers need protection. He claimed no union has ever stepped foot in the MTR factory in Dimona and noted that while he will not prevent organizing, he would ensure no "outside elements" incite the workers (Azulay 2013b).

Moreover, all those who spoke in the courts' defense did so by noting that they sometimes rule against labor; in other words they accepted the idea of balance. Even former NLC president Nili Arad felt it necessary to stress how she acted against workers, reminding her interviewers, for example, that for three months she prevented a general strike among agency workers and disallowed the mass resignation of the resident physicians (Niv and Yoaz 2013).

Labor relations scholar Yitzhak Harpaz, in an opinion piece in *TheMarker* (Harpaz 2013), noted that whether or not the courts "really do" act in favor of labor is not important: when public figures claim this is the case, it makes the public believe it may be so, making it easy to blame the courts for protecting the "strong" committees who are disrupting the "normal" functioning of the state. Indeed, even if threats against the labor courts come to nothing, they still normalize "the option" of doing away with the labor courts, which in itself diminishes their power.

Though I have suggested that the labor court system was established to counter the perceived abuse of the strength of organized labor and tame the workers who were ignoring the authority of the Histadrut in wildcat strikes, labor courts need unions (collective labor relations) perhaps more than strong organized labor needs the labor courts. So while attacking the labor courts is on the one hand a way to curtail the power of strong committees and undermine the last vestiges of corporatism, if the courts were indeed to be canceled, a strong union could perhaps still survive. The real losers would be unorganized workers in the private sector. The work of nongovernmental organizations active among migrant workers and Palestinians from the occupied territories would be particularly affected (see part 3).

To conclude—this chapter has suggested that the labor courts, crucial for the success of organized labor as a political and social force, are at the heart of the institutional struggle, the third plane of struggle defined in part 2, in which vestigial institutions of the corporatist regime are targeted for being significant hurdles in the effort to undermine organized labor. The central institution of collective labor relations, the independent labor court system, finds itself on the defensive, with its legitimacy questioned and proposals put forward for legislation limiting its powers.

CONCLUDING REMARKS TO PART 2

The material presented in part 2 suggests that the challenge to labor's privileged position in the neocorporatist labor relations regime is an important element in the shift in the balance of power away from organized labor and toward capital. Though this regime no longer exists as it did in the 1950s and 1960s, and labor's "privileged position" has been under attack for at least four decades (see the introduction; Maor 2012), various structures and institutions of this regime are still available to workers who wish to use them, as we saw in part 1, protecting labor and delimiting capital's maneuvering space. These institutions are the focus of capital's efforts to undermine organized labor, in addition to its frontline efforts preventing organizing drives in the workplace.

The concept of "balance" is key to the struggle, as articulated in the issue of "balance of rights," which the labor courts have been compelled to adopt, balancing the legitimacy of labor's demands with that of capital's demands. This has effectively negated organized labor's privileged position in the political-economic structure: labor and capital are now to be seen as equal contestants on a level playing field of particularist interests, thus the belief in an a priori power imbalance is rejected. The idea of "balance" has been accepted by the public and taken up by politicians, including by those who speak out in favor of organized labor; thus Shelly Yachimovich, who was once Israel's main center-left politician and former leader of the Labor Party, can crow about new organizing drives with Koach Laovdim even as she condemns the "corrupt, aggressive" Histadrut workers' committees at the ports and Israel Electricity Corporation as being too powerful.[1] Even Koach Laovdim seems to have internalized the idea of balance to a certain extent: in the position paper it submitted to the court in the Pelephone case, it noted it was in favor of permitting employers to speak their mind about organizing drives, on the condition that worker organization representatives are present, and to "correct facts" if the union has distributed inaccurate information.[2] Only the Histadrut was firmly against the idea of balance, but it has the most to lose, because the concept is directed mainly against the ostensibly too powerful committees that are its main pillar of strength.

The attempt to promote the idea of balance is also present in attempts to draw parallels between too-concentrated capital and too-concentrated labor, as seen in the conflation of the idea of the *ports* as a monopoly and the idea of the workers' committees *at the ports* as a monopoly. This conflation enables the "problem" of insufficient competition in the market to be linked conceptually to overly powerful organized labor. Indeed, a recent proposal to restrict the power of the big committees is to declare them a monopoly (Korin-Liber 2014), which would mean that the state could turn to the Trade Restrictions Court instead of the labor court in case of a labor dispute. This would also further undermine the status of the labor court, as it marks another encroachment into its field. By making their monopolistic position an issue, the government is reminding the public that these powerful workers' committees distort competitiveness and efficiency, implying parallels between them and companies like Coca-Cola, which has recently been fending off charges of irregularities in its operations as a monopoly (Hayot 2014). Such parallels also imply that labor is on an equal footing with the state and the employer—ignoring the fact that employers regularly associate to promote common interests in organizations like the Manufacturers Association of Israel. Competition, then, a staple of state policy since the 1980s (Levi-Faur 2000), is also the new panacea that will cure the ills of organized labor.

Furthermore, linking organized labor with a company's lack of competitiveness (and subsequent threat of job losses when the company goes under) implies that workers and employers are all in it together; thus worker interests are aligned with employer interests (the competitiveness of the company) even when no mechanism is in place for profit sharing or worker ownership of company stocks. Interestingly, according to Federation of the Israeli Chambers of Commerce chair Uriel Lynn, even the most fundamental aim of strikes is no longer legitimate—the desire to improve employment terms (Filut, Azulay, and Barkat 2012). Merely having a job is the most workers can legitimately hope for. This is in keeping with the logic of all in it together: workers' strikes against their employer make sense only when a clash of interests is recognized.

The presumption behind the idea of overly concentrated capital is that companies are individual entities that should compete on the open market. This thinking, which turns a blind eye to employer organizations, also equates workers with such entities, as individual entrepreneurs. As Cobble and Vosko put it, "We are entering the world of Me, Inc. . . . a strange new world in which everyone can define themselves as 'independent economic entities' and sell themselves as products on the market," because the expansion of the definition of "capitalist" now includes all of us as entrepreneurs (2000, 308; see also Brown 2015; Helman 2013; M. Peters 2001). According to this logic, monopolistic workers' committees prevent competition among workers, undermining the efficacy of market mechanisms just as monopolies and crony capitalism do—as the economics minister reiterated many times in various ways. Notably, social services were excluded from the range of "essential services" in which the right to strike is being challenged: essential services are now thought to be services that shore up industry and facilitate trade, not services that offer support to those who have failed to transform themselves into individual entrepreneurs and sell themselves on the free market. This reimagining of the entrepreneurial citizen engenders a new normative vision of an ideal public—one that has no need for the safeguards of unionist corporatism and the welfare state, one whose rights must be defended from industrial action.

Indeed, the nurturing of the entrepreneurial citizen is another example of how the public is differentiated from the workers. It contributes to the weakening of neocorporatist labor relations because a fundamental premise of corporatism was that organized labor in some way represented the public. Moreover, it contributes to the weakening of the public sector, not only because of the delegitimization of public services: during labor disputes, workers are necessarily aligned against their employer, and their employer in the public sector is the public. By reimagining this public as having no need of unions in general, the possibility of solidarity between striking workers and the public is further undermined, leaving conceptions of monopolistic workers' committees to go unchallenged. In the private sector, on the other hand, the employer is easily identified with the tycoons, or at least with exploitative employment terms. It is easier for the public to support struggles against such employers.

Moreover, compulsory arbitration was put forward as a way of protecting public property from the big committees and ensuring the public's right to services. It must be noted that in the distinction between the workers and a third party whose interests must be protected, this third party is not necessarily the public. During the labor dispute at the ports in 2005, and again in 2012, for example, the third party was employer organizations representing (in particular) industrialists and those dependent on import and export. When industrialists are the third party, public interest is presumed to be aligned with capital's, while workers' interests are deemed narrow and particularist.

The National Labor Court, too, part of a justice system undergoing liberalization, wittingly or unwittingly adopted a free-market discourse based on an individualist perspective to justify its ruling in the Pelephone case even though the ruling was intended to protect workers and facilitate a collective approach to labor relations. In this case, it emphasized its commitment to the free flow of information at the basis of liberal democracy and the free marketplace of ideas at the basis of liberal capitalism. It therefore implicitly accepted the argument put forward by the Federation of the Israeli Chambers of Commerce, which asserted that limiting the employer's freedom of speech would undermine democracy since workers would be liable to make decisions on incomplete information (see Collective Dispute Appeal 25476-09-12, par. 45).

If we view the broader shifts in the balance of power, we can say that in the years following the establishment of the State of Israel, the state attempted to reduce the power of organized labor that had once been so useful in the settlement project. Indeed, in those early years, then prime minister David Ben-Gurion proposed compulsory arbitration as a way of undermining the Histadrut's monopoly over labor issues and even tried to pass a national health law that would cancel the dependence of workers on the Histadrut's health services (Grinberg 1993, 90),[3] something that finally took place with the National Health Insurance Law of 1995. These attempts were part of the state's move towards *mamlachtiut* (statism), a process of augmenting its autonomy and reducing its dependence on the pre-1948 social structures and institutions: "Under this ideological orientation [*mamlachtiut*], a wide and extensive set of functions and organizations [previously] conducted by non-governmental organizations—such as the political parties and the Histadrut—were transferred to the hands and responsibility of the state" (Levi-Faur 2000, 169; see also Grinberg 1993, 39–55 and 73–91; Harel 2004; Horowitz and Lissak 1978, 186–212).

The establishment of the labor courts and later the Agreed Arbitration Institute, I have suggested, can be seen as part of this same process: the former consolidated labor's power in the political and legal structure but also delimited and constrained it; the latter undermined labor's position as a directly democratic force.[4]

Since the 1980s (taking the Emergency Economic Stabilization Plan of 1985 as a useful watershed; see Shalev 2006), capital has been increasing its power and now appears to be strong enough to challenge the state: in struggles between large corporations and government institutions, the former appear to have the upper hand. The remnants of the corporatist structure, including the labor courts and the big committees, are one of the last barriers to capital's complete freedom of operation—and hence capital's current target. Thus I propose we see the Pelephone ruling as a significant step in the labor courts' efforts to reassert themselves by shoring up organized labor, and thereby collective labor relations, without which they have no raison d'être.

I began part 2 by suggesting that this balance of power can be viewed as a class struggle taking place on three planes that drew on Hyman's (1996, 61) view of union power, a view that encompasses the institutional and political-cultural setting as well as the strategic situation of worker organizations themselves. The first plane I defined was the plane of frontal struggle. Here, capital, in the form of specific employers, is taking steps to prevent organizing drives and the unionization of workplaces—classic workplace unionist activity. The second was the plane of ideological struggle. On this plane, organized labor is defending its image and legitimacy while capital undermines this legitimacy, trying to paint the unions as corrupt interest groups whose activity is disrupting the smooth functioning of the economy. The third was the plane of institutional struggle. Here, capital is attacking the institutions that shore up organized labor and the vestiges of the corporatist labor relations regime. These are the institutions that "fix and to a certain degree legally codify basic social compromises" (Dörre 2011, 21) and that may be used as a source of power when other power resources are declining, as Dörre notes.

Of course, the three planes of struggle are linked: activity on any given plane generally involves activity on other planes. Labor's struggles on the ground, in the workplace, against employer attempts to prevent organizing also involve the use of the courts as well as activities to counter the conceptual delegitimization of organized labor. As we have seen, those involved in the campaigns investigated here made a great effort to emphasize the public aspects of their cause, to explain themselves, particularly in the Forum against the Privatization of the Railway and the social workers' strike: fighting privatization, safeguarding public property, or maintaining the standards of public service. They have had to fight against the idea that they are merely another interest group and reconnect the idea of the public to a public of workers, conflating workers' interests with public interests. Proclaiming that they were bringing the social protest movement into the workplace was one way of doing this and was remarkably successful in recruiting workers and drawing public sympathy, particularly in the private sector.

In short, we can note that success in the frontal struggle, in the workplace, is greatly undermined by the weakening of organized labor in the second plane of ideological struggle and by the attacks on the institutions of collective labor relations (the third plane) that no longer have the backing of the state or government. Organized labor is not just struggling against capital in the workplace, or fending off its attacks, but coping with a fundamental shift in the way organized labor and the place of the worker in society is perceived and being construed. In discussing capital's attempts to weaken labor, then, I do not intend to imply unequivocal causality—that is, I am not simplistically claiming that labor is weak because of the action of employers and their organizations, or not because of that alone, but that such action is part of a complex process that has weakened organized labor and against which labor is struggling. To put it in Hyman's terms: in the face of open resistance in the workplace, organized labor has had some successes (though also suffered some defeats), but its capacity to influence culture and attitudes to create an ideological climate favorable to organized labor has been greatly weakened. Indeed, the strongest labor organization—the Histadrut—is least able to garner widespread public support, though some of the newer and smaller organizations have partly succeeded in positioning themselves as plucky counterweights to big business.

Previously corporatist states around the Western world are undergoing similar changes (Gumbrell-McCormick and Hyman 2013; Hyman 2001; Leisink, Van Leemput, and Vilrokx 1996a; Martin and Ross 1999; Ozaki 1999; Upchurch, Taylor, and Mathers 2009), but in Israel the undermining of organized labor's privileged position in the political-economic structure signifies something more: this is the end, following a long decline, of labor's importance to the Zionist project. Israel has always used private capital for the "good of the country" (see Gozansky 1986 on the development of capitalism in Palestine, for example; see also Shalev 2006); private enterprise "took part in shaping the dominant socialist-Zionist ideology long before the state was established," and capitalist practices applied "ever more intensively immediately after the genesis of the state" (Frenkel, Shenhav, and Herzog 2000, 44, 65). However, as reviewed in the introduction, labor organized within a nationalist framework was crucial as a means of achieving various *yishuv* and state aims, as well as being the center of the settlement movement discourse. Now a very different picture has taken shape. Capital is still crucial for Israel, but workers increasingly less so. Citizens may be consumers, but as workers they are no longer privileged, and they are easily replaceable by cheaper imports: in the doctors' campaign of 2011, the prime minister threatened to bring in Indian doctors to break the strike (Even 2011b); and during the ports dispute in 2013, the transport minister said he was investigating the option of bringing workers from abroad to operate the cargo terminals (Bar-Eli and Coren 2013). These may be merely examples of rhetoric from state representatives facing a workers' struggle, but Israel has no shortage of very real cheap labor in the form of migrant laborers and Palestinians from the occupied territories. Israeli unionized workers, then, are the deadwood that must be cut to facilitate the creation of the streamlined companies that will drive the country's economic growth. Under these circumstances, labor is having to find new ways to make its voice heard in the corridors of power and renegotiate its relationship with the political community and the nation.

Part 3

RENEGOTIATING LABOR'S PLACE IN SOCIETY AND NATION

LABOR REPRESENTATION OUTSIDE UNION STRUCTURES

The corporatist regime included the state as an active and essential partner in the tripartite structure, and organized labor had a place in the political sphere, influencing the forming of decisions and policies. In Israel's case, the link between organized labor and the structures and institutions of the state was particularly strong, especially due to the close relationship between the Histadrut and the Labor Party (in its various incarnations). Now, after more than thirty years in which the state under all governments has acted against organized labor, corporatist channels of influence for unions have been weakened and labor is finding new ways of bringing its demands into the political arena. Part 3 seeks to address these new ways and thus investigate the link between organized labor and the political establishment and explore the relationship between the labor force and the political community or nation following the decline of the labor ethos so crucial to the Zionist project in its formative years.

Since 1967 and Israel's conquest of additional territory, noncitizen Palestinians have entered the Israeli job market. To further complicate the picture, a plethora of relatively new worker groups have joined the labor market since the 1990s, including migrant labor and even asylum seekers from outside the country's borders, as well as increasing numbers of workers in nonstandard employment arrangements within the country. Few of these groups enjoy Histadrut patronage, and new organizations have been established to assist them, paving new paths of influence on the political sphere and carving themselves a place in the polity. These organizations include new unions that turn to workers neglected by the Histadrut or excluded from the Zionist corporatist arrangement, as well as nongovernmental organizations (NGOs) whose main concern is workers' rights, the labor market, and the economy (Mundlak 2007, 133–134).

One such organization is the Workers Advice Center (WAC), which acts in many ways like an NGO and operated as such for much of its existence, but has a strong unionist ideology and was granted recognition as a union by the labor courts in 2011. In keeping with its classically unionist and broadly Marxist approach, it has close ties with a socialist labor party (Daam). However, this is a small party that has not yet obtained the threshold number of votes required for a seat in the Knesset. In the vast majority of its operations, WAC works through the courts and lobbying, gaining invitations to various Knesset committees and nurturing personal connections in government ministries.

Another such organization is Kav Laoved, an NGO established in 1991 particularly to assist Palestinian workers from the occupied territories but that rapidly expanded its sphere of activities to include all workers requiring assistance in ensuring their rights; in practice, this means migrant laborers, asylum seekers, and Arab citizens of Israel in particular as well as Palestinians. These two organizations are introduced here as the basis for the following discussion.

WAC: From NGO to Classic Unionism

WAC is involved in a wide range of activities through various modes of operation and holds to a classic unionist outlook that includes links with a political party (the Organization for Democratic Action, known as Daam in Hebrew and Arabic) and a socialist, internationalist, class-based ideology. WAC is firmly opposed both to the neoliberalization of the labor market and to the Jewish/Arab divide, which it tries to bridge also via the political party. This aspiration to internationalist, class-based solidarity can be seen in WAC's efforts to maintain links with unions abroad, which has included organizing various visits of union delegations.[1] In several cases, WAC has invited representatives of European unions to tour the country to understand the labor issues in Israel and meet representatives of organizations with which WAC has sometimes cooperated and representatives of state bodies such as the Finance Ministry and Labor Ministry (*Challenge* 85, May–June 2004).[2] WAC representatives also travel abroad to develop links, including a trip to Egypt to meet striking workers during the wave of labor unrest from 2006 to 2008, particularly in the industrial city of Mahalla al-Kubra (*Challenge* 109, May–June 2008), Turkey for the LabourStart conference of 2011 (Adiv and Agbarieh-Zahalka 2011), Berlin for the LabourStart conference of 2014, and various European states on several other occasions.

WAC's unionizing activities grew out of its experience as a workers' advice center (hence the organization's name). In 1992, a group of (mostly Jewish) activists established the al-Baqa Center in the Israeli Arab town of Majdal Krum (additional centers in Jaffa and Nazareth were opened later). These activists were linked to Derekh Hanitzotz, an Israeli Marxist movement outlawed for its connections with the Democratic Front for the Liberation of Palestine. The al-Baqa Center assisted Israeli Arab workers, offering advice regarding labor, property, and housing issues, ran a mothers' school and children's summer camps, and held various cultural activities. It was associated with Daam, which was not a political party at the time (it was registered as such in 1996).

WAC national coordinator Assaf Adiv and WAC funding coordinator Roni Ben Efrat (both founding members) said that WAC kept its doors open to all workers but concentrated on those areas it believed were neglected by the Histadrut, and thus in practice was involved mostly (exclusively, at first) with Israeli Arabs (Adiv, Ben Efrat, interviews). In the early years, its main goal was simply to assist Israeli Arabs to get jobs in construction, where migrant labor was already being used. At this stage, there was little thought of acting as an independent union since the Histadrut was considered too dominant, and WAC had a "radical, dangerous" image that made working with employers difficult (Ben Efrat, interview). Furthermore, according to Adiv (interview), the founding members did not have the experience to organize workers, and the population they wanted to work with (from an ideological and practical point of view, as the populations considered most likely to lead to radical change) was "not ready" for unionization.

In the mid-1990s, thousands of Israeli Arabs were being replaced by migrant labor. Local workers were sometimes being laid off and rehired via labor contractors outside the framework of collective agreements. Migrant laborers were also excluded from collective agreements, according to an agreement signed by the Histadrut with the Israel Builders and Contractors Association in 1999. WAC tried to assist Israeli Arabs to get taken on within existing collective agreements. At first, it concentrated on corresponding with government ministries, employers, and the National Insurance Institute (NII) to ensure the rights of workers, which led to various successes such as compensation for dismissals.

Attempts at more unionist-style activities began when eight workers walked off their job in a Kufr Kama textiles plant over a wage dispute. The Histadrut seemed unwilling or unable to help settle the dispute. Due to its work with Israeli Arabs in construction, as an organization WAC was familiar to the textile workers, who approached it for assistance. This led to various attempts at setting up ad hoc workers' committees and providing legal assistance, with some individual successes though little tangible progress collectively (see *Challenge* 32, July–August 1995; *Challenge* 33, September–October 1995; *Challenge*

40, November–December 1996). Toward the end of 1997, WAC members discussed the need for a new democratic union to address issues not covered by the Histadrut, particularly low-paid Israeli Arab workers such as those in the textile industry. In 1998, as a first step, it changed its constitution to become an elected institution, funded in part by membership dues, open to all workers. That same year, it turned its attention to the issue of unemployment, because of the growing phenomenon of hidden unemployment (via part-time or temporary employment frameworks) and working poor, and because Israeli Arabs were disproportionately affected. The following year, it opened an office in Nazareth to concentrate on this issue.

However, little union progress was made in the following decade, though it expanded its work as a labor rights organization. In the year 2000, it began activities in East Jerusalem, offering assistance to jobseekers at the East Jerusalem Employment Bureau, advising, helping with submitting claims, following up irregularities and the cessation of benefits, and working vis-à-vis the NII. The organization took this step after activists noticed apparent cooperation between construction firms who did not want Israeli Arabs, preferring migrant laborers, and the Employment Services who were quick to register Israeli Arabs as "job refusers" thereby denying them social security benefits and opening the way for the construction firms to obtain migrant labor permits (Adiv, interview).[3] It was also a central partner in Wisconsin Watch, a coalition of rights organizations against the so-called Wisconsin program.[4]

In fact, as a union, WAC was able to do very little alone, and it saw real possibility for union work only in 2008, as organizing began to be seen throughout the economy. Developments that opened the way for WAC's work included the establishment in 2007 of the new independent union Koach Laovdim, the campaign (2007–8) at the Coffee Bean chain of cafés taken up by the Histadrut as a flagship case, and the three organizing-related paragraphs of the 2009 package deal agreement negotiated with the government by the Histadrut. Moreover, in 2007 Israel was put on an accession roadmap to become a member of the Organisation for Economic Cooperation and Development (OECD) (it was accepted as a member in 2010), which put pressure on the government to put labor market and inequality issues on the public agenda. For example, in a summary of 2009, the OECD's Employment, Labor and Social Affairs Committee was critical of low rates of labor force participation among Arabs, especially Arab women (OECD 2010). WAC updated its constitution again in 2010 to reflect this new emphasis on unionizing, and added an appendix outlining the principles of organizing.[5]

In its subsequent work in the haulage industry, WAC deliberately set out to establish itself as a union and distributed its own newsletter, "The Union," in three languages (Hebrew, Arabic, and Russian, reflecting the main languages spoken by truckers). It received recognition in the case of Hamenia Derekh Hayam Ltd., in which the employer claimed WAC was not a workers' organization and not the representative organization at the company. The Tel Aviv Labor Court recognized WAC as a union, confirming that WAC meets all the criteria for a workers' organization as defined by the High Court: it is a permanent and democratic organization, independent from employers; its main aim is determining terms of employment via collective negotiation; it has established regulations outlining its objectives and modus operandi; and membership is voluntary. The court also confirmed that WAC's connection to Daam is legitimate and noted that union links to parties were a historical fact (TALC 5630-12-10).[6]

WAC's first steps in collective negotiations were taken in 2008 at the Minshar College of Art, but its role was supportive, not representative, and no permanent workers' committee was established. Its first collective agreement as a representative organization was signed in 2010 with Musrara College, and another agreement soon followed at the Jerusalem School of Visual Theatre.

Kav Laoved: The NGO-ization of Workers' Rights

Kav Laoved was established in 1991 to fight for the rights of noncitizen Palestinians in Israel, particularly in construction where "Russian" immigrants (immigrants from the former Soviet Union with some link to Judaism who were granted Israeli citizenship on arrival) and later also migrant laborers were competing for work formerly carried out by Palestinians. During the first Gulf War, all Palestinians in Israel were sent back to the occupied territories and returned only to find that many of their former jobs had been taken (see Farsakh 2005, 121 and 138–139, who notes that fluctuating numbers of Palestinians in Israel's construction industry was mainly a function of closure policies and not directly dependent on the number of migrant laborers). At first Kav Laoved worked mainly with "illegal" Palestinians, those without a permit to work inside Israel, who were unaware of their basic rights (laws on minimum wage, maximum work hours, and severance pay, for example, are applicable also to workers without a permit) and had no way of claiming on these rights. It soon began assisting migrant workers, subcontracted workers, and new immigrants, both inside the Green Line and in the occupied territories.[7] Today it provides legal assistance to Palestinians, Israeli Arabs, refugees and asylum seekers, and migrant laborers in agriculture, caregiving, and construction in particular, representing and assisting them in court and in their dealings with the authorities and working on issues of principle in the form of legal action and advocacy in Knesset committees. According to the organization's website, by 2012 it had provided services to over thirty-five thousand workers and regained a total of over NIS 16 million that had been illegally withheld from workers by their employers.

In its various projects and initiatives, Kav Laoved has joined forces with a wide range of civil society and workers' rights organizations, including Itach-Maaki (Women Lawyers for Social Justice), Kayan-Feminist Organization (for Palestinian women in Israel), ASSAF (Aid Organization for Refugees and Asylum Seekers in Israel), Mesila (aid and information center for the foreign community), Physicians for Human Rights, Hotline for Refugees and Migrants, and the Workers' Rights Clinic of Tel Aviv University.

In 2011, founder Hannah Zohar said that the organization intentionally avoided union work, though there was one early attempt at unionizing that did not succeed (interview). However, it has cooperated with Koach Laovdim on a number of issues, such as petitioning the Population, Immigration and Border Authority concerning migrant laborers' right to visit their home country during their period of employment (in 2010, together with the Association for Civil Rights in Israel). In 2013, it went a step further and joined Koach Laovdim in an initiative to organize migrant workers in agriculture (who are mostly Thais, especially since the bilateral agreement Israel signed with Thailand in 2012).[8]

The Changing Nature of Representation: Experts in the Field

These two organizations are clearly very different from the established unions of the corporatist regime. Whether, like WAC, they are officially unions or, like Kav Laoved, officially NGOs, they combine unions' focus on labor issues with NGO tactics and broad alliances with other nonunion organizations. The most notable aspects of their activities are expertise and law enforcement or monitoring; it is in these fields that they receive the greatest official recognition from state bodies and are able to develop the closest ties with the political establishment.

In agriculture, for example (one of WAC's flagship projects), WAC has consolidated its position and developed close ties with key figures in the political and administrative establishment. With the decline of the textile industry, agriculture became one of the few fields that remained open to Israeli Arab women, of whom only some 22 percent officially participate in the labor force (Yashiv and Kasir 2013). Many are employed via the *ra'is* system of labor contracting, whereby a man (often known to the workers, even a family member or friend) finds work for the women, negotiates with the employer, organizes their transport, and takes a cut of their wages. Many Israeli Arab women working in agriculture are not registered and receive no proper wage slip. From the NII's point of view, they do not exist, which means they cannot benefit from social security or insurance benefits. Wages are low, sometimes below the minimum, and there are huge social pressures not to complain for fear of getting the *ra'is* into trouble. In 2004, WAC initiated a campaign to assist such women into organized agricultural work with full rights.

WAC sees the employment of Israeli Arab women as an important way of easing poverty in the Arab sector, when a single wage earner in a family is seldom sufficient, but also as a way of changing Israeli Arab society: by assisting women to leave the home, WAC believes, it will promote their interaction with the wider world and augment their independence from husbands and family.

WAC began by contacting potential workers, potential employees, and government bodies that may be interested in promoting the employment of Israeli Arab women, and developed ties with the Ministry of Agriculture and the Ministry of Industry, Trade and Labor (the Economics Ministry). Over the course of a decade it was increasingly invited to meetings, including Knesset committee meetings, at which prominent decision makers were present such as the deputy governor of the Bank of Israel and Finance Ministry officials. For example, WAC has been in ongoing contact with the Finance Committee, the Foreign Workers Committee, the Directors-General Committee, and the Knesset Research and Information Center. It also maintains contact with representatives of various units within the Agriculture Ministry and Labor Ministry, the director-general of the Employment Services, and chairperson of Peripheral Farmers Forum.

Various people in key positions have asked for its opinion, including requests for official position papers, as well as requests for reports from the field and suggestions for possible courses of action. For example, the deputy director of planning at the Agriculture Ministry agreed to cooperate with WAC's efforts, and officials at the Labor Ministry agreed that WAC would submit a document outlining the potential of taking on Israeli workers. The head of the Foreign Workers Committee who is also a Knesset member (MK) requested a detailed position paper from WAC. (He then submitted a private member's bill for encouraging Israeli workers in agriculture, but the bill received no support from the Finance Ministry and was dropped.) WAC also organized tours of farms for various officials involved in initiatives to reduce migrant labor quotas. In this way, WAC became the link between government bodies responsible for regulating the agricultural industry and the Israeli Arab workers. Likewise in the haulage industry, in 2009, the Ministry of Labor's chief labor relations officer requested that WAC prepare a report detailing violations of drivers' rights that result from the collective agreement then in force (the report was submitted in 2010).

Similarly, Kav Laoved has become known as an expert in the field, to which people come for information and advice, including government representatives

(Zohar, interview). This has enabled it to nurture ties with ministries and Knesset committees, particularly the Foreign Workers Committee, and in 2013, the Ministry of Justice recognized Kav Laoved's status in accordance with the Class Action Law of 2006, enabling the organization to submit class action suits on labor issues. It collates reports and position papers for submission to official bodies and addresses international bodies such as UN organizations and the International Labor Organization and EU organizations such as EU-OSHA (European Agency for Health and Safety at Work). It also organizes conferences, workshops, and lectures, sometimes in collaboration with other rights organizations, aimed at raising awareness of specific problems among the workers themselves as well as for lawyers and students; this too contributes to its status as a depository of knowledge and expertise. Its power to effect change is dependent on the organization maintaining a nonpartisan approach, which is enhanced by its reputation as expert.

Advancing Case Law through Targeted Struggle

In their law enforcement role, much of the organizations' work is on an individual level (court cases over specific claims), but in some cases they are able to force a point of principle that paves the way for progress in case law. An example of this is WAC's case in 2009—the first of its kind—to enforce the application of paragraph 12a of the amendment to the Employment of Employees by Manpower Contractors Law of 1996.

In this case WAC represented twenty-one Palestinians employed via the manpower company Brik in salvage projects for the Israel Antiquities Authority (IAA). Many Palestinian residents of East Jerusalem work as unskilled laborers in such projects. These rescue digs, usually short projects, are initiated when an area designated as archeologically significant is slated for development, such as construction. The contractor in charge is legally obliged to call in the IAA, which does rapid exploratory digs to check whether a more comprehensive excavation is justified.[9] Previously, workers for such projects had been employed directly by the IAA, though they were not represented by the archaeologists' workers' committee (which is within the Histadrut). In the first decade of the millennium, the IAA began employing workers for its salvage projects via manpower companies, including dozens of workers from East Jerusalem. According to senior archaeologist Rudi Haim (interview), workers on the manpower company list are called up as projects are commenced. If there is any problem, they are simply not called. Some have worked on such projects for many years in this way, maintaining a precarious livelihood.

In 2009, some workers employed by Brik began organizing, with support from a few archaeologists and silent approval from others, in the hope of being instated as direct employees of the IAA. The company heard of the initiative and fired some of the workers. Three of the workers involved contacted the Histadrut, which granted them a meeting with Histadrut representatives but took no further steps to assist (Haim, interview). The initiators then contacted WAC, which agreed to represent twenty-one workers in court.

The workers claimed they had been illegally dismissed so that the IAA could avoid taking them on as regular employees. According to paragraph 12a of the amendment to the Employment of Employees by Manpower Contractors Law, any worker employed via a manpower agent who has worked for nine months in one position must be taken on by the client company (the firm ordering the services of the manpower contractor) as a regular worker.[10] The court ordered the IAA to take on the twenty-one workers, thus recognizing the IAA as their de facto employer (JLC 1307-09), but the IAA continued to refuse to cooperate with WAC as the workers' representative organization, insisted it had no intention of taking on the workers (WAC 2012), and appealed to the National Labor Court.

In March 2013, four years after the initial case was submitted, the National Labor Court rejected the appeal submitted by the IAA and Brik and ruled that the IAA must take on the workers as regular employees. However, WAC failed to set up a stable workers' committee in this case and was not recognized as a union: at one point during a meeting with the IAA, WAC had offered to assist with logistics, getting workers to work, organizing, and registering them with the IAA until they are taken on as regular workers, but the court asserted that a state body (the IAA) could not cooperate in this way with a "private organization" (the IAA had anyway declined the offer).

Hybrid Identities: Between NGO and Union

WAC, then, occupies a position somewhere between union and NGO. Its members today number only a few hundred and "turnover" is high because many view WAC as a "service provider" and join only for the time they require its services (Ben Efrat, interview). On the one hand it addresses groups who have failed to gain Histadrut support, but on the other its main success as a union (collective bargaining and agreement) has been with workers who have generally been typical of the kind of (Jewish) groups favored by the Histadrut, such as the teachers at the colleges. Groups generally excluded from Histadrut arrangements, such as Israeli Arab women in agriculture, have benefited mostly from WAC's legal and project-based work.

Indeed, WAC is involved in various activities not directly related to labor issues, though these too are all linked to its socialist, class-based agenda and its support for those it perceives to be at the bottom of the labor market hierarchy. One such project is "Youth for Social Change," a series of workshops and meetings between Jewish and Arab youth that aims to raise awareness of their common ground from a class perspective (Ben Efrat, interview). Another example is WAC's empowerment workshops for Israeli Arab women, whom WAC considers to be oppressed as women in a patriarchal society, as Arabs in a Jewish-dominated society, and as workers in a neoliberal capitalist society. These workshops aim to raise awareness of these issues while offering a secure forum for discussion and building personal confidence, in keeping with WAC's broadly Marxist beliefs that change will come from the oppressed classes (Ben Efrat, interview). WAC is also linked to sister organizations including a fair trade organization (Sindyanna of Galilee) that manages a cooperative plant and shop for olive oil products, a publishing venture (Hanitzotz), and a documentary film unit (Video48). These links are based on personal ties (in many cases it is the same people active in the different organizations) and the general aim of promoting the status of workers and the status of Arabs in a Jewish-dominated society.

Thus on the one hand it uses corporatist structures, including of course the labor courts and legislation that enables organizing, for its unionist work; and it has also been dependent on other unionizing developments in the labor market for its ability to act at all in this field. It is openly political, choosing its projects and organizing drives according to what extent they can be partner to, or help promote, a much broader political agenda and not according to how urgently any particular group requires organizing or assistance. On the other hand, it addresses its target populations directly, using various nonunion projects and organizations to promote its agenda; and its most notable success is in individual representation of workers in nonunion frameworks.

In fact, in its efforts to strengthen organized labor, and in its fundraising efforts (from charitable organizations overseas, among others), WAC draws on discourses of human rights as well as legislation that in themselves reflect the decline of organized labor and collective labor relations. Law enforcement, consequently, is a large part of its work and is of course a field that requires fewer resources than organizing. In the case of Brik, WAC's entire case was based on law enforcement; the workers who had started the organizing initiative (some of whom submitted claims independently) were not represented by WAC at all. Similarly, in two organizing attempts in Mishor Adumim, the workers succeeded in setting up committees under WAC's auspices and in gaining recognition from their employers, yet their main demand was that their employers comply with basic labor laws; they did not address more unionist issues such as pay scales, improved wages, benefits, and the like. WAC also has an ongoing project to promote awareness of safety at work, particularly in construction, which has a high rate of work accidents; a significant part of this work is holding employers to statutory safety standards.

Though it has gained recognition as a union, WAC is clearly perceived by both the workers it assists and government figures more as an NGO, as an expert professional organization representing specific population groups with their own particular problems. It is as such, and not as a members' organization, that it has been able to develop ties with specific figures in the political sphere, including ministries and Knesset committees. For example, in December 2009, WAC took MK Nitzan Horowitz on a tour of farms employing both Israelis and Thais. Upon becoming chairperson of the Foreign Workers Committee, Horowitz invited WAC to a committee meeting in November 2011 to discuss reports prepared by various government ministries on the reduction of migrant labor. WAC has had particular success in the Knesset Research and Information Center. The center's Dr. Gilad Nathan uses WAC reports and personal contacts with WAC in writing his own reports on the agricultural sector, and in November 2010, he personally requested WAC's presence at a Foreign Workers Committee debate, where Finance Ministry representatives spoke in favor of WAC's position while the committee's chairperson MK Yaacov Katz was against any reduction in migrant labor quotas. A report from the beginning of 2011 prepared by Nathan for Katz outlines manpower needs and the employment policy in the agricultural sector and favorably mentions WAC's "Women in Agriculture" project.

Kav Laoved, of course, makes no claims to unionism. According to Zohar, the founders did not consider establishing a union at the time Kav Laoved was established: many civil society organizations were being set up at that time, and there was a clear need to assist the new worker groups in the labor market, so they set up an organization to do this (interview). For Kav Laoved, too, most of its work is legal, including individual representation and legal action on precedent-setting cases such as the Givat Zeev case discussed below, which led to labor law being applied to Palestinians employed by Israeli businesses in the occupied territories. It also lobbies for changes to legislation ("closing loopholes" in existing legislation, as Zohar put it—loopholes that the organization can identify because of its position "close to the ground"; interview) and promotes legislation in cooperation with MKs. Much of its work is also aimed at raising awareness of these laws and assisting workers in using them. Thus, in addition to compiling reports, publishing newsletters, and carrying out its own research, it holds workshops to raise awareness, sometimes in collaboration with various Palestinian unions (in

Qalqilia, Tulkarem, Jenin, and Jericho; Kav Laoved 2012, 7), and supplies ledgers to workers so they can record their work hours in an orderly fashion (these ledgers have been accepted as valid by the labor courts when the employer has been unable to supply an orderly account of hours worked; Kav Laoved 2012, 38–40). It also acts to name and shame employers and issues information leaflets in various languages on a wide range of topics, including general workers' rights, sexual harassment at the workplace, work-related accidents, vacation, and sick leave.

PLURALISM AND THE CHANGING NATURE OF POLITICS

Individualization, Juridification, and Instability

The activities of organizations like the Workers Advice Center (WAC) and Kav Laoved must be understood in the context of a changing approach to labor regulation, the move toward what Mundlak (2007) calls a pluralist system. Nongovernmental organizations (NGOs) active in the field of labor and workers' rights are not officially recognized by the state (beyond being registered as NGOs) and have no status within any formal established frameworks for negotiation, though some NGOs have been granted (temporary) status as social partners in specific cases. Though being unrecognized grants them autonomy, it also means they are subject to unstable alliances and changing configurations of interests specific to a particular time. Indeed, NGOs may derive power by taking an uncompromising stand exactly where unions need to compromise (White 2004), because unions rely on membership and seek long-term cooperation with other social partners (Mundlak 2009), while the NGO is compelled to demonstrate notable (and perhaps media-friendly) success.

According to the Employment (Equal Opportunities) Law of 1988 (the same law that allows the labor minister to include public representatives in the traditional tripartite representation structure), "a lawsuit may be filed by the discriminated worker, a trade union, or an organization that represents rights pertinent to the person who claims to have been discriminated against" (Mundlak 2007, 134); the NGO does not need to earn any representative status in the way a union must. This explains why legal strategies are particularly attractive for such NGOs and contributes to the increasing juridification of labor relations (see IDI 2004; Tager 2006).

Mundlak (2007, 138) links these trends to changes in the legislative process as it moves away from corporatist bargaining: "The pluralist regulatory phase is characterized by interest groups' proposals that are endorsed by groups of legislators that are formed ad hoc around the issue at stake," groups that can cut across the typical left–right political spectrum. Statutory reforms can be "characterized as a majoritarian achievement in the legislative process rather than a reflection of consensus." Similarly, court decisions that advance the rights of specific groups are not intended to uphold the labor market status quo, to maintain the corporatist bargaining structure and labor's active role in shaping policy, "but are instead aimed at changing the behavior of the labor market's participants" (Mundlak 2007, 138). The social partners increasingly prefer legislation to promote their positions: "The locus of effective power [has] shifted from bargaining power to political power by means of lobbying and litigation" (Mundlak 2007, 114). This is what Bendor (1998, 277) calls the "legalization of government" or the "legalization of politics"—the growing tendency in Israel to see politics as law: not a question of "what is just" or "what is desirable," but "what is legal," or even, "what will pass judicial inspection."

Furthermore, unlike unions, Kav Laoved and WAC in a large proportion of its activities are not members' organizations; this raises issues of democracy, representation, and accountability. In a brief overview of NGO accountability, Keohane (2002) notes two kinds of accountability: internal, to their members; and external, to their "clients," the people whose lives they affect. He also notes that their members (activists, volunteers, paid staff; also contributors and supporters) are often the least affected by the organization's activities. Indeed, the people they claim to represent are often the least able to directly affect the policies and activities of the organizations. Mundlak (2007, 134–135) notes that NGOs are rarely grassroots organizations and there is a gap between the organization and its "constituency." Workers are "clients" who receive individual assistance and have no control over the organization's agenda; the organization is not directly reliant on them, though of course it may be influenced by them in the natural course of human interaction. The funders, even if passively, have significant influence since staff shape projects to suit funding opportunities and the broad targets of charitable foundations, which are often foreign and have little stake in the results of the projects their contributions are funding. According to Kav Laoved's website, it receives funding from various charitable organizations such as Christian Aid, and unions such as UNISON (the UK public service union), as well as Tel Aviv-Jaffa Municipality and the Economics Ministry. In WAC's case too, very little funding comes from membership in the union. Its main support is from various foundations and donors that contribute to specific projects, such as the "Youth for Social Change" program and the women's empowerment workshops. The organizations also need to show effectiveness in the field for which they have received funding (Mundlak 2007, 134). Keohane (2002) suggests that the public can hold NGOs to account since they depend on credibility and good publicity and are unable to sustain ongoing criticism; however, the public can be a conservative influence if the NGO's aims are wide of some consensus.

If the Histadrut has found itself ejected from the political sphere, dependent now on personal relations and political contingency, the new organizations presented here have an even more contingent and unstable link to political decision-making forums. Both WAC and Kav Laoved must develop a reputation for expertise and ensure their usefulness to state or governmental bodies in order to get invited to Knesset committee meetings or to submit reports and position papers. Their role as experts is very different from a union representative's role as spokesperson for a group of workers with interests and demands: experts have insider knowledge about populations that state institutions are interested in approaching in one way or another, and they have positions on what must be done to alleviate problems; indeed, they frame and interpret those problems. This is very different from the formation of a broad consensus around disparate workers' demands channeled through organizational frameworks that bring them together on common ground—which is what a union does at its best.

Being experts also means addressing external bodies (such as UN or EU bodies, as Kav Laoved does) whose interests are not directly affected by labor–capital relations in Israel. These bodies are a potential source of power, able to pressure the Israeli government into making legislative or policy changes (such as the Organisation for Economic Cooperation and Development's requirement that Israeli Arab women's participation in the workforce be increased), but their mandate is human rights, not the equitable distribution of resources or democratic participation and voice that were at the heart of the labor movement.

The Decline of the Mass Party

These issues are linked to much broader changes in Israeli politics and society. The severing of the party–union link and the rise of NGOs using (predominantly) legal strategies is connected to the decline of the political party, or at least its radical transformation. As Gutmann (1998) notes, the classic party was a members' organization with some kind of internal democracy, a clear ideological orientation, and almost exclusive status as the representative of its members' material and ideological interests. This model, he suggests, has been undermined internally and externally: internally, members are less willing to contribute time and money to the party, which may indicate dissatisfaction with the party or the entire party system; externally, parties are losing their significance because they direct their efforts toward the political establishment and try to control political institutions (especially parliament), yet in pluralist modern societies, the main policy decisions are no longer in the hands of this establishment. Ram (2008, 121–123) places this in the context of globalization, noting that politics remains national while economics has become transnational, leading to a disconnection between economics and politics, or the depoliticization of economics: "It is not globalization as such that generates social disruption but rather the social complexion of it, namely, it being ruled 'from above' by the megacorporations and their neoliberal political counterparts, whereas the checks and balances situated 'from below'—by trade unions and social-democratic parties—are being severely hampered" (Ram 2008, 124).

Gidron, Bar, and Katz (2004, 155) explicitly link the rise of NGOs in Israel to public dissatisfaction with the party system:

> Many of these changes [the growth of civil society organizations and their professionalism] stem from the aftermath of the Yom Kippur War [1973] when large numbers of Israeli citizens became disillusioned with the political system; these feelings intensified over time until the 1990s when many Israelis felt a sense of powerlessness in terms of their ability to influence government policy.... This distrust may explain the significant levels of citizen involvement in non-governmental organizations and movements as a means to influence policy.

Arian (1998) notes that voters no longer depend on parties for welfare or services that are now all administered by the state and have withdrawn from involvement; voters have become (not necessarily active) consumers looking to what party leaders promise to do, and not considering party history or worldview. The voter as consumer undermines the public sphere and corrodes the formation of collective public interest and the ethos of public service (Beetham 2004, 85). Thus the party becomes a mediator between voters and organized interests instead of being an organizer and presenter of those interests.[1] Arian (1998) also notes a public opinion survey from 1990 that reveals low esteem for parties, below that granted many other political and public institutions.

D. Koren (1998) asserts that achievements in the Knesset are increasingly the result of deals, not the promotion of an agenda; they are attempts at getting a bigger slice of the pie for their voters, nothing more. Private members' bills are a means of gaining media time for individual members of the Knesset. Parties no longer have any power to impose unity or discipline—members regularly vote against their own party platform. Thus perhaps the most significant change is that parties no longer shape and constitute a common position among their members and no longer offer a comprehensive worldview positioned against the worldviews of competing parties.

Thus the "end of ideology" announced over fifty years ago (Bell 1960) in fact heralded the end of the party as a members' organization. Indeed, in the Israeli labor context, Lissak (1998) traces this process to the 1950s, when the instrumental aspects of Mapai's activities grew more prominent while the cultural-ideological aspects grew weaker, leading to the blurring of the labor movement's identity. This, he says, was part of Ben-Gurion's statism that tried to erase class, ethnic, and religious differences. This led to what Ram (2008, 150–152) later called the "Americanization" of politics: a move from deep class and doctrinal divisions expressed through party and parliamentary democracy to U.S.-style diffused ideological differences and oscillation around the center of the political spectrum; from class-based divisions to community/identity-based divisions ("communalization"); and from an orientation on ideology (a comprehensive worldview) to an orientation on "sporadic choices" of issues ("commercialization"). The media has also changed and plays a pivotal role in sustaining the new politics: party media has almost entirely disappeared and in its place is heterogeneous mass media controlled by a small number of wealthy families mediating between voters and the "professionally packed messages" (Ram 2008, 152) of politicians seeking votes. Ratings demand the "empty" clashes between personalities, not discussion over genuinely differing positions (Lissak 1998).

The disillusionment with parties, the weakening of the unions, and the feeling of powerlessness have led to the rise of "identity politics" as the "victims of this process . . . rearray struggles for equality as struggles for identity or . . . prefer the politics of recognition over the politics of (re-)distribution" (Ram 2008, 124). These circumstances further undermine the legitimacy of the workers' struggle as an inclusive movement speaking in the name of (acting for) a broad public, a legitimacy already weakened by the influx of women and ethnic minorities into the workforce that has shaken up the homogeneous identity of the traditional working class (Piven 1991). NGOs might target Sudanese refugees, Palestinians from the occupied territories, or Thai agricultural laborers, for example, whose immediate interests are often manifestly in conflict with those of other specific groups. This is why WAC, positioning itself firmly against the import of migrant laborers, emphasized that it believed migrants were no less victims of the global capitalist system than the Israeli Arabs whom they were undercutting and developed links with a Thai union as part of its efforts to avoid appearing anti-Thai in its activities in agriculture. As human rights and workers' advocacy groups grow in importance, "class-based protection from dismissals, rooted in collective agreements, [are] gradually replaced by identity-based protections to discriminated groups and individuals" (Mundlak 2009, 768).

Moreover, the declining importance of political parties is part of a move away from political (democratic) institutions in general and a reliance on expert institutions, including the courts, which Barzilai (1998, 19) links to the "growing impact of liberal values on the political culture, combined with the lack of a written constitution in a highly divided, polarized, and fragmented setting." He notes that "while social rifts have become more severe, political polarization more prominent, and political corruption more frequent, the [High Court of Justice] has continued to be perceived as one of the most reliable institutions in the country, more reliable than the parties, the parliament, or the government" (Barzilai 1998, 19).[2]

Severing the Political Community from the Labor Force

I suggest that these connected processes—the rise of organizations such as WAC and Kav Laoved, the disintegration of the party–union link, and the decline of the mass party—reflect the breakdown of a core premise of the corporatist regime. This premise was the idea that being a worker was congruent with being a citizen: the union could count on the labor party to fight in its corner in the political sphere because the union's members were also members of the political community. In fact, the corporatist compromise could only work if the laborer was a citizen—labor agreed to play the capitalist game in return for political representation. The severing of the union's link to a labor party and the rise of nonmember organizations in the field of workers' rights reflect the fact that the political community is no longer congruent with the worker community—the labor market. It was not by chance that WAC was established to give political voice to Israeli Arabs who were included economically—participated in the workforce—but excluded politically. Similarly, Kav Laoved aimed to assist a population (firstly Palestinians, then also migrant laborers) that was increasingly in demand as labor but adamantly rejected as members of the political community.

This situation can be conceived as two trends that to a certain extent contradict each other. On the one hand, the decline of the mass labor party and its links with the union reflects the fact that national politics are no longer congruous with the labor market. This is in keeping with Ram's assertion that the institutions of local politics (unions, labor parties) are fighting an unequal struggle against powerful transnational or international organizations and firms (2008,

124); however, my focus here is on the blurring of the national labor market borders, which are spreading outward geographically and being penetrated inward by migrant labor and refugees seeking work. On the other hand, national politics is becoming ever more insular, and its conceptual borders are hardening. Labor—workers—is being embraced into the economy but rejected from the political community, as an increasing portion of this labor is not considered eligible to be part of the Israeli (Jewish) society. A labor party struggling in the national arena could in theory lobby for better conditions for all workers present in the country, regardless of nationality, but, first, it cannot represent them as members and voters, and second, the continuing insularity of Israeli nationalism makes interest representation of non-Jewish workers through parliamentary channels almost impossible. Moreover, the Labor Party has always been part of that nationalism, as has the Histadrut.

The Palestinians, whether inside Israel's borders or in the occupied territories, have long been subject to the contradictory demands of the two trends of economic incorporation and political exclusion. Before 1948, as reviewed in the introduction, the main thrust of Zionist efforts was to maintain an insular labor market whose borders coincided with the Jewish community. After 1948, the Palestinians who remained within the new state's borders were granted increasing access to the labor market, though the military administration left no doubt as to their political belonging. After 1967, the occupation once again expanded the reach of the labor market, together with Jewish nationalist geographic expansion, while the Oslo Accords opened the way for outsourcing and moving plants overseas. The most recent stage has been the influx of migrant labor, once again swelling the ranks of workers who have no political representation. These developments will be discussed in the following chapters.

BETWEEN NATIONAL COMMUNITY AND CLASS SOLIDARITY

This chapter overviews the relationship between Israel, its Palestinian Arab citizens, and noncitizen Palestinians in the field of labor to show how the labor market—the workforce—was increasingly expanded. The material covered here will also emphasize the Histadrut's role as a national institution, unwilling (at least until very recently) to act on behalf of noncitizens and unwilling to do much for non-Jewish citizens. The chapter charts the increasing influx of non-Jewish workers into the Israeli political economy, from Palestinian citizens after 1948, through the occupation of additional territory in 1967 and the Oslo Accords, as well as the expansion of the labor market's borders. This material supports the assertion, presented in the following chapter, that the labor market is increasingly porous while the political community remains insular, embracing Jews alone, and that NGOs are currently the most successful way of ensuring at least a minimal level of workers' rights.

Developing the Borders of the Political and Economic Community

Broadly speaking, the *yishuv* leadership tried to create a separate Jewish political-economic community in Mandatory Palestine. Colonizing a region of cheap labor raised employment problems for the newcomers who were unwilling to work for such low wages; this led to the call for Hebrew labor and the (imperfect) separation of the Jewish labor force from the local population including separate unions (Bernstein 2000; Lockman 1996; Shafir 1989).

Under the Mandate, Arab waged workers were employed mainly in public works and services such as the railway and ports. As the region developed, the Arabs underwent a rapid process of proletarianization, and by the outbreak of World War II nearly half the Arab labor force was waged, which also meant an increasing Arab interest in unionization. The Jewish organizations involved in assisting Zionist immigration and developing the Jewish *yishuv* perceived the development of a separate Jewish economy to be the only way to enable high wages for Jewish immigrants and thus ensure they stayed in Palestine. This policy was at the heart of the Histadrut attitude to organizing Arabs: even in mixed Jewish-Arab workplaces such as the railways, the Haifa oil refinery, and the Nesher quarry and cement factory there were fears that Arab organizing would undermine Jewish Zionist objectives.

The "Arab issue" was greatly discussed within the Histadrut, but the goal remained to maximize Jewish labor in mixed workplaces—all the Jewish political parties except the Communist Party prioritized Zionism above socialism. Nonetheless, as long as Arabs remained unorganized, the threat of Arab workers undercutting Jewish wages remained. This led to various attempts at cooperation (see Bernstein 1996; Grinberg 2003; Lockman 1996); indeed, the dominant Zionist position was that some issues were common to both Jews and Arabs (such as basic employment terms) while other issues such as culture and national aspirations were unique and must remain autonomous. This approach led to the logic of separate unions. Struggles were sometimes held in cooperation, but Arabs were not permitted to join Jewish unions, which enabled the Histadrut to continue its immigration and settlement activities in cooperation with other Zionist bodies.

Thus, for example, the Histadrut offered cheaper credit to farmers who employed only Jews and financial assistance to Jews willing to work in rural areas. In addition, those leasing land from the Jewish National Fund (JNF) were obliged to use only Jewish labor. The Histadrut even acted to break the boycott of Jewish workers declared by the Farmers' Association and the agricultural committees of moshavim to protest high Jewish wages, which it was able to do since by 1939 it controlled all the labor exchanges (Wolkinson 1999, 77).

In the years following the establishment of the Histadrut, a small number of Arabs asked to join but were rejected.[1] Instead, the Palestine Labor League (PLL) was established in 1932 under Histadrut auspices to prevent any other unionizing initiative that might have organized Arabs to the detriment of Zionist goals. It was also hoped the PLL would weaken Palestinian nationalism, though the conservative Jewish Agency feared the Histadrut was instilling socialist ideas in the Arab masses. Moreover, the PLL was a source of intelligence for Jewish organizations about what was going on in Arab villages.

Most significantly for the Arab population, the PLL gave Arab workers access to some of the services of the Histadrut's HMO (Clalit). British-supplied welfare services were limited and were mostly distributed to the two populations via their own organizations. The Histadrut was involved in providing these services and also managed services funded by Zionist organizations; thus it played a central role in the development of welfare and developed an extensive but exclusive system of mutual aid whose overriding objective was encouraging Jewish settlement (pioneering). Funds were allocated according to contribution to national cause, making welfare a mechanism for political recruitment and support. It was also a form of subsidy to expensive Jewish labor. This led to the development of an extensive Histadrut bureaucracy with the power to mobilize resources and ensured the dependence of immigrants on Zionist institutions (Rosenhek 2002b).

Israel's Arab Citizens after 1948: Structures of Separation and Inclusion

The Histadrut's role as a national institution promoting Zionist objectives above class or labor considerations continued after the establishment of the state. During and immediately after the 1948 war, hundreds of thousands of Palestinian Arabs fled or were pushed out of Israeli-controlled territory, and tens of thousands more became internal refugees (Morris 1987). The Palestinian Arab population lost much of its land through expropriation (which accelerated the proletarianization of the remaining Palestinians), the Jewish Agency and JNF continued to prevent Arab labor on their lands, and rapid industrialization efforts initiated by the state mostly ignored Palestinian towns (Haidar 2008; Lewin-Epstein and Semyonov 1993, 40–61).

The Palestinians who remained within the new state's borders were granted citizenship but were governed through a military administration and were subject to a system of permits for travel and work. The Histadrut was used as a conduit for granting favors, thus ensuring Arab votes for the ruling labor political bloc. The loyalty of the Arab population was assured through government concessions and subsidies and through the employment of Arab professionals in the public sector.

Full employment and labor shortages in the early 1960s led to the relaxation of the military administration's permit system and an increase in the number of Israeli Arabs in construction, agriculture, and services (Shalev 1989, 108–109). Most work was in Jewish towns, which for Arabs meant long journeys to and from Arab towns. Not all of this commuting was formally permitted by the administration, but as the need for labor grew, it turned an increasingly blind eye to such breaches. The dependence on the establishment led to the development of the *ra'is* system, whereby an Israeli Arab with the right contacts recruited (Arab) workers, transported them to the (Jewish) workplace, and took a cut from their wages. Even after the military administration was dismantled completely, in 1966, the *ra'is* system continued to flourish, partly because it offered a safe path to employment for the small but increasing number of Israeli Arab women seeking waged work (Haidar 2008).

The Histadrut continued to see the PLL as the vehicle for Israeli Arab organizing but also set up an Arab Labor Department within the Histadrut to handle specifically Arab issues. In 1952 the Histadrut Central Committee urged affiliated unions to accept Arab workers, though the Histadrut itself did not: Arabs were not admitted to the regional labor councils or Histadrut conventions where policies were formed, became Histadrut members only in 1959 (Wolkinson 1999, 83–85), and became full members with voting rights only in 1965 (Shalev 1989, 109).

The Arab Department was charged with assisting those whose primary language was Arabic, and it sought to encourage full integration into the Histadrut through setting up cultural centers, libraries, and sports clubs, and even cooperatives for water, transportation, and small industry; however, it was grossly underfunded and had little success, partly because Israeli Arabs were now able to join the Histadrut and receive full representation, and they benefited from all collective agreements and extension orders relevant to the economic branch in which they worked.

In 1980, the Arab Department was replaced by the Department of Integration, which worked toward similar goals. In 1985, the department still represented some twenty-four thousand Israeli Arabs; the rest had been integrated in local labor councils and worker committees (Wolkinson 1999, 85–86). The Histadrut's own investigations noted that integration was not particularly successful and that labor council secretaries often failed to visit Israeli Arab towns or address concerns submitted by Arabs. The councils noted the need to maintain Arab labor at the same wage as Jewish labor so that employers would have no incentive to prefer Israeli Arabs over Jews. But no efforts were made to employ Arabs in plants where none were employed. Furthermore, union officers attached to the labor councils addressed grievances of those living in their area of jurisdiction, but Arab workers rarely lived where they worked (Shalev 1989).

As Shalev (1989, 110) notes, the state needed Arab labor in the so-called business (private) sector in particular. This sector was in dire need of subsidies that the new state did not have the resources to supply; it was able to shore up Hebrew-only labor in the public and Histadrut sectors alone. Moreover, if the state had insisted on Hebrew-only labor throughout the economy (continued separation of the Jewish economy as much as possible from the Arab), it would have had to find another way of providing employment to its Arab citizens. Public works would have been too expensive, while encouraging Jewish investment in the Arab sector, it was feared, may have led to job losses in the Jewish sector. However, an autonomous Arab economy was not considered an option because there were fears that this would lead to calls for political autonomy as well. Thus the Histadrut was a means of limited integration and partial exclusion: by preventing full Arab membership in the Histadrut until 1965 and preventing Israeli Arabs from becoming Labor Party members until 1976, the state technically prevented Israeli Arabs from holding any senior Histadrut positions and suppressed Arab activism within the organization. Moreover, the Histadrut remained the biggest employer after the state, but many Histadrut enterprises were closed to Arabs (Wolkinson 1999).

In short, the period from Israel's establishment up to the early 1980s saw incremental incorporation of Arab citizens as laborers, but limited access to political institutions, including the Histadrut and Labor Party. The Histadrut remained an extremely dominant national organization involved in efforts to consolidate Jewish settlement and strengthen the new state. It was also a useful tool for ensuring Arab loyalty via the political system, but without granting them any significant political voice. The separation of the Arab population from the Jewish population can be seen in the Histadrut's Arab Labor Department and its tardy acceptance of Arabs as members; the development of the Arab sector and the defense of Arab wages was justified in terms of the needs of the Jewish state. At the same time, we see the use of Arab labor to regulate the strength of Jewish labor, and the inclusion of Arab labor in labor-intensive sectors as well as the use of nonstandard employment frameworks such as the *ra'is* system even in the 1950s and 1960s.

1967 and the Palestinians: Economic Incorporation, Political Exclusion

The war of 1967 greatly affected the position of Arabs in the workforce and the economy as a whole by opening a huge pool of cheap labor and a captive market (Davidi 2012). It also provided a path out of the recession of 1966 without the danger of full employment—a path from which the Histadrut also benefited: for the Histadrut as an employer, it provided a flood of low-waged workers; for the Histadrut as a producer, it led to an increase in military spending; and for the Histadrut as a union, it increased its power over workers in the private sector, who now faced the threat of cheap labor (Grinberg 1996, 67). As Shalev (1989, 118) puts it, the Histadrut could "hardly have relished the prospect of a return to the inflation, wildcat strikes, and difficult-to-manage conflicts among rival groups of workers which had characterized the years of full employment earlier in the decade."

The Israeli government's immediate concern was security (quiet). The security establishment and all political leaders believed this could be obtained by limiting unemployment and maintaining or even raising living standards in the newly occupied territories (Shalev 1989).[2] Direct economic development of the territories would have been a drain on Israeli resources, and there were also fears that the territories would become an economic competitor. Providing employment in Israel for the Palestinians was seen to be the best option (see also Farsakh 2005, 194), though Israel also initiated some public works (particularly in construction and forestry), thus providing employment for some twenty thousand people (Semyonov and Lewin-Epstein 1987, 11).

Security, then, was the reason for integrating Palestinians into the labor force, but maintaining the integrity of the Jewish political community was the driving motive behind the institutions and legislation set up to regulate this integration. According to the Employment Arrangement Act of 1969, for example, Palestinians had to obtain a permit and be employed through the state's Regional Employment Bureaus, and only forty thousand were allowed to enter each day. Moreover, Palestinians were forbidden to be in Israel between midnight and 6:00 a.m. However, the law was ineffectual and not strictly enforced. By 1985, some one hundred thousand Palestinians were entering Israel each day, and many were spending the entire week in Israel, returning home only on the weekends (Portugali 1993, 5). There is no shortage of anecdotal evidence of poor living conditions, of landlords taking advantage of Palestinians' precarious legal status to raise rents, and of Palestinian workers sleeping in building sites and basements (see Ben Efrat 2008; Portugali 1993, 7–10). Still, for Israeli society the immediate social consequences of using Palestinian labor were limited compared with the use of migrant labor: "Israel manages to reap the benefits of employing foreign labor without experiencing the full social burden of incorporating them residentially and institutionally into the society" (Semyonov and Lewin-Epstein 1987, 112).

While the physical movement of Palestinians into Israel proper (inside the Green Line) was controlled, the economy of the territories was welded to Israel. Soon after the 1967 war, the external borders of the territory now under Israeli control were closed, while the internal borders practically disappeared as economic transactions crossed the Green Line (Arnon 2007). Until 1993 and the Oslo peace process, the public sector of the Palestinian economy (taxation, services, investment in infrastructure) was under Israeli control and managed according to Israel's needs (see Tamari 1992, who calls this the deliberate development of "dependency"). The Israeli shekel was the main currency, and Israel closed the local banking system (it reopened to a limited extent in the 1980s), while a few Israeli banks began limited operations in the territories. Financial activities were also limited and carried out mostly via the Jordanian banking system. Huge differences in development and gross domestic product between Israel and the Palestinian territories remained, and in fact continue to this day (Arnon 2007, 576).

Israel's official policy was to ensure Palestinians working inside Israel earned the same wages as Israelis, to prevent Israelis from losing jobs to Palestinians. To regulate this, wages were paid to the Department of Payments, set up in 1970, which then transferred them to the Palestinian workers (Zohar and Hever 2010). A network of employment bureaus was set up in the territories, through which Israeli employers were to seek labor only if none could be found locally (i.e., if no Israelis were available). The bureau then sought a suitably qualified Palestinian and issued a permit (valid for a specific employer only). However, enforcement of the system was limited: in 1987, an estimated one third of Palestinians working in Israel were "illegal" (Semyonov and Lewin-Epstein 1987, 14; another study suggests that between 1970 and 1987, some 40–60 percent were not registered; Farsakh 2005, 119–120). Again the *ra'is* system was widely used, and those responsible for transport developed a dynamic network able to get Palestinian workers to various and constantly changing workplaces while bypassing roadblocks and checkpoints (Portugali 1993, 75–91). By 1982, Palestinians from the territories were to be found in 80 percent of Israel's occupational categories and comprised some 7 percent of Israel's workforce (Semyonov and Lewin-Epstein 1987, 1).

Palestinians working legally in Israel were covered by collective agreements relevant to their place of work, though in practice little was done to ensure their wages were correct, and with most working by the day, they were not eligible for industry-related extras or company-specific increments, or bonuses, overtime payments, and seniority increments. Those without a permit suffered from even lower wages and poorer employment terms, but on the other hand tax and other deductions were not made from their wages, and they could avoid the bureaucratic process. Thus, in practice, there were significant wage differences between Palestinians, whether legal or illegal, and the Israelis working by their side (Semyonov and Lewin-Epstein 1987, 86–88).

The Histadrut avoided addressing specifically Palestinian labor grievances, claiming that it (the Histadrut) was a quasi-state organization whose members were Israeli citizens. However, it did collect agency fees of 0.7 percent of wages;

it dealt with employment issues on an individual level but did not represent Palestinians vis-à-vis the Finance Ministry or the Department of Payments, and they were not permitted to be members (Zohar and Hever 2010, 12–13). Mostly, the need to keep Palestinians quiet was the main consideration behind employment policies regarding the territories; the employment services became an arm of the occupation (Rosenhek 2003, 240) as did the Histadrut, too. Palestinian trade unions, acting in particular via the Palestinian General Federation of Trade Unions (PGFTU), continued to operate (ineffectually) in the territories but until the Oslo peace process could do nothing for Palestinians working in Israel (Sovich 2000).

In short, this period saw increasing incorporation of Palestinians in the Israeli economy according to both security concerns and the requirements of Israel's (Jewish) economy (or those of the institutions within it, such as the Histadrut—not necessarily those of Jewish workers). At the same time, an elaborate system of permits defended the borders of the Jewish community, with the Histadrut collaborating in this aim. Workers who chose (or were compelled to take) an illegal path to employment lacked even the basic protection granted by legislation and the Histadrut, but whether illegal or legal, Palestinians had no representation in the political sphere, of course.

Oslo: The "Peace Dividends"

The Oslo Accords ushered in a new era in economic relations, as laid out in the 1994 "Protocol on Economic Relations between the Government of Israel and the PLO [Palestine Liberation Organization] Representing the Palestinian People," generally known as the "Paris Protocols."[3] These protocols noted that the two sides (Israel and the Palestinians) view the economic dimension of the peace process as crucial and would work toward a mutually beneficial economic base to relations, laying the groundwork for strengthening the Palestinian economy and enabling Palestinians to make autonomous decisions in accordance with their own development plans and priorities. Labor movement was not to be hindered, but as Arnon (2007) notes, things took a different turn: after 1994, Israel unilaterally imposed increasing separation, increasing restrictions on movement of goods and labor, and increasing limitations on movement within the territories (due to security and political concerns). Moreover, the Paris Protocols put Israel and Palestine in a common customs envelope and maintained the use of the Israeli shekel as the Palestinian currency while imposing trade and manufacturing restrictions on the Palestinian side, thus protecting Israeli businesses from competition (Who Profits 2013).[4]

The West Bank and Gaza, then, remained economically dependent on Israel, and work in Israel remained crucial to Palestinians in the occupied territories. The Paris Protocols "actually participated in locking the [occupied territories] into a labor reserve economy by failing to guarantee the freedom of labor movement within the [territories] and towards Israeli areas" (Farsakh 2005, 159). As Farsakh (2005) shows, unemployment in the West Bank was directly related to access to Israeli markets for Palestinian workers, especially for the unskilled, since Israel's main demand was for unskilled workers. Before 1994, some 30 percent of the Palestinian labor force in the West Bank and 40 percent of that in the Gaza Strip worked in Israel; by 1996, these figures had dropped to 18 percent and 6 percent respectively. Remittances from work in Israel dropped from about 30 percent of Palestinian gross domestic product in the 1980s to about 20 percent in 1996 in the West Bank, and 50 percent to less than 10 percent in the Gaza Strip. Unemployment in the territories also rose, though it went down again after 1996 when restrictions were eased (Arnon 2007, 587; Farsakh 2005, 77–78).

Entry to Israel still required a permit, based on a system of quotas according to the stipulations of the Paris Protocols, with the number of quotas issued for each sector decided separately according to economic, security, and foreign policy considerations. A Kav Laoved report from 2012 notes that at the end of 2011, a total of thirty-three thousand permits were issued; however, with 16.6 percent unemployment in the West Bank that year, the number of Palestinians seeking work in Israel was far higher—some 125,000 (Kav Laoved 2012).

Palestinians are dependent on the employer for obtaining a permit, and also because they have few other options for earning a living. Violation of labor law is common, and enforcement, the responsibility of the Ministry of Industry, Trade and Labor (now the Economics Ministry), is insufficient and slow. Violations are hard to prove in court, and workers fear retaliation from their employer. Moreover, some violations are subject to a statute of limitations. Most cases end in compromise, leaving workers with less than they should have received and giving employers no incentive to act according to the law.

The Histadrut, for its part, continued the path it had taken before the Oslo Accords, from the time it was established, limiting Arab representation and membership and making few efforts to ensure equality. It remained a national (Jewish) institution, cooperating with the state to manipulate Arab participation in the labor market to benefit state objectives and Jewish labor, and rejecting class-based solidarity with Palestinian unions. In 1994, the Histadrut held talks with the PGFTU, but it was not clear what role the Palestinian unions would have.[5] The Palestinians expected the PGFTU would be permitted to operate in Israel, but the Histadrut was opposed. Avital Shapiro, then Histadrut coordinator of PGFTU relations, said "What country allows a trade union from another country to recruit inside its borders?" (during an interview with Sovich: 2000, 76). The Histadrut was to provide four Israeli Arab lawyers authorized to take on cases of Palestinians in Israeli courts. The lawyers had offices in the PGFTU's West Bank premises and the Ministry of Labor in Gaza, but the Histadrut paid them and controlled their activities. PGFTU lawyers and leaders could not enter Israel without permits, and these were usually obtained via the Histadrut. The result is that the Histadrut controlled representation of Palestinians in Israel, but entirely neglected the collective, organizing aspect of a union's activities, emphasizing only the legal, individual aspect.

In 2008, the Histadrut signed another agreement with the PGFTU that settled the issue of organizing fees collected by the Histadrut since 1993. At the same time, however, Palestinians were categorized as daily or temporary workers, further reducing the benefits they would otherwise have received as regular workers protected by Histadrut collective agreements (Zohar and Hever 2010, 13).

The Textile Industry: An Illustrative Case

The textile industry is a perfect synecdoche for the Israeli labor market and the changes brought about by Oslo. It was developed by the state in the 1950s to provide jobs for new Jewish immigrants and to enable the dispersal of the population to strengthen the state's hold on less-populated regions close to the new borders (Levi-Faur 1995). From the beginning, the textile industry was characterized by poor employment terms and insufficient law enforcement (Bar-On 2007), and the Histadrut was of little help. As the state's commitment to full (Jewish) employment waned, the textile industry became a source of employment for Israeli Arab women, an increasing number of whom, in the 1970s, were seeking employment to meet expectations of higher standards of living or to compensate for unemployed male family members (Ashqar 1997)—thus a pool of cheap, reliable, and replaceable workers developed.[6] In Jewish plants, the management remained Jewish even as the workforce became increasingly Israeli Arab, but in Israeli Arab towns, new Arab-owned plants also grew up, mainly subcontracting for the Jewish-owned firms (Drori 2000). Conditions in the plants were poor, and many employers took advantage of the lax law enforcement. Many women were employed via the *ra'is* system (Ashqar 1997).

By the 1990s, Arab women in textiles constituted 51 percent of the Arab industrial workforce. In the Galilee, 86 percent of all textile workers and 98 percent of production workers were Israeli Arab women. By 1995, textiles made up about 30 percent of all Arab industry (Drori 2000). This was by far the largest industry in the Arab sector and almost the only industry in the Druze sector (Ashqar

1997). Thus Arab Israelis were particularly affected by the transformation of the industry brought about by liberalization and the peace process of the 1990s.

Possibilities for changes to the textile industry were explored even before the Oslo Accords of 1992 made economic cooperation with neighboring countries feasible. For example, a study in 1987 by the Armand Hammer Fund for Cooperation in the Middle East investigated the advantages of cooperation between Israel and Egypt for the textile and clothing industries of both countries, suggesting that the division of labor would increase competitiveness and improve access to markets. As this was part of hopes for broader regional peace, the United States and the European Economic Community were expected to approve such cooperation, though it was noted that "cooperation" basically meant that Israeli firms would set up subsidiaries in Egypt to take advantage of cheap labor (Tovias and Wolpert 1987). In the 1990s, restrictions on textile imports were reduced, but the minimum wage rose, partly due to high salaries in the rapidly expanding high-tech sector, which affected the minimum wage because of the way Israel calculates this wage. This led major companies such as Delta, Polgat, Kitan, and Gibor Sabrina to move some of their operations to Turkey, Jordan, and China (Lavie 2006).[7]

A conference of Israeli, Egyptian, Jordanian, and Palestinian textile industrialists and merchants in Jerusalem in 1994, organized by the Textile and Fashion Association (part of the Manufacturers Association of Israel) and the Center for Jewish-Arab Economic Development, was entitled "Sewing towards Peace." The participants noted the higher wages of the West Bank and the Gaza Strip compared to Jordan and Egypt and the fact that the industry was less developed there though it was a leading sector in terms of numbers of employees (some ten thousand at the time) and number of factories (Gargir 1995). Nonetheless, the advantages of using Palestinians were clear—as one industry publication noted, subcontracting in the territories was a means of avoiding Israel's minimum wage law and the peripheral benefits Israeli workers were entitled to, while employers would save on the transportation costs and "headache" of bringing Palestinians into Israel (*Yalkut* 1994).

As factories moved abroad, subsidies were reduced, and protective tariffs dropped, conditions in plants located in Israel became even worse. The Histadrut's Textile Workers Trade Union did not concern itself with the poor conditions and (often illegal) contractor employment frameworks in textile plants in the Arab sector. In 1996, then Histadrut chief Amir Peretz noted that the process of textile outsourcing was "inevitable" and said his organization must concentrate on making the transition go smoothly (see *Challenge* 48, March–April 1998).

Between 1991 and 1996, the portion of Israel's labor force in textiles declined by about 11 percent. In the first half of 1998 alone, over 1,500 seamstresses were fired. Dismissals continued throughout the 1990s, and by the year 2000, some twenty-five plants had relocated from the Galilee to Jordan and Egypt, and many others had simply shut down. In 2012, when the iconic Kitan factory in Dimona finally closed after two years of repeated waves of dismissals (from 350 workers in 2008 to 40 in 2012), *Globes* (Azulay and Niv 2012) reported that about eleven thousand Israelis were employed in textiles compared with over one hundred thousand some twenty years before.

In the first years of the new millennium, West Bank textiles continued to be undercut, particularly by China, but Palestinian textile plants offered the advantage of faster turnaround, the ability to meet small orders, higher standards, and geographic proximity enabling oversight by the client company. According to Tariq Assous, head of the Palestinian Textile Union quoted in *Globes* (Y. Ben-Israel 2013), the industry in the West Bank today is operating at less than 40 percent capacity. At the beginning of 2012, the Peres Peace Center initiated "Partners for Peace, Partners for Business" with EU funds to increase business cooperation, and the textile industry was one of the project's main aims (Y. Ben-Israel 2013). The textile industry, then, epitomizes the increasing use of workers who are not accepted as full members of the political community (Arab Israelis) or noncitizens (Palestinians in the occupied territories),[8] and the increasing outsourcing abroad of Israeli industry or the transfer of entire plants overseas.

POROUS LABOR MARKET, INSULAR POLITICAL COMMUNITY

Expanding the Reach of Labor Legislation

I have suggested that since 1948 Israel has increasingly struggled with the conflicting demands of economic incorporation and political exclusion of its Palestinian citizens and, in a different way, of Palestinians in the territories it occupied in 1967. In 2007, this process took a significant new form when the High Court issued a landmark ruling in the so-called Givat Zeev case (HCJ 5666/03), submitted by Kav Laoved. In this case, the High Court determined that Israeli labor law is applicable to all settlements and the industry around them, overturning a ruling from the National Labor Court that saw no reason why Palestinians in the occupied territories should be subject to Israeli law. This important High Court ruling, which came after more than ten years of hearings, established the legal framework for improving employment conditions for Palestinians working for Israeli companies; indeed, following the ruling, some firms made moves to align themselves with labor regulations (Heruti-Sover 2013).[1]

This led to another important case, in 2011, when the Maaleh Adumim municipality agreed (after labor court mediation) to pay its Palestinian employees the same wages, with the same peripheral benefits, as its Israeli employees (Hasson 2011). A further development came in June 2013 when the Jerusalem Labor Court ruled in favor of ten Palestinians employed in the Mishor Adumim industrial zone. Though they held a permit issued by the Civil Administration, their employer claimed they had been recruited via the *ra'is* system and that they had agreed to work according to West Bank labor norms. This case had roots in 2006, when Kav Laoved had contacted the employer after workers had complained the firm had withheld wages, failed to pay minimum wage, failed to properly insure its employees, and failed to meet safety standards. Kav Laoved also submitted a complaint to police. However, nothing was done to enforce labor standards. In 2013 the court noted that the firm pays municipal tax to Maaleh Adumim, and is therefore an Israeli settlement and part of the Israeli economy, and ruled in favor of the workers (Bior 2013b).

While the High Court ruling of 2007 confirmed that Israeli law is applicable, it noted that law enforcement was minimal. According to a report in *TheMarker* (Heruti-Sover 2013), a huge number of firms in the industrial zone is characterized by poor working conditions, failure to meet safety standards, wages of less than minimum, a lack of proper wage slips, and no holidays or sick pay. Wages are often paid by check and exchanged for cash through a local dealer who takes a commission. If workers complain, they are easily fired. Moreover, a firm can submit a complaint against a worker, who is then liable to lose his permit to enter Israel to work. Indeed, this is what happened in the Tzarfati Garage case, taken on by the Workers Advice Center (WAC) in the summer of 2014 (see WAC 2014). Here, according to WAC, the chair of the workers' committee who had been very active in unionizing the workplace was banned on a security pretext from continuing his work despite some fifteen years of employment at the garage. Thus security was used not only to silence an individual but also to thwart an organizing drive.

The Economics Ministry, however, said it had no authority to act outside the Green Line (Heruti-Sover 2013). Thus an industry of lawyers has grown up around suits filed against firms in Mishor Adumim. A Kav Laoved (2012) report makes similar claims, noting that things have barely improved despite the ruling: enforcement of labor law remains minimal, there is no routine monitoring, and the two bodies charged with administrative enforcement—the Employment Staff Officer in the Civil Administration and the Economics Ministry—respond rarely and sluggishly to complaints.[2] Even when cases get to court, a settlement is usually reached that leaves the workers with less than they are entitled to and offers no incentive to employers to operate according to the law. The same report claims that some factories that had issued wage slips prior to the ruling stopped doing so in order to conceal working practices if a case were made against them (Kav Laoved 2012, 40). Employers can evade some of their responsibilities by using manpower agencies, though in 2010 the Jerusalem Labor Court ruled that in case of labor law violations, both the contractor and the employer bear responsibility (Kav Laoved 2012, 41).

Maintaining the Borders of the (Jewish) Political Community

Thus the borders of the labor market are increasingly porous. Palestinians and migrant laborers enter the market while labor legislation (and thus, in a very tangible way, the legitimate labor market) is extended outward to encompass Palestinians working for Israeli businesses outside the Green Line. At the same time, the national borders of the political community are guarded as diligently as ever. Arabs and migrant laborers are welcomed as labor but rejected as participants in the Israeli (dominant Jewish) political community.

WAC, for example, has encountered difficulties as an "Arab organization" with a radical, dangerous image, which has made work with potential employers difficult (Ben Efrat, interview). Its links to Daam add to this image: Daam, a Jewish-Arab party fielding an Arab candidate, is beyond the pale for many Jewish Israelis.[3] The perception of WAC as an Arab organization is also a major hurdle in its attempts to organize mixed (Arab and Jewish) workplaces and was raised by Hamenia (the employer) in its case against WAC in the haulage industry. In the Tzarfati Garage case noted above, too, ethnic tensions arose. Thus the sanctity of the political community's borders is invoked to prevent full (union) representation for those included in the labor force but outside the political community.

According to WAC members (Ben Efrat, Adiv, interviews), its Arab image was also behind attempts to close WAC by the registrar of nongovernmental organizations (NGOs). In 1998, the registrar refused to register WAC and for two years refused to explain the reasons for the rejection. Only in 2000, with assistance from the Association for Civil Rights in Israel, was WAC able to receive details of the rejection and counter them in court. In 1999, the registrar struck Hanitzotz Publishing from the list of NGOs but responded to WAC's challenge by settling out of court. In 2001, the registrar opened an investigation into WAC, claiming it was a cover for Daam, but after a long public campaign, the charges were dropped in 2006. WAC claims that the registrar who initiated these proceedings targeted mainly Arab NGOs, over seventy of which were struck from the list in 1999 (Adiv, interview). Ameer Makhul, who was head of Ittija (the Union of Arab Community-Based Organizations), said none of these NGOs had received warnings of the closure. He also said the registrar's office regularly "loses" reports from Arab NGOs, while Adallah attorney Jamil Dakwar noted that procedures for registering Arab NGOs can drag on for months (*Challenge* 61, May–June 2000).

The government's zigzagging policy on migrant laborers also illustrates Israel's ambivalence toward cheap but non-Jewish labor—an ambivalence that WAC has encountered in its efforts to place Israeli Arab women in agricultural positions. Arab workers, if employed legally as any other Israeli citizen, with wage slips and benefits, are significantly more expensive than Thais. Moreover, farmer associations are strong and have an effective lobby through the Peripheral Farmers Forum and the Israel Farmers Federation, with contacts in relevant bodies.[4] It insists that there are no Israelis willing to do the work, while WAC claims it has lists of hundreds of Israelis who want agricultural jobs. In 2007, the Labor Ministry's migrant labor officer Shalom Ben Moshe claimed migrant labor agencies are making it impossible to regulate the import of laborers and that attempts to work with the UN's International Organization for Migration to lower agency fees are torpedoed by agencies who fear to lose out on profit (see A. Cohen 2007). When a delegation from the Labor Ministry went to Thailand to discuss the issue, an agency delegation went too, to try to stop the initiative (Ben Simhon 2007). In 2010, farmers' organizations including the Israel Farmers Federation, the Growers' Union, and the Poultry Farmers' Association threatened to strike to protest plans to reduce migrant worker quotas.[5]

The government, committed in theory to increasing Israeli Arab participation in the labor force, charted a convoluted course through competing interests, promising to reduce the number of migrant laborer permits it issued even as it approved the increase of migrant laborer quotas. In 2005, then director-general of the Labor Ministry noted that placing Israelis in agriculture was too expensive. But the following year, the head of the Planning and Research Administration in the Labor Ministry said the demand for migrant labor was exaggerated by farmers seeking cheaper workers. The agricultural minister in the same period was in favor of importing migrant laborers, and in June 2006 a committee of ministry directors-general headed by the Prime Minister's Office (PMO) director decided to increase migrant labor quotas even as the government declared its commitment to decreasing these quotas. The deputy governor of the Bank of Israel went further, calling for a reduction of migrant labor to zero (see Finance Ministry 2007).

The result of this governmental indecision was a series of programs to reduce farmers' dependence on migrant labor and increase Israeli Arab participation in the agricultural workforce, all of which failed through lack of financial and institutional support. To take just one example, in 2012 the state comptroller investigated two agreements made in 2009 between the Agriculture Ministry and the farmer organizations, with Finance Ministry support. The agreements involved funds for special support for agricultural issues, including mechanization to reduce reliance on labor, especially migrant labor. However, the Agriculture Ministry defined the grants as "administrative," which enabled it to avoid certain stipulations including the ceiling on the sums bestowed. Furthermore, the grants were not made dependent on farmers' commitment to stop using foreign labor. The ministry claimed that if that had been a condition, farmers would not have taken the grant. Thus from 2009 to 2011, the state invested some NIS 100 million to reduce migrant labor, yet in those years the number of migrant laborers rose (Litman 2012).

A similar situation can be found in construction. In December 2001, with unemployment in Israel of over 10 percent, the government decided (Decision No. 642) to reduce migrant labor permits in construction from forty-five thousand to twenty-three thousand, but in January 2002 agreed to postpone the decision until February and then again until April. The president of the Israel Builders and Contractors Association (IBCA), Shmuel Ulpiner, proposed his own program to take on Israeli workers in construction, including a commitment to employ one Israeli for every one hundred migrant laborers (*Challenge* 73, May–June 2002). The same year, the Foreign Workers Committee increased permit quotas for 2002 to 30,000. By 2005, they were reduced again to 17,500, and the director of the Employment Services at the time, Esther Dominissini, initiated a program to train Israelis for the industry (see *Ynet* 2007; see also Ministry of Industry, Trade and Labor, Justice Ministry, and Finance Ministry 2004). However, the program, which involved the Labor Ministry, the IBCA, and the Employment Services, was rejected by the construction firms. By 2007, and again in 2011, more migrant laborers for construction were imported (see Boso 2011). The Bank of Israel has spoken out repeatedly against the use of migrant labor, holding that claims of a lack of labor are false and noting too that cheap labor has led to a technologically backward sector (Adiv 2011; see also Finance Ministry 2007), yet workers for construction are still imported in coordination with the IBCA, despite government commitments to reduce migrant labor in this sector to zero (Boso 2011).

The Doubtful Benefits of Begrudged Inclusion

Thus we see pressure to increase Israeli Arab rates of participation in the workforce yet continued import of migrant laborers competing with them directly in the sectors most likely to take on Arabs; and indeed, in general Israeli Arabs are underrepresented in labor market participation. According to a study from 2013 (Yashiv and Kasir 2013), Palestinian citizens of Israel, who make up some 20 percent of citizens and 18 percent of those of working age, comprise only 13.1 percent of the labor force. Arab women in particular have low participation rates of just 22 percent (though this is rising), while both men and women retire early. Nonparticipation is high relative to Jews: 37.4 percent for men and 57.9 percent for women among those aged twenty-five to sixty-four. Unemployment among Arab men has been consistently higher than that among Jewish men, though the difference has varied (see also Sa'di and Lewin-Epstein 2001). Among Arab women, it was lower than Jewish women (though participation rates were also far lower, as noted) until the 1990s, when unemployment rose dramatically, partly due to the decline of the textile industry. In general, Arab Israelis are overrepresented in low-skilled work and in education, health, and welfare (parts of the public sector that are not perceived to be "sensitive" from a national security point of view). They also earn less on average than their Jewish counterparts. Services in Arab towns are generally poorer than those in Jewish towns, including transport and childcare, which makes it especially difficult for women seeking work outside the home.

Furthermore, Arab Israeli poverty rates are significantly higher than Jewish rates. According to a Kav Laoved report (2013), in 2011, 53.5 percent of Arabs lived below the poverty line, making up almost 40 percent of those below the poverty line. This same report noted continued discrimination in work opportunities, pay, and conditions, as well as unequal labor law enforcement among Jews and Arabs. In 2008, of the forty towns with the highest unemployment rates, thirty-six were Arab towns. In sensitive sectors such as high-tech, banking, insurance, and finance, as well as state monopolies such as electricity and water, Arabs were significantly underrepresented. Using data from the mid-1980s and 1995, Wolkinson (1999) found little overt discrimination against Israeli Arabs in these sectors, but various mechanisms reduced Arab employment: security concerns or the claim that army service is required in some branches, and employers' use of employment bureaus in Jewish areas. Furthermore, there are insufficient employment bureaus in Arab towns, and Arabs are more likely to seek work through friends or family (Haidar 2008).

The Kav Laoved report notes how various laws are ignored, such as the Equal Opportunities Law of 1988 that states that employers shall not ask for the military profile of applicants or employees, and Arabs are regularly excluded on the grounds that they have not served in the army. A connected issue is the Pension Insurance Agreement (2007) negotiated by the Histadrut that obliges employers to pay into a pension fund for employees without such a fund, but excludes males under twenty-one and women under twenty, thus denying Israeli Arabs pension contributions for two or three years, since they enter the labor force earlier (Kav Laoved 2013, 11–12).

Efforts have been made to increase the inclusion of Israeli Arabs in the sphere of labor, including initiatives by former president Shimon Peres such as Maan-Tech, the opening of additional employment centers in Arab towns, budget allocation for public transport and industrial zones in the Arab sector, and assistance from foundations such as the Abraham Fund Initiatives. However, these efforts are couched in neoliberal terms of individual opportunity and responsibility:

individually, Israeli Arabs are encouraged to participate in Israel's growth, while social and political reasons for low rates of participation are glossed over. In an op-ed piece in *TheMarker*, Economics Minister Naftali Bennett noted that the beauty of Israel was its variety, especially in the labor market (Bennett 2013). Speaking in terms of benefits to the individual and the economy, the minister stressed the importance of equal opportunities as the basis for success for all in this multicultural and heterogenic country, without mentioning decades of neglect and underinvestment or the lack of basic services and infrastructure. Similar language is used in the "Growth for Partnership" conference and in similar conferences held since 2007.

Efforts to integrate Arab citizens in the workforce can be divided into two main areas: high-tech on the one hand and low-paid, insecure work in nonstandard employment frameworks on the other. Both these areas grew rapidly as a result of the neoliberal changes to Israel's economy. Thus Peres's initiatives to integrate Israeli Arabs into the high-tech sector are in partnership with high-tech companies who, according to the former president himself, have more power than the government to affect the labor market. There are no laws discriminating against the Arabs, Peres claimed, only "economic gaps" that can be solved through the high-tech industry, a kind of magic panacea that will lift the Israeli Arabs into the twenty-first century (Ministry of Foreign Affairs 2011). These initiatives are relevant to only a small percentage of the Arab population in Israel.

Many, though encouraged to work by the government, participate in the labor force through manpower companies, the *ra'is* system, and state projects like the so-called Wisconsin program (a welfare-to-work program, since discontinued), which leaves them outside collective agreements and with only the minimum protection from labor law. In agriculture, as we have seen, Israeli Arab women—ostensibly the target of countless government initiatives to increase labor force participation—continue to struggle against competition from migrant labor, lacking daycare services and public transport, subcontracted through the *ra'is* system, and earning the minimum wage (or often much less, since many are not legally employed from the state's point of view). A similar picture of low wages and minimal employment terms emerges from the construction industry and the light industries of the industrial zones in the West Bank.

Bank of Israel governor Karnit Flug talks in a similar language. In her first speech as governor, she said, "The Arab population in Israel contains immense untapped potential from the standpoint of the Israeli economy's growth capability. Beyond the economic potential, the issue also contains highly significant social potential." She noted that the integration of Palestinian citizens into the economy, particularly the labor market, "is a very important, even essential, component of the Israeli economy's ability to continue to grow, and to support a higher standard of living for all Israelis" (Elis 2013). Flug spoke at the Prime Minister's Conference on Minorities, at which the finance minister also spoke, pledging to invest some NIS 4 billion over the next two years to advance the "Arab sector" (*NRG* 2013). However, in the same speech, the finance minister also noted that in Israel there would never be separation between religion and state and reiterated that Israel was defined—both by law and according to the opinion of the "majority of its citizens"—as Jewish and democratic. Indeed, the Supreme Court has given this approach its seal of approval: in a case filed by an organization known as "I am Israeli" (Ani Israeli) the court rejected the claim that there was such a thing as an "Israeli" as opposed to Jewish or Arab citizens of the State of Israel; it thereby separated Arab citizens from Jewish citizens once again (Hovel 2013).[6] Furthermore, the ideology of Hebrew labor has not disappeared: companies in Israel's "Yellow Pages" hint at their preference for Jews; in June 2010 notices posted around Bnei Brak (a town in the greater Tel Aviv area) warned residents against hiring Arabs; and opposition to migrant labor is often couched in Jewish-nationalist terms. Indeed, an Agricultural Ministry program to encourage Israelis to work in agriculture was dubbed "Hebrew labor" (Agricultural Ministry 2008). In February 2013, *Globes* (Azulay 2013a) ran an article on an agency that "imports" Jewish workers, the Fund for Promoting Israeli Labor.[7] According to the article, this agency, a commercial venture, has a database of workers who have "already proved their Judaism." It has already brought workers to Israel, some of whom have begun the process of applying for citizenship, and the owners have held meetings with the Jewish Agency and government representatives to win the support of these institutions for their initiative.

East Jerusalem Palestinians: The Epitome of Politically Excluded Labor

The Palestinians of East Jerusalem live this contradiction every day: Israel's annexation of East Jerusalem shortly after the 1967 war left them caught squarely between physical inclusion and employment in the secondary labor market and a political exclusion far more ostentatious than that endured by Israel's Arab citizens, as well as efforts to remove them from the bounds of the city.

In 1980, with the Basic Law: Jerusalem, Israel declared the "complete and united" city to be its capital. Palestinians in East Jerusalem were granted residency but not full citizenship, and thus are not eligible to vote in national elections (M. Klein 2008). As of 2012, between three hundred thousand and four hundred thousand noncitizen Palestinians lived within the city's jurisdiction (Sasson, Maimon, and Luster 2012). An increasing though still miniscule number are applying for full Israeli citizenship, but the state also finds ways of reducing the number of Palestinians in the city through draconian rules on marriage and permanent presence (see Ir Amim 2010). The Oslo Accords affirmed their identity as Palestinians, and they were permitted to vote in Palestinian Authority (PA) elections for the Palestinian Council, but the PA is not active in East Jerusalem and receives no taxes from the Palestinian residents there; in any case, few actually vote in the PA elections. Furthermore, their vote has little effect on their lives because Israel controls all decisions regarding Jerusalem, which is subject to the Ministerial Committee on Jerusalem Affairs (and hence the Knesset) and various developmental authorities answerable to the PMO and the Interior Ministry. The Jerusalem Development Authority, for example, has broad powers concerning planning and budgeting for the city, and noncitizens cannot serve as board members.[8]

The Palestinian part of this ostensibly united city suffers from underfunding and a lack of basic services, including employment-related infrastructure such as employment bureaus. Though residency in theory grants Palestinians in East Jerusalem employment in Israel, services, and their share of socioeconomic resources, in fact there are huge differences between Jewish and Palestinian neighborhoods. Before the first intifada,[9] Israel ensured East Jerusalem's dependence on West Jerusalem by maintaining freedom of movement westward and employment in the west, while failing to develop East Jerusalem. The intifadas, especially the second intifada and the separation wall,[10] have meant Palestinians in East Jerusalem are even more restricted, but there is still no development of the east (M. Klein 2008), which is now "a city of physical, social and budgetary neglect, forsaken by the Israeli authorities in every facet of life" (Sasson, Maimon, and Luster 2012, 41).

Thus the Palestinians of East Jerusalem may be seen as embodying the Israeli inclusion/exclusion conundrum. They have no citizenship but are a permanent presence. There is little investment in their parts of the city and no development of the infrastructures and services, yet they are included within the workforce and in theory benefit from Israeli law, including labor law, though there is insufficient enforcement. They are a physical presence within Israel's self-declared borders, but Israel makes no attempts to integrate them or recognize their place within the state, and from Israel's point of view they belong to the largely fictive Palestinian state that has almost no presence and no influence on their daily lives.[11]

CONCLUDING REMARKS TO PART 3

In part 3, I suggested that the decline of the union–party link and the rise of nongovernmental organizations (NGOs) active in the sphere of labor are connected to the gradual undermining of one of corporatism's central premises: the congruence of the labor market with citizenship. Since the establishment of the State of Israel, following attempts to create an insulated Jewish labor market in Mandatory Palestine, the labor market's borders have continually expanded and become more porous, embracing increasing numbers of Palestinians and later migrant workers. The borders of the national political community, on the other hand, have remained firm, and the Jewish nationalism that guides the state's policies is as strong as ever.

In such a situation, a party representing labor in parliament could choose to fight for the interests of all workers. However, there are a number of barriers to choosing this path, some particular to Israel's case: the decline of the party as an important institution in the nation's politics; the fact that these workers have no electoral power (since they are not citizens); the Labor Party's acceptance of the neoliberal rules of the game, which prevents it from putting forward an alternative; and the party's continued identification with the Jewish citizenry to the detriment of other workers in the Israeli economy. The Histadrut too has been associated almost exclusively, throughout its history, with Jewish labor (though this may be changing now, as noted in chapter 5, particularly as the Histadrut has been accepting migrant laborers as members since 2010). The greater the proportion of non-Jewish labor in the labor market, the less the Histadrut could claim to represent labor as a whole.

Moreover, the Labor Party, which once claimed to speak for all workers and by extension (within the labor movement ideology of the state) a huge proportion of the population, has come to be seen as a party of narrow interests: the public is no longer a public of workers, and organized labor's potential to speak in a universal voice has been greatly weakened. (This is not to claim that the Labor Party or the Histadrut did in fact speak for all Jewish workers at any time; see Shafir and Peled 2002 for differential inclusion in the Israeli polity.) Being merely the voice of sectarian interests, organized labor is no longer anchored in the institutions and legal frameworks of the state and is increasingly reliant on temporary political contingencies, opportunistic alliances, and personal relations. This is true even of the Histadrut but much more so for NGOs active in the field of workers' rights, whose links with the political establishment are unstable, heavily dependent on personal connections, and unsupported by solid institutional frameworks. In targeting distinct client groups as being in need of special assistance, such organizations also contribute to identity politics and the breakdown of an alternative discourse of solidarity and of a universal class of workers that was once the dominant discourse in many unions under corporatist regimes. On the other hand, these same NGOs are able to address the concerns of noncitizens that the Histadrut has been reluctant to do. Indeed, the two organizations discussed in part 3 mostly concentrate on those excluded entirely from the political community (Palestinians from the occupied territories and migrant laborers), or reluctantly accepted but only as second-class citizens subject to discrimination (Arab citizens of Israel). Not by chance were these NGOs established as union strength reached a nadir and noncitizen labor increased dramatically.

Rejecting unionism (Kav Laoved) or less successful in unionist activities than in other activities (Workers Advice Center, WAC), these organizations have adopted the human rights discourse that resonates with foreign donors. This discourse also resonates with the Israeli courts upon which they are so dependent, since their main work in representing workers is carried out on the legal plane, drawing on the liberalization of legislation led by the Supreme Court (Hirschl 1997; Mautner 1993; Raday 1994). Thus it was the High Court that extended labor law to the occupied territories in the case submitted by Kav Laoved, overruling the labor court's decision; the labor court still holds to a corporatist conception of collective labor relations that includes collective bargaining and is based on equal political rights. As Justice Eliezer Rivlin noted in that case, "The National Labor Court had in fact removed from Palestinian workers the cover of protection which Israeli legislators saw fit to grant Israeli workers. This removal constitutes . . . discrimination and creates an irrelevant and immoral distinction between the employment terms of Israeli workers and those of Palestinian workers" (Osherov 2011). The High Court, taking a liberal approach, cannot accept formal discrimination, but the rights it insists apply to Palestinians are legislative only and include no right to political voice. As Barzilai (1998, 20) notes, on political issues pertaining to Palestinian self-determination and control of their own lives, the court provides only an illusion of democracy: "in most cases the [High Court] has dismissed the appeals of Palestinians, legitimating the military occupation." In other words, the High Court extends human rights to all, in line with its liberal outlook, but does not concern itself with political rights.

Thus too Kav Laoved makes extensive use of the Freedom of Information Law of 1998 in its court cases, using this liberal legislation to crack open the secretive procedures and lack of transparency surrounding restrictions on Palestinian movement and the reasons for refusals to issue entry or work permits. In addressing the concerns of Palestinians (after Oslo), the Histadrut too concentrated on individual representation, not collective representation as members of the union: collective representation within a national union is barred from those excluded from the political community—those who have no political rights.

The human rights discourse also resonates with another neoliberal discourse: individual responsibility (Maman and Rosenhek, forthcoming) and the obligation to work (Sharone 2007; M. Peters 2001), the ideals embodied in the Wisconsin program (Helman 2013). Israel's economic elites believe that their continued success depends on reducing the unproductive population—hence the mantra reiterated by then finance minister Yair Lapid: "sharing the burden" means increasing the employment rates among the two fastest-growing population groups, the Arabs and the Haredim, who will make up some 50 percent of Israel's citizens by 2059 if current trends continue (Weissberg 2013). The state is no longer willing to bear the "burden" of supporting such "non-productive" populations, who are now being shoehorned into a labor market that offers few opportunities for meaningful employment and is saturated by cheaper labor intentionally imported by the state in response to powerful employer lobbies. The drive to encourage Arab citizens to participate in the labor force pushes them into nonunion positions: the young and trendy world of high-tech, in practice relevant for only a few, and grueling employment in agriculture, construction, or the growing market of manpower agencies and outsourced services. The sector that still enjoys union protection with all the advantages this brings, such as employment security, good wages, and peripheral benefits, is a remnant of the corporatist arrangement and includes the railways, the electricity and water companies, and banking. These branches constitute the last Histadrut strongholds, albeit here too organized labor is being undermined, and they remain mostly closed to Israel's Arab citizens (Yashiv and Kasir 2013; Wolkinson 1999).

Moreover, the individualization of representation and the reliance on legal activities to ensure basic rights and the enforcement of existing legislation disconnects the workers from broader political issues: NGOs, as Grinberg (2011, 227) has it, are an apolitical substitute for the political and dynamic interaction between civil society, political parties, and state. The obligation to be an economically viable, self-reliant human being includes the right to legal protection but does not include the right to challenge or shape the rules of the game, or to put forward an alternative vision for society. As experts, NGOs are outsiders, able to provide government agents with insider knowledge but not representatives of the demands of their "clients" in the way unions represent their members' demands. The human rights discourse on which they base their work is not a political discourse of equitable (re)distribution or democratic participation.

The activities of NGOs in the field of labor can also be viewed as the outsourcing of enforcement. Where unions enforced the agreements they had had a hand in shaping, NGOs struggle to apply the legislation and agreements that they have no structured way of influencing even if under certain circumstances they are able to promote amendments. Thus Kav Laoved receives funding from the Economics Ministry and Tel Aviv-Jaffa Municipality, an acknowledgement of its work in areas from where state agencies are retreating. Indeed, as Kav Laoved founder Hannah Zohar herself noted (interview), Kav Laoved's work can be seen as a kind of "privatization" of workers' problems, or the outsourcing of these problems (see also Gidron, Bar, and Katz 2004). Furthermore, since much funding comes from abroad, it is as if foreign organizations are subsidizing work that the Israeli government should be carrying out (as Hannah Zohar also noted; interview). Similarly, in upholding safety at work, WAC is taking on the role of Labor Ministry safety officers. Indeed, WAC's "Safety at Work" conference in August 2011 was held in cooperation with the National Insurance Institute's Manof Fund for Funding Activities for Prevention of Work Accidents and the Labor Ministry's deputy chief labor inspector Varda Edwards and with the participation of the Israel Institute for Occupational Safety and Hygiene (the official representative of the International Labor Organization Information Center in Israel). WAC, in its efforts to uphold paragraph 12a of the amendment to the Employment of Employees by Manpower Contractors Law of 1996, can even be perceived as acting in place of the Histadrut, which appears to have little interest in ensuring the enforcement of legislation (which the organization itself promoted) among populations with no political voice.

The decreasing congruence between laborer and citizen, the undermining of labor's universal discourse, the rise of NGOs in law enforcement and representation of individual workers, and the emphasis on individual responsibility for economic viability and the obligation to work—these trends suggest a partial reorientation of organized labor's battlefront, from a face-off with capital to an appeal to the public and state. While Kav Laoved, for example, may hook up with

Koach Laovdim for some unionizing activities, such as organizing Thai workers in agriculture, we see an increasing number of broad alliances where the union is just one among many organizations acting in concert to influence legislation and improve conditions for a certain worker population. The Coalition for Direct Employment, discussed in part 1, is one example: in the cleaners' campaign, organizing was the least successful aspect. The cleaners had a minimum level of union representation via the Histadrut,[1] which they rejected, and a collective framework through Koach Laovdim. Yet the campaign was begun outside union frameworks and involved a wide range of organizations whose main focus was influencing policymakers via nonunion channels including naming and shaming and lobbying.[2] The Coalition continues its efforts to put an end to the triangular employment relationship in various workplaces, but the employer is often a secondary player if addressed at all. Indeed, the workers at the center of the issue being addressed are also secondary players: for them, participation in the campaign is as concerned citizens like anyone else, not as workers with a stake in the result. Thus the conflict with the employer, centered on employment conditions and based on the ideal of equitable distribution, gives way to a narrow issue-specific appeal to state bodies to impose changes on the labor relationship.

Similarly, the Forum against the Privatization of the Railway was an alliance of various union-affiliated activists who downplayed their union identities to enable a broad appeal directly to the public and the state. So too in Wisconsin Watch, the alliance against the so-called Wisconsin program: WAC acted together with a wide range of NGOs including Association for Civil Rights in Israel, Rabbis for Human Rights, Yedid, Laborer's Voice, and Community Advocacy. These are labor issues in which the employer is bypassed and the importance of the conflict with the employer diminished. The organizations involved are also active in many areas not directly related to labor though bearing significantly on workers' lives. Kav Laoved emphasizes freedom of movement, for example, while WAC (through its various affiliated organizations) focuses on poverty, discrimination, and empowerment for women. The same liberalization that enabled the expulsion of workers from collective frameworks also enabled the inclusion of workers (regardless of citizenship status) within the human rights regime.

The conflict between labor and capital, institutionalized and legitimized through class compromise, has been delegitimized and deinstitutionalized. Furthermore, we are persuaded that no such compromise is needed (Gutwein 2012). Where the capital/labor conflict was once built into the basic structure of the corporatist regime and could not change without changing the entire political structure (Mundlak 2007, 134), the conflicts of these new broad alliances are not anchored in such institutional structures; they are changeable, subject to strategic considerations and internal organizational politics, tentative, unstable, contingent on political expedience and the figures involved. Individual unions can still use the corporatist scaffolding, but they find themselves representing interest groups facing other interest groups (Leisink, Van Leemput, and Vilrokx 1996b) as opposed to a worker population whose interests tally with at least some conception of the public good.

As Mundlak (2007, 133) has it, "The general representation of interests in society has been transformed. Rather than being based on the sole distinction between labor and capital, it is currently a more dynamic and segmented form of representation that corresponds to the growing disposition to multiculturalism in Israeli society."

Labor disputes are no longer perceived within an ethical framework of class, but one of human rights and equality of opportunity; the "labor–capital axis has no priority over other social cleavages" (Mundlak 2009, 767). In fact, the possibility for confrontation in the sphere of labor relations and equitable distribution is diminished: an NGO like Kav Laoved is dependent on state funding and on the legitimacy granted by its expertise as well as on its presence in Knesset committees; it has no electoral power and cannot threaten to strike. Its ability to get results draws workers, but that ability is dependent on working together with government bodies through a careful balance of confrontation on specific points and cooperation over time. Thus it must develop what the organization's website calls "cooperative partnership" with state authorities: "monitoring current policies, encouraging effective enforcement over employers, and supervising the granting of employment licenses and work permits," maintaining an uneasy "partnership" with the same state institutions it is also trying to influence (see also Chandhoke 2004, who discusses the dependency of NGOs on the state). Much of WAC's work is carried out in a similar uneasy partnership, such as its cooperation with state bodies in its "Safety at Work" project.

Conclusion

In this final chapter, I bring the threads of previous chapters together to take a broader view of organized labor in Israel today. In the tumult of labor campaigns, the diverse organizations emerging on the ground, and the efforts of government and capital to thwart organizing initiatives, those who are "rather friendly towards labor" (Baccaro 2010, 341) may find some causes for optimism. Indeed, a central insight of this broad study is that the fragmentation of labor and labor representation, despite the weakening of organized labor in general, also enables those who were once excluded from the neocorporatist regime to be included in at least some frameworks for collective representation. Moreover, within the cracks of neocorporatism, workers are finding ways to oppose processes associated with neoliberalism, taking advantage of both vestigial neocorporatist frameworks and new liberal legislation to impede the blanket application of neoliberal policies. In some cases, the workplace has become a site of resistance or focus of activism for groups that address broader concerns, beyond the traditional remit of classic unionism. However, organized labor has moved from being a legitimate, even dominant political player to being on the defensive. The central premises of corporatism have been rejected by the state and eroded by labor market developments that have been promoted by political and economic elites. The corporatist structures at all levels—including on the ideological plane—are being undermined, leaving organized labor fighting a rearguard battle: it no longer has a privileged position in the political sphere, it is not an automatic partner to socioeconomic policy decisions, and even the right to organize is no longer self-evident. Moreover, much of this new organizing, particularly activism in the framework of nongovernmental organizations (NGOs), does not re/build or shore up the collective institutions and frameworks that once gave a voice to organized labor. Therefore, despite the impressive energy in the recent wave of organizing, the overall picture for organized labor is far from optimistic.

The chapter discusses the broad themes of this study in general terms. The first section discusses the hurdles with which labor activism has to contend in its bid to establish itself as a democratic, participatory force. The next section addresses labor activism as opposition to policies associated with neoliberalism, commonly thought to weaken organized labor. In some cases such policies are successfully hindered while in other cases the application of such policies has strengthened certain groups of workers. The third section overviews the status of organized labor within the socioeconomic regime, in particular in light of increasing labor-oriented activism among nonunion organizations. It reiterates the idea that the workplace has become a site of resistance, attracting activists who use existing collective frameworks to promote their agenda, but also casts doubt on the ability of this new activism to rebuild or sustain these very frameworks—particularly in light of the fact that organized labor appears to be losing the ideological struggle for legitimacy. The subsequent section discusses a more optimistic possibility: that the cracks in neocorporatism may create paths to political participation for those who have been economically incorporated but politically excluded. Finally, I discuss the significance of these developments specifically for Israel, in light of the country's singular labor history.

Labor Activism and the Revitalization of Organized Labor

As noted at the beginning of this book, I was drawn to investigate organized labor by what appeared to be a wave of organizing. I embraced the premise of worker agency, unlike most of the literature of the 1980s and 1990s that viewed change to the socioeconomic regime through an institutional lens and offered mostly structural-functionalist interpretations. As Molina and Rhodes (2002, 314) assert, the "institutional bias" in neocorporatist theory meant that such interpretations "underplayed actors' rational calculation of their interest and objectives in creating corporatist institutions" and left "little room for political contingency." The "wave of organizing" demonstrates that workers and labor activists too have some belief in their own agency, and it behooves us to understand the implications of this activity, its aims, the opportunities it can use, and the hurdles it encounters.

The research undertaken for this book supports the impression that this wave is not merely a few isolated incidents of particularly media-savvy worker committees: from the second half of the new millennium onward, there has been a new interest among workers in both unionized and nonunionized workplaces to make their voices heard, to be involved in shaping their workplace and society at large. Something in the "turbulent environment" of neoliberalism, to use Molina and Rhodes's words, seems to have indeed triggered "a search for new modes of concertation" (2002, 315). In that sense, the frameworks associated with organized labor still hold some appeal for those seeking to have their voices heard and their opinions taken into account. However, the question that must be addressed is to what extent this framework offers a real path to change, a real participatory democratic opportunity to shape society.

Relevant to this question, one particular problem emerges from the cases studied: a prominent characteristic of this new labor activism is the clash between new groups, mobilized workers, and new organizations, on the one hand, and what we might call the old guard of the Histadrut and its long-established connections with the political elite, on the other. In short, the new may not be completely compatible with the old, and the case of the Histadrut supports the literature that suggests mobilization of the rank and file may be incompatible with the partnership approach of established worker organizations (Badigannavar and Kelly 2011; Heery 2002; Turner 2005). While mobilization and worker activism can be a response to the failure (or perceived failure) of historical partnership with other social partners, the strategies for action adopted by the rank and file may neutralize or contradict strategies being followed by the leadership, and the bureaucratic structures of established organizations can dampen the activism on the ground. In this sense, unions do not necessarily nurture democracy as often asserted (from Webb and Webb 1897 to Fick 2009), if democracy is understood as voice, participation, and influence on the representative organizations—and this may be for structural and historical reasons, not just because of leadership personality.

From the cases studied, it appears the leadership of such organizations may withhold their support for activism in three situations: (1) if they believe it will undermine their organization's good standing with social partners; (2) if the demands of activists threaten the stability of past agreements (whether tacit or written) in which the organizations have made concessions on an issue now being brought to the fore, such as privatization or outsourcing; and similarly (3) if activists' messages of social justice undermine their organization's ability to make sacrifices in certain areas of welfare in return for voice and representation at peak levels. In such situations, the union is perceived to act against the workers it represents (see Preminger 2013 for a discussion of these issues). The legitimacy of a workers' representative organization among its members is crucial so that it can decide how to best balance different mutually competing interests of workers, yielding on some issues for the sake of gains in other areas (Offe 1981). If its legitimacy is doubtful, its ability to control members or demand greater sacrifice from them is reduced. Rank-and-file activism, if it is seen to influence the leadership, may increase the union's legitimacy and enable it to regain the ability to control its members. However, activism threatens to undermine another important source of legitimacy for a workers' organization, and that is legitimacy in the eyes of the political regime as a whole.

Thus, as organized labor's role in this regime is undermined if not rejected outright, peak-level workers' organizations are having to choose between increased control of members in exchange for continued legitimacy with social partners and state representatives, or increased support for members' activism at the risk of losing this legitimacy. While activism could be harnessed to increase pressure on social partners, this would be a risky tactic when organized labor is losing support among the general public. As workers are increasingly differentiated from the public, when the public does not identify itself as a public of workers, labor cannot aspire to be a universal category or subject of emancipation, as some labor movements once hoped. Indeed, far from being the subject of emancipation, unionized workers in strong labor organizations (like the Histadrut's big committees) are held up as the privileged elite from whom the public needs to be defended, and the public for the most part has accepted this as a given. In this situation, as we have seen, it is easy for the other social partners (including the government) to paint a union as irresponsible if it is seen to be encouraging too much disruptive activism.

In short, organized labor as an overarching concept has lost its legitimacy: only certain kinds of workers are permitted to organize; others, already organized, are deemed to have too much power and are therefore illegitimate. The idea that capital represents universal interests (the good of the economy) and that workers are interest groups whose power must be limited has been internalized. Under these conditions, organized labor is having to concentrate its efforts on explaining to the public—in other words, conducting its struggle particularly on the ideological plane. Workers, then, may find themselves up against both the public and their own representative organization.

Labor Activism as Opposition to Neoliberalization

The cases discussed in this book provide evidence to suggest that the demand for participation and internal democracy in representative organizations is at least partly the result of the perception that these organizations are colluding with the adversary and accepting privatization, outsourcing, and other policies associated with the postcorporatist, neoliberalizing economy. Hyman (2001, 51–52), taking a broader view of unions' place in the socioeconomic structure, suggests that states' renewed interest in unions in the 1990s was part of their search for ways of managing the fallout from neoliberal policies; thus the new social partnership that some have lauded (Baccaro 2003; Baccaro and Howell 2011) came to mean that unions were being asked to share responsibility for dismantling (legitimize the dismantling of) the gains achieved in the 1950s and 1960s. Thus unions' legitimacy is being thrown into question at least partly because members suspect they are no longer representing their interests. This makes internal democracy doubly attractive, both as a way of influencing the leadership and as a way of increasing transparency—to ensure the leadership really is striving for members' interests. As unions—the Histadrut, in Israel's case—offer fewer benefits and are being compelled to legitimize cuts to public services, procedural fairness becomes increasingly important to members (Baccaro 2003, 691). In light of this frustration with this aspect of the role of representative organizations, I suggest we view many of these struggles as various cases of resistance to what can broadly be called neoliberalism, expressed in terms of a demand for change within organizations that (are perceived to) have failed to resist it themselves. Moreover, labor campaigns can themselves become rallying points for popular opposition to neoliberalization, as noted in other studies (e.g., Camfield 2006, 40), particularly—in Israel's case—following the perceived failure of the social protest movement of 2011.

There is widespread recognition that the neoliberalization project is multifaceted, varying from state to state (Hermann and Flecker 2012; Schulten, Brandt, and Hermann 2008), but also broad agreement on certain policy outcomes including the acceleration of privatization, the deepening of marketization, and an increase in competition as governing practice (Flecker and Hermann 2011; J. Peters 2012). The overall effect on organized labor includes weakened unions and deteriorating working conditions, especially in the public sector (Gill-McLure 2007; Schulten and Böhlke 2012; Schulten, Brandt, and Hermann 2008). However, the cases analyzed in this book show that not all labor activism is necessarily directed against the concrete manifestations of policies associated with neoliberalism, such as privatization. Differing modes of privatization in different sectors lead to different outcomes for industrial relations in those sectors and for the strengthening or weakening of unions. Some sectors subject to privatization, marketization, and increased competition are undermined as part of the state's attempts to shake off previous commitments, leaving workers in those sectors with no situational or structural power (E. Wright 2000, 1994) at all. Others, however, become sources of profit, especially if they have links with other profitable sectors; neoliberalization in these sectors can enhance workers' situational or structural power. But for this to be transformed into associational power, there must be some industry-wide solidarity based on a shared sense of grievance and drawing on a history and culture of organized labor.

This oscillation between collusion and resistance is in keeping with what Peck and Theodore (2012, 178–179) call neoliberalism's "lurching dynamic, marked by serial policy failure and improvised adaptation, and by combative encounters with obstacles and counter-movements." As others have noted, the policies and mechanisms that push neoliberalization forward can be contradictory, appearing improvised and opportunistic, not always successful, and far from inevitable (Goldstein 2012; Harvey 2005; Hilgers 2012; Kalb 2012; Schmidt 2009; Wacquant 2012). Thus in some areas organized labor is asserting itself, or reasserting itself, or maintaining its strength, and even in areas without unions workers are being assisted by organizations with considerable influence in the legislative and legal spheres. However, these challenges are taking place within frameworks created by neoliberal processes and to a certain extent condoned by their agents. In Israel, there is a broad political consensus over the basic tenets of neoliberal social and economic policy, to which even the Labor Party subscribes. Challengers use the results of neoliberalization such as liberal legislation (the Freedom of Information Act, for example) and take advantage of political tolerance of pluralism in civil society to mitigate the wounds caused by neoliberalism itself, but have been unable to create a framework for nurturing an alternative social vision: the demise of the labor party/trade union project for social change continues unhindered, yet no stable alternative project has been put forward.

Where Israel differs from other states is in its much-lauded history of solidarity and the hegemonic role of the labor movement in the official state narrative. In many cases studied here, including the railway campaign, the social workers' strike, and even the medical residents' breakaway campaign, the history of organized labor in Israel has been invoked as justification for the campaign, as rhetoric for recruitment, and as a legitimizing idea. It is this rich history that assisted those with situational and structural power to bring together their fellow workers and shape collective demands. This is somewhat paradoxical, given the hostility to strong organized worker groups that are in a sense left over from a time of greater labor power. However, it is in keeping with the tendency of the social protest movement to hark back to what is perceived as a better time of equality, substantial welfare, and national solidarity (Rosenhek and Shalev 2013), no matter how many inequalities this period of history may in fact have contained (see Shafir and Peled 2002, for example).

Labor Activism and Organized Labor as a Privileged Interest Group

Another broad issue we must address is the relationship between these new organizing drives, new worker groups, and new organizations active in the field of workers' rights and the neocorporatist regime—or more accurately, the labor-relations regime that remains following over thirty years of decline of neo-corporatism. Is organized labor succeeding in retaining its privileged position above other civil society groups, despite its weakened state? Viewed in light of this question, the emerging activism noted in part 1 is somewhat paradoxical. On the one hand, workers are creating a new, activist identity rooted in labor organizing and based in the workplace and are drawn to democratic labor organizations such as Koach Laovdim; there can be no doubt that the results of this activism have included increased public attention to labor campaigns and increased awareness of labor issues and the possibilities that labor organizing offers. Yet on the other hand, work and workers are increasingly mixed up in other issues and struggles, as labor rights are increasingly intermingled on a conceptual and practical level with other concerns drawn from the human rights discourse. The traditional boundaries of organizing and representation—within which unions once staked their claim—are increasingly porous, and it becomes increasingly hard to define "labor" as a separate sphere with its own particular interests and demands. In organizing and representing workers, the union is no longer the only, nor even necessarily the dominant, organization. In seeking "associational power" (E. Wright 2000), workers are looking beyond unions, or—increasingly—their cause is being taken up by nonunion organizations.

As these nonunion organizations spread into traditionally union territory, the privileged position of the workers is undermined; even those workers at the core of the conflict, such as the cleaners or the laborers at the archeological digs, are merely the galvanizing focus of a broader campaign of policy or principle, not the prime drivers of a labor-focused struggle. If workers choose to participate, they do so within the framework of an individual decision to be active, to be one of the many people within the group of activists working on the campaign.

Similarly, these organizations are often staffed not by unionists or workers, but by professional NGO staff or volunteers; thus in Israel, too, we see the development of a class of activists, "freely [crossing] the lines between union, anti-sweatshop, antiwar, human rights, and environmental campaigns" (Turner 2005, 393), using labor issues to tackle broader concerns. These activists surge from one campaign to another, turning up at each other's demonstrations and organizing solidarity strikes, "liking" each other's Facebook pages, using each other's lawyers, and adding their signature to each other's letters to parliamentary committees.

Familiar with Israeli labor law, norms, and history and also international labor issues, they are, however, unencumbered by commitments made in past agreements or by considerations of future partnerships and cooperation; they take advantage of leftover corporatist frameworks but also adopt less unionist tactics while endeavoring to make their struggle a public battle over principles or policies as opposed to a battle of organized labor against employers. Thus unencumbered, these activists and their organizations enjoy extensive freedom of activity, unlike the union, which is hindered by past agreements and considerations of maintaining good relations with the social partners and has its eye on future compromises that it may have to make.

The core unionist conflict—labor versus employer—is still present, then, but this is often merely one facet of a much broader aspiration for change; most nonunion organizations have their own specific focus where their resources and efforts are directed even when they act within a broad coalition. Likewise, a given campaign can use the corporatist frameworks at the same time as working through other channels such as lobbying, working through the courts, and getting to Knesset committees, but also appealing directly to the public, naming and shaming, and using public opinion to pressure government into changing policies. In December 2013 and January 2014, this logic was taken a step further, when asylum seekers used the ultimate union weapon—the strike—to try to compel the state to change the way it was handling their appeals for asylum. This had nothing to do with employment terms or any clash of interests with their employers; in fact, in this case, they had the support of many small businesses in Tel Aviv. The strike was just one of a wide range of tactics used to promote their cause, including hunger strikes, vigils in front of foreign embassies and the Knesset, and demonstrations (see Zonszein 2014, for example).

The workplace, then, has become a site of resistance open to, and potentially useful for, activists or organizations running a range of campaigns that do not necessarily address workplace-specific employment issues directly. This was noticeably so after the social protest movement of 2011: many workers interviewed in the course of this research noted that their struggle was a direct embodiment of the protest's aim of social justice, and others noted the protest's influence on their decision to take an active part in the struggle. However, unions and nonunion organizations struggle on different levels. Unions seek agreements for ongoing partnership; even radical unions accept the basic structure of collective industrial relations, whether corporatist or pluralist, because their legitimacy and legality depend on it. They are also concerned with day-to-day enforcement of laws and agreements and day-to-day grievances of workers. In contrast, many nonunion organizations, particularly coalitions of such organizations, aim for broad social change, raising awareness and promoting legislation. They adopt different tactics and draw on different resources, with notable results on an individual level as well as some important legal and legislative precedents, but they do not have the resources for the daily grind, and without a workers' committee they have no daily contact or on-the-ground presence. Working extensively through the courts, they depend on post-factum enforcement to deter future violations but cannot address problems in real time.

Moreover, while old structures continue to be used (workers or activists drawing on institutional power), these structures are mostly the result only of past struggles and negotiations (see Dörre 2011, 18–22), not of recent conflict; these same structures are not being renewed by current organizing activity through new representative organizations. Similarly, the success of nonunion organizations in promoting legislation has had a positive effect on the lives of many workers, and in some cases it has even opened sufficient space for union work, but this kind of rights legislation does not actively contribute to continued collective labor relations or shore up the institutions that maintained them.

Alternative visions of society require collective action; individual action, on the level of legal protection, cannot include such visions and does not foster political participation. This means that nonunion organizations are able to mount only a limited challenge to pervasive ideologies and discourses, especially given that they have little foundation in institutional structures and are often reliant on contingent cooperation or partnership with state bodies. The human rights discourse within which these NGOs work poses no serious challenge to the neoliberal outlook adopted by the state, within which capital has a strong position and a clear voice: its interests are public interests—a flourishing economy—that organized labor only hinders. The human rights discourse is one of entitlement but not of empowerment; rights-based claims are made by supplicants, not by partners who have a hand in shaping policy. It is a persuasive language that appeals to the Israeli judicial system, yet it bypasses the workers themselves who are left with expert representation but no voice or participation. This discourse, which has even influenced labor court decisions, rejects "labor" as an empirically relevant concept; instead, it emphasizes identities such as ethnicity and thus shifts the focus toward discrimination as opposed to exploitation, and toward individual difficulties as opposed to collective and structural location.

This discourse is in keeping with the reconfiguration of rights and duties that has seen the whittling away of the social rights defined by Marshall (1963), a crowning development of the Western world in the twentieth century that was linked to the rise of the welfare state. Citizens remain with only civil and political rights while noncitizens who are nonetheless included within the labor market are left with civil rights alone.[1] Social rights—which, in practice, mean the right to economic security among other things—are being transformed into duties:

the duty to work, to manage one's employment path and nurture one's employability even as jobs remain scarce and good jobs (with good wages, peripheral benefits, tenure, and so on) even scarcer. Since the status of being a citizen has been disconnected from employment, the labor market can be extended to those deemed undesirable as members of the political community; at the same time, the political rights granted to citizens are utilized (through voting) to maintain an insular political community.[2]

Able to draw on only weakened, leftover institutional structures, lacking legitimate and stable links to the political establishment, and having lost the ideological struggle, organized labor is unable to offer an alternative that appeals to society beyond the workplace. In E. Wright's (1994, 93–101) terms, we can say that labor still has considerable institutional power resources, and some groups of workers such as the doctors and high-tech employees have significant situational power, but most worker groups have no situational power at all: labor power has been fragmented and is distributed increasingly unevenly, and representation has been decentralized, leaving many workers reliant on NGOs. Though some worker groups may be in a strong position, organized labor as a whole has lost all systemic power—the logic of the social system itself affirms only capitalists' interests. Organized labor is in a transitional and unsettled period: the new initiatives, new organizations, and new alliances that have blurred the boundaries of the sphere of organized labor have not (yet) consolidated into clear structures of representation or even into accepted patterns of political behavior.

Labor Activism and Citizenship in the Political Community

As Crouch (2006, 52) notes, neocorporatism can only hold if there is a "relatively bounded universe linking fiscal and monetary policy, labor markets and labor market organizations and the scope of firms." As Ram (2008, 138–150) has noted, this relatively bounded universe certainly no longer exists—the Israeli variant of neocorporatism is severely cracked. These cracks are partly the result of a long process of what I called the imperative of economic inclusion that has undoubtedly contributed, sometimes intentionally, to the undermining of organized labor as a whole. However, we have seen how this has affected different groups of workers in different ways—even empowering some, though perhaps at the expense of broad solidarity. Most significantly, the cracks in neocorporatism may also engender opportunities for those previously excluded from this regime or for new worker groups who do not benefit from the protections of neocorporatism. The logic behind policies associated with neoliberalization opens paths to challenging this exclusion.

Two cases analyzed in this book illustrate two aspects of that challenge: the cleaners at Ben-Gurion University, and the High Court ruling of 2007. In the former, those with formal citizenship but with few concrete rights or protections as workers are included in the political community through labor activism; in the latter, labor activism enables those formally excluded to take advantage of existing frameworks to claim a level of effective citizenship where formal belonging is denied (see Preminger 2017). It should be emphasized that in both cases, effective citizenship was the result of struggle, of labor activism. In fact, as Isin (1999) notes, citizenship and the rights associated with it have always been the result of struggle and contestation; the idea of citizenship associated with the Western welfare, corporatist regimes (see Isin and Turner 2007) not only included and protected but also excluded and deprived (Anderson 2010), spurring the excluded to challenge the social order that excluded them.

In the first case, the Coalition for Direct Employment that coalesced around the cleaners drew on ideas of community organizing, appealing to a wider public while using standard unionist frameworks—a form of organizing that has been effective elsewhere, most famously in the Justice for Janitors campaign in the United States (Erickson et al. 2002; Howley 1990) and more recently in living wage campaigns (Hannan, Bauder, and Shields 2016). According to Lopes and Hall (2015, 208), "community organizers and union activists were able to organize and mobilize a largely apolitical group of migrant workers" by successfully mobilizing the wider community. Since Justice for Janitors, union cooperation with nonunion organizations or social movements has come to be considered a central component of what is called social movement unionism (Walsh 2012). Lopes and Hall (2015, 212) note that this "broad-based organizing," sometimes known as community unionism, differs from "traditional models of organizing [that] center on the workplace and the ongoing struggle of workers with managers" as it is centered "on the community and the particular space or locale [the workers] occupy" and aims "to bring people of otherwise disparate views together on an issue of fundamental importance" (see also Vosko et al. 2013).

While the Coalition for Direct Employment did not provide the cleaners with specific channels to participation in the campaign, it drew on ideas of community organizing to include those excluded but present (the cleaners) into the community (the campus community). Though the cleaners were noncitizens (despite formal citizenship) in terms of workplace democracy, the Coalition insisted that they be "part of a local community at the specific workplace" (Davidov 2015, 29) and thus belong at the communal level. The Coalition effectively widened the circle of responsibility for the workers beyond the employer (see C. Wright 2013) by appealing to students and faculty, thus creating "a communal sense of obligation to support collective action" (Heckscher and McCarthy 2014, 629)—making the cleaners a community concern.

Unlike union solidarity premised on shared interests, this is mutual obligation that arises from a sense of social injustice. Heckscher and McCarthy (2014) define this moral appeal of obligation around a shared cause as one of the two "pillars" on which solidarity rests. The other "pillar," they suggest, is the social relations that stem from daily interaction—the kind of interaction industrial unions relied on and that has greatly declined in so-called postindustrial societies. The Coalition was able to re-create at least some such interaction by involving both the cleaners and the other members of the community (the campus community) in common protest activities.

In short, the campaign around the university cleaners injected a radical social justice discourse into a workers' struggle (in fact, the Coalition created a workers' struggle where none had been waged), while taking advantage of existing collective labor relations frameworks (vestigial institutional power, in Dörre's 2011 terms) to promote a broader agenda of social justice. Despite the potential weaknesses of this strategy as noted in chapter 2, including its dependence on an educated milieu of faculty and students at what is considered a politically left-leaning academic department, the result was increased inclusion of formerly invisible workers into the local community and into a framework that facilitated political activism. This is a level of effective citizenship where formal workplace participation or industrial democracy has been denied.

The second example, the High Court ruling of 2007, illustrates another path to effective citizenship on a certain level where formal participation—and in this case formal citizenship, too—have been denied. Responding to an appeal led by an NGO, and drawing on a logic that decoupled formal citizenship from concepts of individual equality, the High Court permitted the use of neocorporatist structures as frameworks for political participation even where (potential) participants lack formal citizenship. In other words, the extension of labor law over Palestinians in the West Bank grants a path toward political agency for those outside the corporatist regime, an opportunity to practice at least one aspect of active citizenship: to claim not just "first-generation" rights (Frost 2005), which can be demanded using ethical arguments (the right not to be tortured or freedom of religious belief, for example) but also second-generation rights that can only be claimed using government-sanctioned structures, including the right to unionize. This is citizenship as practice (Kemp et al. 2000; Sassen 2002), regardless of formal inclusion in the political community, and is a fine example of how economic inclusion might challenge political exclusion while taking advantage of the discourses that have undermined organized labor. This development may even tentatively herald the emergence of labor solidarity beyond the national collective, as evident from the Workers Advice Center's recent work in Mishor Adumim.[3] Indeed, as the old solidarities become weaker or less convincing, new solidarities may be forged at levels other than the level of nation or state—solidarities that enable politics to happen (see Keating 2009).

Moreover, in taking advantage of existing frameworks and making their case in the labor courts, the organizations involved in the university cleaners' campaign and the NGO that assisted the Palestinian claimants are taking an active and political role. This means we may need to reappraise our thinking about the role of NGOs in general and particularly in labor relations. It is common among critical labor scholars to decry the NGO-ization of labor issues. Streeck (2006, 29–32), for example, notes the growth of NGOs as one outcome of the state's use of corporatist organizations as service providers where the government is trying to avoid responsibility for social programs. This is more like pragmatic joint problem-solving than social partnership, since there is little sharing of state authority, and the state remains above, directing events. It has led to concerns about the "privatization" of service provision, as "official agencies of development . . . accord a significant and often directive role to NGOs in development projects and programs" (Kamat 2004, 156). This is not just a question of the state delegating roles and conferring authority, with all the problems of democratic transparency and accountability. As Kamat notes, we should see these NGOs "in relation to the global economic and political process that involves an overall restructuring of public good and private interest. At stake is not the struggle between state and civil society, but a revaluation of private interest and public good" (2004, 156). This is no less than a privatization of the public sphere, she suggests, carried out by pluralizing the public sphere (at the national or global level) and depoliticizing the private sphere (at the community level) (Kamat 2004, 157). However, the role of Kav Laoved in representing the Palestinians' appeal at the High Court and the role of the various organizations in the Coalition for Direct Employment suggest that NGOs may have the potential to be more than merely "apolitical substitutes" (Grinberg 2011, 227) for political interaction between civil society, political parties, and the state—even though their contingent and unstable status, as discussed above, still obtains.

Labor in Israel: Beyond Nationalism and Neoliberalism?

In the context of Israel's singular labor history, the issues discussed above mark an extremely significant development, one that has taken over forty years to unfold, but is now unequivocally completed. Almost one hundred years after Zionism took on a socialist hue,[4] we can confidently say that it has fully abandoned organized labor as the vehicle for the national project. Nowhere is this more clearly observable than in the agricultural branch, since it was here that Zionist ideologies of redeeming the land and settlement were combined with strategies of Hebrew labor and the physical task of taking over tracts of land. The philosopher-farmer pioneer still has a glorified place in Israel's self-image and mythologies, but agriculture has become a business like any other, with diminished state assistance and reduced export subsidies, and reliant on imported labor. Here, as in many other sectors, the Israeli worker is perceived as deadwood, weighed down by legislative protection and historical collective agreements, which must be lopped off to enable economic growth: labor is no longer necessary for the achievement of state objectives.

Thus, paradoxically, the weakening of the neocorporatist regime in the Israeli context also frees organized labor from the historical burden of nationalism and the settlement project. As noted in chapter 1, the assumption at the heart of the neocorporatist regime was that labor's (workers') interests were different from capital's (employers') and that a working compromise between them could nonetheless be achieved: labor would "play the capitalist game" in the sphere of production, and in return it would be granted political rights (Molina and Rhodes 2002; Schmitter 1974). But the corporatist premise that the workers are a recognizable group, distinguishable from employers or capital, never fully held in Israel (Grinberg 1996, 1993; Shalev 1992). Now, the ethos that linked worker identity to national identity, and the workers to national goals, has all but disappeared, and this has clarified the distinction between labor and capital, opening the way to real class-based organizing. Freed from the national burden, workers are creating a new worker identity, growing from the bottom up, and recognize their situation as waged workers regardless of their role in the national story. This is a very different kind of worker identity than that nurtured within the context of Zionist settlement and the strengthening of the Jewish state.

However, just at the historical juncture in which the decline of Israeli corporatism frees organized labor from nationalism, labor representation is fragmented and struggling to maintain its relevance as a political concept. The lacuna in Israel's labor history—the lack of a class-based, grassroots organizing tradition—is being felt as new organizations as well as the Histadrut attempt to develop unionizing skills and establish a unionizing culture but fail to engender a broad labor movement extolling class solidarity. The creation of such broad solidarity has been made extremely difficult by the continued existence of a strong nationalist rhetoric even as the common political framework between labor and capital, the nation-state, has been subverted, with capital spreading beyond the national borders and labor being brought into them from outside.

Thus the *Israeli* variant of corporatism has been completely eroded, even as some vestigial corporatist structures and frameworks remain strong enough to offer channels for new struggles, and workers as well as activists are taking advantage of them to promote their agendas and interests. Organized labor, now viewed as an illegitimate remnant of a bygone era, has been shunted outside the political structures of representation and is renegotiating its place vis-à-vis the old social partners, the new organizations, and a public that, for the most part, does not identify itself as workers and does not accept labor's claim to represent it. It remains to be seen whether, perhaps together with other civil society organizations, it will be able to forge new institutional structures with sufficient political legitimacy and strength to challenge the dominance of capital.

List of Interviewees

Interviewees are listed alphabetically (by family name) with the position they held at the time the interview was conducted and the date of the interview.

Adiv, Assaf, WAC National Coordinator, 14 November 2011

Adler, Steve, former National Labor Court president, 19 January 2014

Amos, Orna, community organizer, among the leaders of the initiative to organize cleaners at Ben-Gurion University, 16 December 2013

Avitan, Itamar, chair of Pelephone workers' committee, 1 October 2013

Basha, Amir, labor lawyer at Benny Cohen Law Offices, 15 October 2013

Ben Efrat, Roni, WAC Funding Coordinator, 7 December 2011

Berezovsky, Jacob, HOT technicians' committee member, 9 December 2012

Bior, Haim, labor relations journalist at *TheMarker*, 13 September 2012

Boaron, Hadas, activist and workers' committee member at Pelephone, 28 August 2013

Cohen, Shay, organization secretary and founder, Koach Laovdim, 20 August 2013

Dolev, Eran, among the founders of Arbel, 25 February 2013

Dvir, Rom, chair of the Histadrut's Workers Organizing Unit, 7 October 2013

Edra'i, Gila, former chair of the workers' committee at Israel Railways, 27 November 2013

Farber, Tami, social worker and among the leaders of Osot Hasharon, 5 April 2012

Feuer, Dror, columnist at *Globes* and among the founders of the Journalists Organization, 11 October 2012

Goldman, Tal, social work student, founder and one of the chairs of Osim Shinui, 9 April 2012

Haim, Rudi, former archeologist at the IAA, 25 October 2013

Kimhi, Rafi, northern branch coordinator at Koach Laovdim, 16 October 2012

Levine, Ilan, former wages officer at the Finance Ministry, 30 December 2012

Linder-Ganz, Ronny, health sector journalist at *TheMarker*, 7 December 2012

Matar, Hagai, journalist at *Maariv* and workers' committee member, 19 December 2012

Niv, Shay, labor relations journalist, *Globes*, 27 September 2012

Raz, Roni, chair of Clal workers' committee, 11 December 2012

Raznik, Tomer, among the founders of the Forum against the Privatization of the Railway, 4 October 2013

Shlosberg, Inbal, social worker, former chair and among the founders of Atidenu, 16 April 2012

Tarchitzky, Yair, chair and among the founders of the Journalists Organization, 25 December 2012

Vatury, Ami, among the founders and chairs of Koach Laovdim, 1 December 2013

Weissbuch, Yona, chair and founder of Mirsham, 19 March 2013

Zohar, Hannah, founder and chair of Kav Laoved, 8 November 2011

Notes

INTRODUCTION

1. Zionism: the movement for the establishment of a Jewish homeland. For an overview of Zionist settlement in Palestine, see for example Shafir (1989); Shafir and Peled (2002).

2. Kibbutzim were communal, originally mainly agricultural, settlements established by Jewish immigrants to Palestine from 1912 onward. In the more radical kibbutzim, all property was owned in common by their members including means of production and the kibbutz's various economic branches, salaries were equal regardless of work being done, and decisions were made through structures of participatory democracy involving general meetings and committees (see Palgi and Reinharz 2014, for example).

3. I focus here on the Histadrut as the hegemonic labor organization, but the same general description is true of its nearest (though still distant) rival, the National Histadrut, whose political allegiance was to the Revisionist movement led by Zeev Jabotinsky. This movement did not support the idea of labor as the vehicle of a Jewish national resurgence in Palestine.

4. Mapai, forerunner of the Labor Party, was long considered the natural party of government and was also the party of Israel's first prime minister, David Ben-Gurion.

5. Palestinian Arab citizens of Israel are known by various terms, including Israeli Arabs, Arab Israelis, and Palestinian Israelis, each of which carries its own political baggage. All are Israeli citizens, in contrast to the Palestinians in the territories occupied by Israel in 1967, who are not citizens, with the exception of the Golan Heights. The Golan Heights were formally annexed and all its residents granted Israeli citizenship. See Levy (2005) for a critique of the term "Israeli Arab."

6. The two Basic Laws, Freedom of Occupation and Human Dignity and Liberty, are discussed more fully in part 2.

7. After 1948, about 20 percent of the population within the new state's borders were Palestinian and granted Israeli citizenship. After 1967, Israel occupied what is known as the West Bank and the Gaza Strip, bringing noncitizen Palestinians under its control. These developments are discussed more fully in part 3.

8. Note that these figures are from 2007; but see also Mundlak et al. (2013) who give slightly different figures in their detailed analysis of union density in relation to coverage of collective agreements.

1. NEOLIBERALISM, NEOCORPORATISM, AND WORKER REPRESENTATION

1. There is another conflict Offe does not specify here: the radical labor aim of bringing capitalist exploitation to an end, which can conflict with the workers' day-to-day aim of maintaining a living wage.

2. This is generally the case when capital faces labor. When capital seeks to influence policy, there may be conflicting interests; for example, exporters may demand a different currency exchange rate than importers. Hence the Marxist claim that though the state always acts to the benefit of the capitalist class as a whole, it may act against individual capitalists.

3. Much of the material, including court documents and the vast majority of media sources, was in Hebrew. Unless otherwise stated, all translations are mine.

4. All interviews were conducted in Hebrew except the interview with former National Labor Court president Steve Adler, which was conducted in English. All translations are mine.

2. THE RISE OF LABOR ACTIVISM

1. Israel Railways Company Ltd. ("the railway") was made into a limited company in 2003, in accordance with the amendment (2002) to the Ports Authority Law of 1961. The state is the sole shareholder. At the time of the strike, the railway employed some 2,000 workers; the Histadrut claimed 1,900 were Histadrut members (see Inter-Organizational Dispute 9685-07-12, par. 2).

2. The National Coalition for Direct Employment of Cleaners included representatives of organizing initiatives in various universities and colleges, Koach Laovdim, student union representatives, the Coordinating Forum of the Senior Staff Associations, the Coordinating Forum of the Junior Staff Associations, Itach-Maaki: Women Lawyers for Social Justice, Shatil, Social Alternative Movement, and the Mahut Center; the National Coalition for Direct Employment established in 2012 includes also Adjunct Faculty Organization, WAC-Maan, Maagalei Tzedek, Association for Civil Rights in Israel, Better Israel, Open Knesset, Hadash, Atidenu, Kav Laoved, Rabbis for Human Rights, and others (Amos and Baharav 2012, 118–119).

3. Putting the focus on the client company was the tactic initiated by the Justice for Janitors campaign. This campaign began in Denver, Colorado, in the late 1980s and has since spread throughout the United States and also to some parts of Canada, led by the Service Employees International Union (see Erickson et al. 2002).

4. Agency fees: the fees workers pay to a union when they are covered by a collective agreement achieved by that union but are not members of the union.

5. Eini was Histadrut chair from 2005 to May 2014, after which Avi Nissenkorn was elected to the position.

6. Haifa Chemicals was established as a government-owned company in 1967. Its primary product is fertilizer, of various kinds, and it has done particularly well in recent years due to the importance of fertilizer following rising food requirements as populations increase around the globe. The company was privatized in 1989, when it was bought up by Trance Resource Inc., a holding company controlled by the Trump Group. In 2008, the Trump Group brought in a new CEO, Nadav Shahar, known for American-style antiunion management, who split up Haifa Chemicals into two subsidiaries, North and South, under a holding company.

3. THE CORRUPT OLD STRUCTURES

1. The impression that Koach Laovdim is somehow "cool" (*magniv* in Hebrew) was noted by many people I spoke to informally in the course of this research.

2. During a private conversation, 25 October 2011.

3. Speaking at the Rosa Luxembourg Foundation seminar, "Labor Relations and Left Strategies of the Union Movement," Tel Aviv, 29 November 2011.

4. In referring to Mizrahim, religious workers, and Arabs, Raznik is emphasizing that railway workers tend not to come from elite population groups, unlike journalists, doctors, and teachers.

5. Following the campaign, the IMA appointed a committee led by Judge Dalia Dorner (the "Dorner Committee") to recommend changes to the organization's structure and decision-making processes. One recommendation was to increase representatives

from among the resident physicians on the IMA's local committees; see Public Committee Inquiring into the Structure and Functioning of the Medical Association of Israel (2013).

4. TAKING THE STRUGGLE BEYOND THE WORKPLACE

1. "Sharap": Hebrew acronym for "private medical services." It is currently offered only in two hospitals, but the state is under continuous pressure to extend the service to other hospitals (the hospital receives a percentage of the fee collected by the doctor). The Finance Ministry is mostly against it, for fear this will lead to increased wage demands in the public sector. This also illustrates the play-off between privatization and cuts to public expenditure, reflected in the different modes of privatization sought by the state (see also Achdut and Bin Nun 2012; Preminger 2016).

2. See *TheMarker* (Linder-Ganz 2011d) for an overview of the IMA's quiet support.

5. RENEGOTIATING THE ROLE OF THE HISTADRUT

1. Eini's first term as chair was unelected, because the previous chair, Amir Peretz, had had to step down due to a new law that forbids the chair from being an MK at the same time.

2. As head of the Finance Ministry's Budget Department in 2004 when Netanyahu was Finance Minister, Yogev noted that his greatest achievement had been breaking organized labor and called for reducing union density to below 20 percent (Gutwein 2012, 72).

3. Alon Hassan is chair of the Mechanical Equipment Workers' Committee at Ashdod Port and has become a symbol of Histadrut corruption and a headache for its leadership.

4. The Alignment: the name given to two governing coalitions (1965–68 and 1969–77) dominated by parties from the labor movement that later became the Labor Party.

5. In its privatized incarnation, Mankoor became ORS, now one of Israel's largest manpower agencies.

6. The issue of bargaining units is critical in Israeli labor relations. In order for a union to gain status as the representative organization, it must have as members at least one third of the workers within the bargaining unit (and more than a rival union, if there is one). This means that the size of the bargaining unit, as determined by the labor court in cases of dispute, can make or break a unionizing drive. This can be seen in the HOT case, where the labor court effectively brought the organizing drive to an end by ruling that HOT technicians should not be considered a separate bargaining unit (Collective Dispute 15391-12-11; Request for Appeal 18551-12-12).

7. Weinblum (2010) also notes the possibility of incompatibility between the approaches.

7. THE FRONTAL STRUGGLE

1. Israeli corporate tax in 2013 stood at 26.5 percent (compared to 35 percent in the United States), up from 25 percent in 2012 but down from 36 percent in 2004 (Swirsky 2013).

2. See http://www.oecd.org/social/inequality.htm. Ram (2008, 139) notes that inequality data do not include the huge number of low-income, noncitizen workers in Israel, such as the Palestinians from the occupied territories and migrant laborers; thus actual inequality among all those working in the Israeli economy is probably much greater.

3. Bezeq was founded as a state-owned corporation in 1984, taking over Israel's telecommunications that had been directly operated by the Communications Ministry. It was partially privatized in 1990–91 and fully in 2005, and the controlling shareholder is now B Communications, part of the Eurocom Communications group.

4. Clal Insurance Enterprises Holdings Ltd., part of the IDB Group (at the time controlled by Nochi Dankner).

5. Pelephone's company livery is blue and white. There may also be a suggestion that these were the real patriots, since blue and white are also the colors of the national flag—in Israel, saying you are "blue and white" is code for declaring your patriotism.

6. Migdal Insurance and Financial Holdings Ltd., controlled by Shlomo Eliahu since 2012.

7. Note that Adler had previously held the opinion that the employer has the right to speak about organizing but changed his mind (Adler, interview; see also Adler et al. 2012, 517–561).

8. Hassneh, previously a Histadrut company, was dissolved in 1992 with heavy debts. Most of the insurance policies it had managed were transferred to Migdal and Clal.

9. The Pelephone ruling was referenced in the Migdal case (Collective Dispute 13125-12-13) and the HOT case (Collective Dispute 11241-08-13).

10. HOT Telecommunication Systems Ltd.

8. THE IDEOLOGICAL STRUGGLE

1. According to the same survey, 26 percent of respondents thought organized labor harms a business's efficiency, while 53 percent disagreed with this. Some 42 percent believed a workers' organization reduced economic disparities.

2. Bibi: Prime Minister Benjamin Netanyahu; Katz: Transport Minister Yisrael Katz.

3. Hassan was at the center of allegations of corruption again in the spring and summer of 2014.

4. Since the "cottage cheese wars" between two major producers, the price of cottage cheese has become symbolic of Israel's high cost of living and was used in the slogans of the social protest movement of 2011.

5. Open Skies, signed in 2013, essentially removed some of the privileges granted to Israeli airlines and opened the way for budget airlines to operate in Israel.

6. There is a play on the Hebrew word for "ants" and the similar word for "ports."

7. Special committees set up with representatives of management and workers to determine operational issues in keeping with changes to work patterns and new technologies.

8. The limitation clause in the 1992 Basic Laws forbids infringement of declared rights "except by a statute that befits the values of the State of Israel, for a worthy goal, and not exceeding what is necessary" (translation from Hirschl 2000, 191).

9. Later Supreme Court President (1995–2006).

10. This possibility was first opened up with the 1972 amendment to the Settlement of Labor Disputes Law of 1957 (see IDI 2004, 39).

11. Indeed, this differentiation is enshrined in the 1977 amendment to the Settlement of Labor Disputes Law, which stipulates special provisions for public services (including the entire civil service, local authorities, education, health, water, and electricity) that are not differentiated from "essential services." According to this amendment, if a strike does not meet special requirements, it will be considered "unprotected," and thus the provision in the Collective Agreements Law (that participating in a strike will not be considered a breach of personal obligation) and the provision in the Civil Wrongs Ordinance (that strikes and lock-outs will not be regarded as breach of contract for purposes of tort of causing breach of contract) will not apply (Goldberg 1994, 94–95).

12. In the Bezeq case, when workers struck against threats to break Bezeq's monopoly on international calls, the labor court had to decide whether the strike was political or economic. The court ruled it was economic because it affected employment terms, but the

High Court overruled and created a new category of strike, "quasi-political," which was legitimate but must be limited to short periods of time (Mundlak 2007, 166–169).

13. R. Ben-Israel (1994, 2–3) notes that changes to the economy have meant greater integration and interdependency, which has made some services "essential" that were not considered so before: "Public concern over industrial action does not grow just out of a prejudice against unions. Public anger and anxiety over strikes arises from a wider concern with the private exercise of massive organizational power within a highly interdependent, industrial society." She fails to note, however, the huge capacity for collective action wielded by employers.

9. THE INSTITUTIONAL STRUGGLE

1. This institute has rarely been used in practice; see Finkelstein 2003.

2. Headed by Yitzhak Zamir, former attorney general and judge.

3. The presence of public representatives has sometimes been seen as merely symbolic, but Adler noted that during his term they often played a crucial role in the court's efforts to reach compromise proposals (interview).

4. In this paper, Navot and Peled argue that the balance may be shifting once more to elective institutions since the nationalist right wing is losing patience with the court's concern for Palestinian rights following the failure of the Oslo Accords and the second intifada.

5. Note that in this case the interests of the IEC management, which wanted to prevent reforms, lined up with the interests of the workers, who feared their excellent employment terms would be whittled away; see Bar-Eli 2014b.

10. CONCLUDING REMARKS TO PART 2

1. In a further twist to the relationship between the Labor Party and the Histadrut, at the beginning of 2017 Yachimovich announced that she would run in the elections for Histadrut chair, to be held in May of that year. However, she also declared her plans to make this organization "incorruptible" and "truly democratic" (Niv 2017).

2. See Collective Dispute Appeal 25476-09-12; the National Histadrut was also sympathetic to this position.

3. Mapai, the dominant party, prevented both moves since it was dependent on the Histadrut for its power; see Grinberg (1993) for a discussion of the symbiosis between the two.

4. In fact, only potentially; as noted, the institute has rarely been used.

11. LABOR REPRESENTATION OUTSIDE UNION STRUCTURES

1. It was also reflected symbolically in WAC's joint project with activist and labor artist Mike Alewitz, who painted a mural in the Israeli Arab town of Kufr Qara entitled *No Walls between Workers* (Ben Simhon 2003).

2. In 2014, the Labor Ministry, whose full name was the Ministry of Industry, Trade and Labor, changed its name to the Economics Ministry. *Challenge* was a WAC publication reporting on the union's activities and related issues. Past issues are available at the WAC offices.

3. See *Yedioth Aharonoth* Saturday supplement for 8 December 2000 for an exposé of "night-time meetings" between employment bureau officials and contractors.

4. This program, which was launched as a pilot program and has since been discontinued, aimed to put the chronically unemployed into some kind of job by training them in basic skills. Critics of the program were mainly concerned with the fact that it was run

by private, for-profit companies and with the structure of financial compensation for the companies that too easily led to exploitation of participants.

5. WAC's constitution may be viewed here: http://www.wac-maan.org.il/he/arti cle__300, and the appendix here: http://www.wac-maan.org.il/he/article__301 (both in Hebrew).

6. However, the court did not recognize WAC as the representative organization because at the time of the hearing an insufficient number of workers had signed up. This, WAC said, was due to employer pressure on workers to rescind their membership (Adiv, interview).

7. The Green Line is the common term for the borders of the State of Israel before the war of 1967.

8. See Kav Laoved position paper submitted to the Knesset Foreign Workers Committee, 1 January 2014, retrieved from: http://www.kavlaoved.org.il/en/foreign-workers-employed-agricultural-sector/.

9. See the Israel Antiquities Authority Law 1989 and the Antiquities Law 1978.

10. The amendment came into effect only in January 2008, after being repeatedly postponed for a number of years by means of the Arrangements Law.

12. PLURALISM AND THE CHANGING NATURE OF POLITICS

1. Korczynski (2003, 268) notes that the consumer has become a "figure of authority at the societal level," while Bauman (1992) places the consumer at the center of his conception of postmodern society.

2. Though, as noted above, Navot and Peled (2009) suggest that right-wing frustration with the courts' respect for Palestinian human rights may be causing a shift of power back to majoritarian institutions.

13. BETWEEN NATIONAL COMMUNITY AND CLASS SOLIDARITY

1. The violence of 1929 further dampened any hopes of cooperation along class lines; see H. Cohen 2015.

2. Unemployment stood at some 10 percent in the occupied territories toward the end of the 1960s (Arnon 2007).

3. "Peace Dividends" is from the title of Nitzan and Bichler's (1996) article.

4. The customs envelope unifies the customs and indirect taxes regime of the occupied territories and Israel. Israel controls external customs points, collects revenues, and reimburses the Palestinians' share through the Revenue Clearance Mechanism.

5. According to Sovich (2000, 68), the PGFTU has strong links with the Palestinian Authority and Fatah and is more involved in power struggles than in protecting workers' rights, more experienced in fighting the occupation (many unionists were active during the first intifada) than in organizing workers. Cooperation with the Histadrut is viewed with suspicion. The PGFTU had no records system and no financial accountability. When talks began, it was not even clear how many members it had or what funds it could muster.

6. In 1970 only 6 percent of Arab women worked outside the home, but by the mid-1990s over 16 percent were seeking work (Ashqar 1997).

7. Delta chairperson Dov Lautman, it should be noted, was Prime Minister Yitzhak Rabin's special advisor on economic issues and the first Israeli to open a factory in Egypt. He was also president of the Manufacturers Association and held meetings with Palestinian industrialists and economic leaders even before the Oslo Accords (see Almog 1993).

8. It should be noted that Mizrahi Jews were also employed in textiles, and in fact this population group was the first to be hurt by changes in the industry (see Bar-On 2007).

14. POROUS LABOR MARKET, INSULAR POLITICAL COMMUNITY

1. It must also be noted that some Palestinians feared the ruling reflected a deepening of Israel's hold on the occupied territories, though the ruling stated explicitly that it should not be seen as such.

2. The Civil Administration is Israel's administration in the occupied territories.

3. Hostility to Daam is in stark contrast to the way Hadash—the other Jewish-Arab party—is accepted. This is not the place to discuss the intricacies of the Israeli party system, but it should be noted that Hadash has a long history as part of the political establishment, and Hadash-affiliated candidates take part in Histadrut elections.

4. A former member of the Knesset is head of the Farmers Federation, and another MK leads the agricultural lobby.

5. The cost of fruits and vegetables in Israel is a sensitive issue (tomato prices are regularly reported in the daily press and compared to different time periods or between regions), and it has become a truism that farmers barely make ends meet. Indeed, during a meeting with the Knesset Committee on Foreign Workers, WAC representative Assaf Adiv suggested the import of Thai workers was a way for the government to placate farmers after it reduced export subsidies and state assistance in case of natural disasters and increased water costs for farmers.

6. This is a complex legal and cultural (not to mention theological) issue that cannot be fully discussed here; the point, however, is to emphasize the deep connection between the state and its Jewish citizens to the detriment of its non-Jewish citizens. See Ornan 2013 and Gross 2013 for a brief overview of the case.

7. Note that in this case, due to the connotations of the Hebrew term "Israeli," "Israeli labor" means "Hebrew labor" as opposed to merely labor in the State of Israel.

8. Palestinian residents are permitted to vote in the local elections under the Local Authorities Law (Elections) of 1965, but few exercise their right to vote because they do not wish to legitimize Israel's hold of the city (Sasson, Maimon, and Luster 2012).

9. "Intifada" is the name given to the Palestinian uprising against the Israeli occupation. The first began in 1987 and the second in 2005. The recent violence (toward the end of 2015) has been dubbed by many as the "intifada of knives" or "third intifada."

10. In 2002, Israel began building a physical barrier between Israel and the Palestinians, which runs roughly along the Green Line but also eats up large swathes of Palestinian territory and divides neighborhoods in East Jerusalem.

11. The various groups known as "Arabs" can be further divided, into Druze and Bedouin for example, and Israel has incorporated them to different degrees at different times, but these subdivisions are not necessary for understanding the main argument here. For a discussion of differential incorporation into the political community, see Shafir and Peled 2002.

15. CONCLUDING REMARKS TO PART 3

1. The Histadrut had reached various collective agreements with the Organization of Cleaning Enterprises and Contractors. This meant the cleaners paid an agency fee to the Histadrut though not a membership fee.

2. The Coalition in this case, for example, included women's groups, lawyers' groups, human rights groups, student groups, faculty workers' committees, and religious groups.

CONCLUSION

1. This is not the place for a discussion of the political process vis-à-vis the Palestinians, but it is worth mentioning in this context that the conflict is being increasingly

framed in terms of human rights as opposed to political emancipation or national self-determination.

2. Note that Kemp and Raijman (2008) assert that the influx of migrant labor is changing the "Jewish state," challenging national borders as migrants become permanent features of society. I do not disagree with this view, but emphasize the efforts to maintain a Jewish political community (and the accompanying nationalist rhetoric) even in the face of migrants' sometimes successful attempts to influence and participate in society through nonparliamentary, nonelectoral channels (see Kemp et al. 2000).

3. In February 2017, in the Tzarfati Garage case, WAC signed the first collective agreement between noncitizen Palestinians and an Israeli employer. This precedential case provides further support to the argument that the decline of Israeli neocorporatism opened up possibilities for those previously excluded (see WAC 2017).

4. The 1921 conference of the American Zionists, according to Frenkel, Shenhav, and Herzog (2000, 47), was a watershed moment in the shaping of socialist-colored Zionist discourse.

References

Achdut, Leah, and Gabi Bin Nun. 2012. *Ben Hatziburi l'Prati b'Maarechet Habri'ut b'Israel: Hamikre shel Sharap* [The private-public mix in the health system in Israel: The case of the private health service in public hospitals]. Jerusalem: Friedrich Ebert Foundation and the Van Leer Jerusalem Institute.

Achdut, Leah, Victor Sula, and Zvi Eisenbach. 1998. *Haasakat Ovdim Be'emtza'ut Hevrot Koach Adam: Hekef Hatofa'a uMe'afyene'ha* [The employment of workers through manpower agencies: Scope and characteristics]. Jerusalem: New General Federation of Labor and the Friedrich Ebert Foundation.

Adiv, Assaf. 2011. "Lemi Do'eg Yor Hahistadrut?" [About whom does the Histadrut chair concern himself?]. *TheMarker*, 7 December.

Adiv, Assaf, and Asma Agbarieh-Zahalka. 2011. "WAC Maan Representatives at LaborStart International Conference in Istanbul." Retrieved from http://www.wac-maan.org.il/en/article__228/wac_maan_representatives_at_laborstart_international_conference_in_istanbul.

Adler, Steve, Yitzhak Eliasof, Nili Arad, Guy Davidov, Sigal Davidov-Motola, Yitzhak Zamir, Orna Lin, and Guy Mundlak, eds. 2012. *Sefer Elika Barak-Ussoskin* [Essays in honor of Elika Barak-Ussoskin]. Jerusalem: Hebrew University of Jerusalem and Nevo Publishing.

Agricultural Ministry. 2008. "Hoda'a La'itonut: Tochnit Hadasha Tenaseh Lehahzir et Ha'israelim le'Avodat Ha'adama" [Press release: New program will try to bring Israelis back to working the land]. 6 July. Jerusalem. Retrieved from http://www.moag.gov.il/yhidotmisrad/dovrut/publication/2008/Pages/avoda%20ivrit.aspx.

Ajzenstadt, Mimi, and Zeev Rosenhek. 2002. "Privatization and New Modes of State Intervention: The Long-Term Care Program in Israel." *Journal of Social Policy* 29 (2): 247–262.

Alberti, Gabriella, Jane Holgate, and Maite Tapia. 2013. "Organizing Migrants as Workers or as Migrant Workers? Intersectionality, Trade Unions and Precarious Workers." *International Journal of Human Resource Management* 24 (22): 4132–4148.

Alford, Robert, and Roger Friedland. 1985. *Powers of Theory: Capitalism, the State and Democracy*. Cambridge: Cambridge University Press.

Almog, Ruth. 1993. "30 Shana shel Textil: Sihot im Dov Lautman" [30 years of textiles: Conversation with Dov Lautman]. *Yalkut* 134:22–24.

Amos, Orna, and Tal Baharav. 2012. "The Organizing of the Cleaners at Ben-Gurion University of the Negev as a Case Study of Coping with Multi-Dimensional Institutional Oppression." In *Haasaka Poganit: Hadara veNitzul Shitati'im b'Shuk Ha'avoda* [Precarious employment: Systematic exclusion and exploitation in the labor market], edited by Daniel Mishori and Anat Maor, 113–128. Ramat Gan: Social-Economic Academy and Achva Press.

Anderson, Bridget. 2010. "Mobilizing Migrants, Making Citizens: Migrant Domestic Workers as Political Agents." *Ethnic and Racial Studies* 33 (1): 60–74.

Appelberg, Shelly, and Michael Rochwerger. 2013. "'Tisporet' shel 1.8 Milliard Shekel: Hapoalim v'Elbit Hadmaya Hatmu al Hesder Hov" ["Haircut" of 1.8 billion shekels: Hapoalim and Elbit Imaging sign debt restructuring agreement]. *TheMarker*, 29 December. Retrieved from https://www.themarker.com/markets/1.2202498.

Arian, Asher. 1998. "Parties in Accelerated Change." In *Ketz Hamiflagot: Hademokratia Ha'Israelit b'Metzuka* [*The Demise of Parties in Israel*], edited by Dani Koren, 91–128. Tel Aviv: Hakibbutz Hameuchad.

Arian, Asher, and Ilan Talmud. 1991. "Electoral Politics and Economic Control in Israel." In *Labor Parties in Postindustrial Societies*, edited by Frances Fox Piven, 169–189. Cambridge: Polity Press.

Arlosoroff, Meirav. 2012. "Oved Nikayon She'yikalet k'Oved Medina Yistaker ad 8,200 Shekel" [Cleaner who is taken on as state employee will earn up to 8,200 shekel]. *TheMarker*, 30 January. Retrieved from https://www.themarker.com/career/1.1629079.

———. 2013a. "Al Tit'u – Hama'avak Ha'amiti hu Lehahzir et Hamafsek leyadei Hatzibur" [Don't be mistaken – the real struggle is putting the switch back in the hands of the public]. *TheMarker*, 16 July.

———. 2013b. "Thilata shel Politica Hadasha" [The beginning of a new politics]. *TheMarker*, 22 April.

———. 2013c. "Tiutat Hok Borerut Hova: Ovdim b'Sherutim Hiyuni'im lo Yochlu Lishbot neged Yitzirat Taharut" [Compulsory arbitration draft legislation: Workers in vital services will not be able to strike against the creation of competition]. *TheMarker*, 23 June.

Arnon, Arie. 2007. "Israeli Policy towards the Occupied Palestinian Territories: The Economic Dimension, 1967–2007." *Middle East Journal* 61 (4): 573–595.

Ashqar, Ahmad. 1997. "Hamizrah Hatikhon Hahadash neged Hatofrot Hafalestiniot" [The new Middle East versus Palestinian seamstresses]. *M'Tzad Sheni* 7:20–21.

Avriel, Eytan. 2013. "Hahesder b'IDB eino Savir" [The deal at IDB is unreasonable]. *TheMarker*, 13 March. Retrieved from https://www.themarker.com/markets/1.1962647.

Azulay, Yuval. 2013a. "Hapitaron l'Mahsor b'Ovdim? Hata'asiyanim Rotzim Leyaveh Ba'alei Miktzoa Yehudim m'Ha'olam" [The solution to the shortage of workers? The industrialists want to import professional Jews from around the world]. *Globes*, 27 February. Retrieved from http://www.globes.co.il/news/article.aspx?did=1000825935.

———. 2013b. "'Lo Eten Lahistadrut Lehikanes l'Mif'al sheli u'La'asot Propagandot'" ["I won't let the Histadrut enter my factory and spread propaganda"]. *Globes*, 21 February. Retrieved from http://www.globes.co.il/news/article.aspx?did=1000824330.

Azulay, Yuval, and Shay Niv. 2012. "Hamif'al Nisgar: Kitan Mafsika et Hayitzur b'Dimona" [The factory is closing: Kitan stops production in Dimona]. *Globes*, 2 December. Retrieved from http://www.globes.co.il/news/article.aspx?did=1000802612.

Baccaro, Lucio. 2003. "What Is Alive and What Is Dead in the Theory of Corporatism." *British Journal of Industrial Relations* 41 (4): 683–706.

———. 2010. "Does the Global Financial Crisis Mark a Turning Point for Labour?" *Socio-Economic Review* 8 (2): 341–348.

Baccaro, Lucio, and Chris Howell. 2011. "A Common Neoliberal Trajectory: The Transformation of Industrial Relations in Advanced Capitalism." *Politics and Society* 39 (4): 521–563.

Badigannavar, Vidu, and John Kelly. 2011. "Partnership and Organizing: An Empirical Assessment of Two Contrasting Approaches to Union Revitalization in the UK." *Economic and Industrial Democracy* 32 (1): 5–27.

Bar-Eli, Avi. 2012. "Rosh Hava'ad Ka'as – Vehaoniya Haturkit Nitke'ah b'Namal Ashdod" [Committee Chair got Angry – and Turkish Ship got Stuck in Ashdod Port]. *TheMarker*, 16 January.

———. 2013a. "Doch: Hanezeq Mehatifkud Halakui shel Hanamalim – 5 Milliard Shach Bashana" [Report: The damage from defective port operations – 5 billion shekels a year]. *TheMarker*, 30 April. Retrieved from https://www.themarker.com/dynamo/1.2007414.

———. 2013b. "Namal Ashdod Muf'al Tahat Iyumim" [Ashdod Port is operated under terror of threats]. *TheMarker*, 17 January.

——. 2013c. "Reshut Hahagbalim: Lehayev Mesirat Retzifei Hanamal Hahadashim l'Zachiyanim Prati'im" [Anti-Trust Authority: Compel new port wharfs to be transferred to private franchisees]. *TheMarker*, 1 May. Retrieved from https://www.the marker.com/dynamo/1.2008449.

——. 2014a. "Beit Hadin Hekpi et Tahanat Hakoach Hapratit Hagdola b'Israel" [Labor court freezes largest private power station in Israel]. *TheMarker*, 27 April.

——. 2014b. "Hatargil shel Hevrat Hahashmal Hetzliah: Beit Hadin l'Avoda Kovel et Hamedina" [IEC trick worked: The labor court ties up the state]. *TheMarker*, 5 May. Retrieved from https://www.themarker.com/dynamo/1.2288981.

Bar-Eli, Avi, and Ora Coren. 2013. "Bennett: Hayalim Yaf'ilu et Hanamalim Hamushvatim; Hassan: Lo Yode'a im Litzhok o Livkot" [Bennett: Soldiers will operate ports during strike; Hassan: I don't know whether to laugh or cry]. *TheMarker*, 19 May. Retrieved from https://www.themarker.com/dynamo/1.2023427.

Bar-Eli, Avi, and Daniel Shmil. 2013. "Lamemshala ein Koach Letapel Bava'adei Hanamalim. Hem Mekablim Kol Ma she'Dorshim" [The government doesn't have the power to deal with the port committees. They get whatever they demand]. *TheMarker*, 16 January.

Bar-Eli, Avi, and Hila Weissberg. 2012. "Va'adat Hakalkala Kiyema Diyun Dahuf al Hashvatat Harakevet" [The Economics Committee held an urgent meeting about the railway strike]. *TheMarker*, 15 February. Retrieved from https://www.themarker.com/dynamo/1.1642021.

Bar-Eli, Avi, Daniel Shmil, and Zvi Zarhia. 2012. "Sar Hatahbura Hodia al Pitzul Harakevet l'Shalosh Hevrot Banot; Eini: zo Hafkerut" [Transport minister announces division of railway into three subsidiaries; Eini: This is irresponsibility]. *TheMarker*, 5 February. Retrieved from https://www.themarker.com/dynamo/1.1656462.

Bar-Eli, Avi, Daniel Shmil, Lior Dattel, Haim Bior, and Hila Weissberg. 2011. "Local Authorities the Biggest Users of Contract Workers." *Haaretz*, 8 November. Retrieved from http://www.haaretz.com/local-authorities-the-biggest-users-of-contract-workers-1.394301.

Barkat, Amiram. 2014. "Gov't, IEC Employees to Resume Reform Talks." *Globes*, 13 May. Retrieved from http://www.globes.co.il/en/article-govt-iec-employees-to-resume-reform-talks-1000938160.

Bar-On, Shani. 2007. "Hozeh she'Hufar: Ovdim u'Medina b'Ofakim 1955–1981" [Violated contract: Workers and state in Ofakim, 1955–1981]. *Iyunim b'Tkumat Israel* 17:287–317.

Barzilai, Gad. 1998. "Courts as Hegemonic Institutions: The Israeli Supreme Court in a Comparative Perspective." *Israel Affairs* 5 (2–3): 15–33.

Bauman, Zygmunt. 1992. *Intimations of Postmodernity*. London: Routledge.

Beck, Ulrich, and Elizabeth Beck-Gernsheim. 2002. *Individualization*. London: Sage Publications.

Beetham, David. 2004. "Civil Society: Market Economy and Democratic Polity." In *Civil Society in Democratization*, edited by Peter Burnell and Peter Calvert, 72–89. London: Frank Cass.

Bell, Daniel. 1960. *The End of Ideology: On the Exhaustion of Political Ideas in the Fifties*. New York: Free Press of Glencoe.

Bellin, Eva. 2000. "Contingent Democrats: Industrialists, Labor, and Democratization in Late-Developing Countries." *World Politics* 52 (2): 175–205.

Bendor, Ariel. 1998. "Political Parties: The Legal Aspect." In *Ketz Hamiflagot: Hademokratia Ha'Israelit b'Metzuka* [*The Demise of Parties in Israel*], edited by Dani Koren, 274–280. Tel Aviv: Hakibbutz Hameuchad.

Ben Efrat, Jonathan. 2008. *Shesh Komot l'Gehinom* [Six floors to hell]. Israel: Claudius Films [film].

Ben-Eliezer, Uri. 1993. "The Meaning of Political Participation in a Nonliberal Democracy." *Comparative Politics* 25 (4): 397–412.

Ben-Israel, Ruth. 1993. "Tafkido u'Mekomo shel Bet Hadin l'Avoda b'Ma'arekhet Hamishpat Ha'Israelit" [The role and status of the labor court in the Israeli legal system]. *Hapraklit*, 50th Anniversary Volume, 431–477.

——. 1994. "Introduction to Strikes and Lock-Outs: A Comparative Perspective." *Bulletin of Comparative Labour Relations* 29:1–29.

Ben-Israel, Yael. 2013. "Textil Politi: Me'atzvim Israelim Meyatzrim Bgadim b'Shithei Hagada" [Political textile: Israeli designers produce clothes in the West Bank]. *Globes*, 13 June. Retrieved from http://www.globes.co.il/news/article.aspx?did=1000852392.

Benjamin, Orly, Deborah Bernstein, and Pnina Motzafi-Haller. 2010. "Emotional Politics in Cleaning Work: The Case of Israel." *Human Relations* 64 (3): 337–357.

Bennett, Naftali. 2013. "Al Tehiyu Frayerim: He'esiku Nashim, Aravim v'Haredim" [Don't be suckers: Employ women, Arabs, and Haredim]. *TheMarker*, 22 October. Retrieved from https://www.themarker.com/career/1.2146112.

Ben Simhon, Dani. 2003. "Mike Alewitz in Kufr Qara." *Challenge* 81. Retrieved from http://www.challenge-mag.com/81/alewitz.htm.

——. 2007. "Rothschild Blof" [Rothschild bluff]. *Haaretz*, 9 July. Retrieved from https://www.haaretz.co.il/misc/1.1423932.

Berger, Suzanne. 1981. "Introduction." In *Organizing Interests in Western Europe: Pluralism, Corporatism and the Transformation of Politics*, edited by Suzanne Berger, 1–26. Cambridge: Cambridge University Press.

Bernstein, Deborah. 1983. "Economic Growth and Female Labor: The Case of Israel." *Sociological Review* 31 (2): 263–292.

——. 1986. "The Subcontracting of Cleaning Work: A Case in the Casualisation of Labor." *Sociological Review* 34 (2): 396–422.

——. 1996. "Brit Poalei Eretz Israel: Irgunim shel Poalim Aravim u'Mediniut 'Ha'avoda Ha'Ivrit'" [The Palestine Labor League and the Hebrew labor policy trap]. *Megamot* 37 (3): 229–253.

——. 2000. *Constructing Boundaries: Jewish and Arab Workers in Mandatory Palestine.* Albany: State University of New York Press.

Bior, Haim. 2012a. "Mapala l'Edra'i v'Koach Laovdim: Hahistadrut Ha'irgun Hayatzig Barakevet" [Fall for Edra'i and Koach Laovdim: The Histadrut is the representative organization at the railway]. *TheMarker*, 15 July. Retrieved from https://www.themarker.com/career/1.1776773.

——. 2012b. "'Ovdei Harakevet Pohadim La'azov et Hahistadrut'" ["Rail workers scared to leave the Histadrut"]. *TheMarker*, 12 July. Retrieved from https://www.themarker.com/news/1.1773985.

——. 2013a. "Alon Hassan Hozer: Hahistadrut Heshiva L'avoda et Yor Va'ad Namal Ashdod" [Alon Hassan returns: The Histadrut reinstated chair of Ashdod Port committee]. *TheMarker*, 30 September. Retrieved from https://www.themarker.com/dynamo/1.2129034.

——. 2013b. "Beit Hadin l'Avoda: Falestinim Hamu'asakim Bahitnahluyot Zaka'im l'Sachar al pi Hadin Ha'Israeli" [Labor court: Palestinians employed in settlements entitled to wages according to Israeli law]. *TheMarker*, 22 June. Retrieved from https://www.themarker.com/career/1.2052563.

——. 2013c. "'Isur Hashvita b'Sherutim Hiyuni'im Yif'al gam l'Tovat Haovdim'" ["Forbidding strikes in essential services will be good for the workers too"]. *TheMarker*, 24 June. Retrieved from https://www.themarker.com/career/1.2053697.

——. 2013d. "Lishkat Ha'irgunim Hakalkali'im: Mekavim she'Beit Hadin l'Avoda Yisager" [Economic Organizations Bureau: We hope the labor court will close]. *TheMarker*, 31 January.

Bior, Haim, and Daniel Shmil. 2012. "Ha'aracha: Beit Hadin Yidhe Bakashat Koach Laovdim l'Hakara k'Irgun Yatzig Barakevet" [Assessment: Court to reject Koach Laovdim's request to get representative status in railway]. *TheMarker*, 8 July. Retrieved from https://www.themarker.com/dynamo/1.1751072.

Boso, Nimrod. 2011. "800 Poalei Binyan shel Hevrat Yilmezler Haturkit Yagiyu l'Israel" [800 construction workers from the Turkish firm Yilmezler will come to Israel]. *TheMarker*, 2 December. Retrieved from https://www.themarker.com/realestate/1.1581488.

Brenner, Neri. 2011. "Hastudentim l'Refo'ah Shovtim: 'Lo Nishtok Od'" [Medical students strike: "We won't be silent anymore"]. *Ynet*, 24 October. Retrieved from http://www.ynet.co.il/articles/0,7340,L-4138029,00.html.

Brown, Wendy. 2015. *Undoing the Demos: Neoliberalism's Stealth Revolution*. New York: Zone Books.

Camfield, David. 2006. "Neoliberalism and Working Class Resistance in British Columbia: The Hospital Employees' Union Struggle, 2002–2004." *Labour/Le Travail* 57: 9–41.

Chandhoke, Neera. 2004. "The 'Civil' and the 'Political' in Civil Society: The Case of India." In *Civil Society in Democratization*, edited by Peter Burnell and Peter Calvert, 143–166. London: Frank Cass.

Cobble, Sue, and Leah Vosko. 2000. "Historical Perspectives on Representing Nonstandard Workers." In *Nonstandard Work: The Nature and Challenges of Changing Employment Arrangements*, edited by Françoise Carré, Marianne A. Ferber, Lonnie Golden, and Stephen A. Herzenberg, 291–312. Champaign, IL: Industrial Relations Research Association.

Cohen, Amiram. 2007. "Misrad Hatamat Ma'ashim: Hevrot Koach Adam Israeliyot Poalot b'Thailand kidei Letarped Haba'at Ovdim Zarim b'Ezrat Ha'Um" [Labor Ministry accuses: Israeli manpower companies acting in Thailand to torpedo import of foreign workers with the help of the UN]. *Haaretz*, 27 June. Retrieved from https://www.haaretz.co.il/misc/1.1421080.

Cohen, Hillel. 2015. *Year Zero of the Arab-Israeli Conflict 1929*. Waltham, MA: Brandeis University Press.

Cohen, Yinon, Yitzhak Haberfeld, Guy Mundlak, and Ishak Saporta. 2003. "Unpacking Union Density: Membership and Coverage in the Transformation of the Israeli IR System." *Industrial Relations* 42 (4): 692–711.

Committee Investigating the Labor Courts (the "Zamir Committee"). 2006. "Doch Hava'ada Lebdikat Batei Hadin Le'avoda" [Report of the Committee Investigating the Labor Courts]. Jerusalem.

Crouch, Colin. 1983. "Pluralism and the New Corporatism: A Rejoinder." *Political Studies* 31 (3): 452–460.

——. 2006. "Neocorporatism and Democracy." In *The Diversity of Democracy: Corporatism, Social Order and Political Conflict*, edited by Colin Crouch and Wolfgang Streeck, 46–70. Cheltenham: Edward Elgar.

Davidi, Ephraim. 2012. "Each Generation and Its Wounded: A Short History of Exploitative Work in Israel." In *Haasaka Poganit: Hadara veNitzul Shitati'im b'Shuk Ha'avoda* [Precarious employment: Systematic exclusion and exploitation in the labor market], edited by Daniel Mishori and Anat Maor, 39–44. Ramat Gan: Social-Economic Academy and Achva Press.

Davidov, Guy. 2015. "Indirect Employment: Should Lead Companies Be Liable?" *Comparative Labor Law and Policy Journal* 37 (5): 5–37.

Delanty, Gerard, and Engin F. Isin. 2003. "Introduction: Reorienting Historical Sociology." In *Handbook of Historical Sociology*, edited by Gerard Delanty and Engin F. Isin, 1–8. London: Sage Publications.

De Vries, David. 2002. "Drawing the Repertoire of Collective Action: Labour Zionism and Strikes in 1920s Palestine." *Middle Eastern Studies* 38 (3): 93–122.

Dörre, Klaus. 2011. "Functional Changes in the Trade Unions: From Intermediary to Fractal Organization?" *International Journal of Action Research* 7 (1): 8–48.

Drori, Israel. 2000. *The Seam Line: Arab Workers and Jewish Managers in the Israeli Textile Industry*. Stanford: Stanford University Press.

Elis, Niv. 2013. "Flug: Israel must Deal with Discrimination against Arabs or Suffer Economic Consequences." *Jerusalem Post*, 29 October. Retrieved from http://www.jpost.com/Business/Business-News/Flug-Israel-must-deal-with-discrimination-against-Arabs-or-suffer-economic-consequences-330038.

Erickson, Christopher L., Catherine L. Fisk, Ruth Milkman, Daniel J. B. Mitchell, and Kent Wong. 2002. "Justice for Janitors in Los Angeles: Lessons from Three Rounds of Negotiations." *British Journal of Industrial Relations* 40 (3): 543–567.

Even, Dan. 2011a. "Menahelei Mahlekot b'Shva u'b'Ichilov Tzfu'im Lehitztaref Lamitpatrim" [Department directors at Sheba and Ichilov expected to join those resigning]. *Haaretz*, 15 November. Retrieved from https://www.haaretz.co.il/news/health/1.1566637.

——. 2011b. "Misrad Habriyut Hediah et Gamzu Minihul Mashber Harefuah" [Health Ministry removes Gamzu from managing health service crisis]. *Haaretz*, 18 November. Retrieved from https://www.haaretz.co.il/news/health/1.1569378.

Farsakh, Leila. 2005. *Palestinian Labour Migration to Israel: Labour, Land and Occupation*. Routledge: Abingdon.

Fick, Barbara. 2009. "Not Just Collective Bargaining: The Role of Trade Unions in Creating and Maintaining a Democratic Society." *Working USA* 12 (2): 249–265.

Filc, Dani. 2004. "Israel Model 2000: Neo-Liberal Post-Fordism," in *Shilton Ha'hon: Hahevra Ha'Israelit Ba'idan Haglobali* [The power of property: Israeli society in the global age], edited by Dani Filc and Uri Ram, 34–56. Tel Aviv: Hakibbutz Hameuchad.

——. 2005. "The Health Business under Neo-Liberalism: The Israeli Case." *Critical Social Policy* 25 (2): 180–197.

Filc, Dani, and Uri Ram, eds. 2004. *Shilton Ha'hon: Hahevra Ha'Israelit Ba'idan Haglobali* [The power of property: Israeli society in the global age]. Tel Aviv: Hakibbutz Hameuchad.

Filut, Adrian. 2011. "B'Hora'at Beit Hadin L'Avoda: Hashvita Haclalit Histayima b-10:00" [In keeping with labor court order: General strike ended at 10:00]. *Globes*, 7 November. Retrieved from http://www.globes.co.il/news/article.aspx?did=1000695450.

——. 2012. "Yachimovitch l'Steinitz: 'Eich Tzrichim Lehargish kol Ha'idiotim Sheshilmu Mas b'Zman? Ata Noten Hatavot l'Hevrot Ha'anak – Lama lo l'Hanut Makolet o l'Phoenicia?'" [Yachimovitch to Steinitz: "How are all the idiots who pay tax on time supposed to feel? You give benefits to giant corporations – why not to the corner store or to Phoenicia?"]. *Globes*, 6 September. Retrieved from http://www.globes.co.il/news/article.aspx?did=1000782967.

Filut, Adrian, and Ela Levy-Weinrib. 2012. "Steinitz Metachnen Hakalot Mas b'Milliardei Shkalim l'Ta'agidei Ha'anak" [Steinitz planning tax breaks of billions of shekels for the giant corporations]. *Globes*, 28 May. Retrieved from http://www.globes.co.il/news/article.aspx?did=1000752317.

Filut, Adrian, Yuval Azulay, and Amiram Barkat. 2012. "Ha'erev: Ma'amatz Lehafsik et Hashvita Hagdola Banamalim" [This evening: Efforts to stop big strike in ports]. *Globes*, 26 February. Retrieved from http://www.globes.co.il/news/article.aspx?did=1000727808.

Filut, Adrian, Amiram Barkat, and Yuval Azulay. 2012. "Ovdei Hanamalim Hazru L'avoda B'tom Yom Ehad shel Shvita" [Port workers return to work after one day's strike]. *Globes*, 26 February. Retrieved from http://www.globes.co.il/news/article.aspx?did=1000728190.

Finance Ministry. 2007. "Doch Hava'ada Le'itzuv Mediniut Banoseh Ovdim Lo-Israelim (Doch Eckstein)" [Report of Committee for Shaping Policy regarding Non-Israeli Workers (the Eckstein Report)]. Jerusalem.

Fine, Janice. 2005. *Workers Centers: Organizing Communities at the Edge of the Dream.* Ithaca, NY: Cornell University Press.

Fine, Robert, and Daniel Chernilo. 2003. "Classes and Nations in Recent Historical Sociology." In *Handbook of Historical Sociology*, edited by Gerard Delanty and Engin F. Isin, 235–249. London: Sage Publications.

Finkelstein, Keren. 2003. "Pitaron Lashvit b'Migzar Hatzibori: Shimush Ya'il Bamosad l'Borerut Muskemet" [Solution to strikes in the public sector: Using the Agreed Arbitration Institution]. Unpublished. Jerusalem: Institute for Advanced Strategic and Political Studies.

Flecker, Jörg, and Christoph Hermann. 2011. "The Liberalization of Public Services: Company Reactions and Consequences for Employment and Working Conditions." *Economic and Industrial Democracy* 32 (3): 523–544.

Freeman, Richard, and James Medoff. 1984. *What Do Unions Do?* New York: Basic Books.

Frege, Carola, and John Kelly. 2003. "Union Revitalization Strategies in Comparative Perspective." *European Journal of Industrial Relations* 9 (1): 7–24.

Frenkel, Michal, Yehuda Shenhav, and Hannah Herzog. 2000. "The Cultural Wellsprings of Israeli Capitalism: The Impact of Private Capital and Industry on the Shaping of the Dominant Zionist Ideology." In *The New Israel: Peacemaking and Liberalization*, edited by Gershon Shafir and Yoav Peled, 43–70. Boulder: Westview.

Frost, Mervyn. 2005. "Global Civil Society, Civilians and Citizens." In *The Idea of Global Civil Society: Politics and Ethics in a Globalizing Era*, edited by Randall Germain and Michael Kenny, 122–138. New York: Routledge.

Gargir, Yaacov. 1995. "Tofrim Leshalom: Shituf Peula Eyzori b'Anaf Hatextil" [Sewing for peace: Regional cooperation in the textile branch]. *Yalkut* 140:4–7, 48.

Gavizon, Yoram. 2013. "Tayasei El Al Mekarka'im et Hasikui Lehatzil Ota" [El Al pilots are grounding the chance of saving it]. *MarkerWeek*, 13 September.

Gidron, Benjamin, Michal Bar, and Hagai Katz. 2004. *The Israeli Third Sector: Between Welfare State and Civil Society.* New York: Kluwer Academic/Plenum Publishers.

Gill-McLure, Whyeda. 2007. "Fighting Marketization: An Analysis of Municipal Manual Labor in the United Kingdom and the United States." *Labor Studies Journal* 32 (1): 41–59.

Globes. 2012a. "Eini: 'Hahistadrut Teshalem Sachar l'Ovdei Pelephone Hashovtim'" [Eini: "The Histadrut will pay the wages of striking Pelephone workers"]. 14 December. Retrieved from http://www.globes.co.il/news/article.aspx?did=1000806359.

——. 2012b. "Israel Katz: 'Od Shvita kazo Ve'ani Soger et Harakevet'" [Israel Katz: "Another strike like that and I'll close the railway"]. 18 February. Retrieved from http://www.globes.co.il/news/article.aspx?did=1000725781.

Globes and Lilach Weissman. 2012. "Beit Hadin Horeh l'Ovdei Harakevet Lahazor La'avod; Hava'ad Hit'akev" [Court orders rail workers back to work; the committee delays]. *Globes*, 14 February. Retrieved from http://www.globes.co.il/news/article.aspx?did=1000724514.

Goldberg, Menachem. 1994. "Israel." *Bulletin of Comparative Labour Relations* 29:83–100.

Goldstein, Daniel. 2012. "Decolonialising 'Actually Existing Neoliberalism.'" *Social Anthropology* 20 (3): 304–309.

Gordon, Jennifer. 2005. *Suburban Sweatshops: The Fight for Immigrant Rights.* Cambridge, MA: Harvard University Press.

Gozansky, Tamar. 1986. *Hitpathut Hacapitalism b'Falestina* [Development of capitalism in Palestine]. Haifa: Mifalim Universita'im Lehotza'a La'or.

Grinberg, Lev. 1993. *Hahistadrut m'al Hakol* [The Histadrut above all]. Jerusalem: Nevo Publishing.

——. 1996. "Ovdim Halashim, Ovdim Hazakim: Zramim Bakalkala Hapolitit Ha'Israelit 1967–1994" [Weak workers, strong workers: Currents in Israel's political economy, 1967–1994]. *Te'oria uBikoret* 9:61–80.

——. 2001. "Social and Political Economy." In *Megamot Bahevra Ha'Israelit* [Trends in Israeli society], edited by Ephraim Yaar and Zeev Shavit, 585–704. Tel Aviv: Open University.

——. 2003. "A Historical Slip of the Tongue, or What Can the Arab-Jewish Transportation Strike Teach Us about the Israeli-Palestinian Conflict?" *International Journal of Middle Eastern Studies* 35 (3): 371–391.

——. 2011. "The Reversal of Citizenship: The Lebanon War and Intifada in the 1980s and the 2000s." In *Democratic Citizenship and War*, edited by Yoav Peled, Noah Lewin-Epstein, Guy Mundlak, and Jean L. Cohen, 217–230. Oxon: Routledge.

Grinberg, Lev, and Gershon Shafir. 2000. "Economic Liberalization and the Breakup of the Histadrut's Domain." In *The New Israel: Peacemaking and Liberalization*, edited by Gershon Shafir and Yoav Peled, 103–127. Boulder: Westview.

Gross, Aeyal. 1998. "The Politics of Rights in Israeli Constitutional Law." *Israel Studies* 3 (2): 80–118.

——. 2000. "The Israeli Constitution: A Tool for Distributive Justice, or a Tool that Prevents It?" In *Tzedek Halukati b'Israel* [Distributive justice in Israel], edited by Menachem Mautner, 79–96. Tel Aviv: Ramot.

——. 2013. "Psak Din Haleum Ha'Israeli: Leumiyut al Cheshbon Ezrachut" [Israeli nation ruling: Nationalism at the expense of citizenship]. *Haaretz*, 3 October. Retrieved from http://www.haaretz.co.il/news/law/.premium-1.2131385.

Gumbrell-McCormick, Rebecca, and Richard Hyman. 2013. *Trade Unions in Western Europe: Hard Times, Hard Choices*. Oxford: Oxford University Press.

Gutmann, Emmanuel. 1998. "A Welcome or Expected Death: The Fate of Political Parties." In *Ketz Hamiflagot: Hademokratia Ha'Israelit b'Metzuka* [*The Demise of Parties in Israel*], edited by Dani Koren, 45–53. Tel Aviv: Hakibbutz Hameuchad.

Gutwein, Danny. 2012. "The Privatization of Labor Relations as the Political Logic of the Dismantling of the Welfare State." In *Haasaka Poganit: Hadara veNitzul Shitati'im b'Shuk Ha'avoda* [Precarious employment: Systematic exclusion and exploitation in the labor market], edited by Daniel Mishori and Anat Maor, 61–74. Ramat Gan: Social-Economic Academy and Achva Press.

Haberfeld, Yitchak. 1995. "Why Do Workers Join Unions? The Case of Israel." *Industrial and Labor Relations Review* 48 (4): 656–670.

Haidar, Aziz. 2008. *The Arab Labor Force in Israel: From Felah'im to Foreign Workers*. Ra'anana: Hebrew University and Harry S. Truman Research Institute for Peace.

Handels, Shuki. 2003. *Me'avtehim Veshomrim b'Israel 1995–2003* [Security guards and watchmen in Israel, 1995–2003]. Jerusalem: Ministry of Industry, Trade and Labor.

Hannan, Charity-Ann, Harald Bauder, and John Shields. 2016. "'Illegalized' Migrant Workers and the Struggle for a Living Wage." *Alternate Routes* 27:109–136.

Harel, Aharon. 2004. *Ben Binyan l'Heres: Hahistadrut u'Tnu'at Ha'avoda 1956–65* [Crisis in the labor movement]. Tel Aviv: Am Oved.

Harpaz, Itzhak. 2005. "Ha'asaka Poganit: Hamea Ha-19 Kvar Can" [Harmful employment: The nineteenth century is already here]. *Mashabei Enosh* 18 (210): 10–13.

——. 2007. "The State of Trade Unionism in Israel." In *Trade Union Revitalization: Trends and Prospects in 34 Countries*, edited by Craig Phelan, 445–460. Bern: Peter Lang.

——. 2013. "Beit Hadin l'Avoda lo Moteh l'Tovat Haovdim" [The labor court is not biased towards the workers]. *TheMarker*, 16 May.

Harvey, David. 2005. *A Brief History of Neoliberalism*. Oxford: Oxford University Press.

——. 2007. "Neoliberalism as Creative Destruction." *Annals of the American Academy of Political and Social Science* 610:22–44.

Hasson, Nir. 2011. "Aharei 36 Shana: Iriyat Maaleh Adumim Takir b'Hokei Avoda Ha'Israeli'im" [After 36 years: Maaleh Adumim to recognize Israeli labor law]. *Haaretz*, 8 November. Retrieved from https://www.haaretz.co.il/news/education/1.1560733.

Hayot, Ilanit. 2014. "Coca Cola Israel Hashuda Shenitzla et Kocha Hamonopolisti" [Coca-Cola Israel suspected of exploiting its monopolistic power]. *Globes*, 12 February.

Heckscher, Charles, and John McCarthy. 2014. "Transient Solidarities: Commitment and Collective Action in Post-Industrial Societies." *British Journal of Industrial Relations* 52 (4): 627–657.

Heery, Edmund. 2002. "Partnership versus Organising: Alternative Futures for British Trade Unionism." *Industrial Relations Journal* 33 (1): 20–35.

——. 2003. "Trade Unions and Industrial Relations." In *Understanding Work and Employment: Industrial Relations in Transition*, edited by Peter Ackers and Adrian Wilkinson, 278–304. Oxford: Oxford University Press.

——. 2009. "Trade Unions and Contingent Labor: Scale and Method." *Cambridge Journal of Regions, Economy and Society* 2:429–442.

Helman, Sara. 2013. "Keytzad Kupayot, Menakot u'Metaplot Siyud hafchu l'Yazamot: Sadna'ot M'revaha l'Avoda Vekinun Ha'atzmi Haneo-Liberali" [How checkout girls, cleaners, and caregivers became entrepreneurs: "Welfare to Work" workshops and the formation of the neoliberal self]. *Soziologia Israelit* 14 (2): 312–335.

Hermann, Christoph, and Jörg Flecker, eds. 2012. *Privatization of Public Services: Impacts for Employment, Working Conditions, and Service Quality in Europe*. New York: Routledge.

Heruti-Sover, Tali. 2013. "10 Shkalim b'Sha'a, bli Tlush u'lelo Zchuyot" [10 shekels an hour, without wage slip and without rights]. *TheMarker*, 9 May. Retrieved from https://www.themarker.com/career/1.2015929.

Hickey, Robert, Sarosh Kuruvilla, and Tashlin Lakhani. 2010. "No Panacea for Success: Member Activism, Organizing and Union Renewal." *British Journal of Industrial Relations* 48 (1): 53–83.

Hilgers, Mathieu. 2012. "The Historicity of the Neoliberal State." *Social Anthropology* 20 (1): 80–94.

Hirschl, Ran. 1997. "The 'Constitutional Revolution' and the Emergence of a New Economic Order in Israel." *Israel Studies* 2 (1): 136–155.

——. 2000. "The Great Economic-Juridical Shift: The Legal Arena and the Transformation of Israel's Economic Order." In *The New Israel: Peacemaking and Liberalization*, edited by Gershon Shafir and Yoav Peled, 189–215. Boulder: Westview.

Holgate, Jane. 2005. "Organising Migrant Workers: A Case Study of Working Conditions and Unionisation at a Sandwich Factory in London." *Work, Employment and Society* 19 (3): 463–480.

Horowitz, Dan, and Moshe Lissak. 1978. *Origins of the Israeli Polity: Palestine under the Mandate*. Chicago: University of Chicago Press.

Hovel, Revital. 2013. "Supreme Court Rejects Citizens' Request to Change Nationality from 'Jewish' to 'Israeli.'" *Haaretz*, 3 October. Retrieved from http://www.haaretz.com/israel-news/.premium-1.550241.

Howley, Jogn. 1990. "Justice for Janitors: The Challenge of Organizing in Contract Services." *Labor Research Review* 1 (15): 61–71.

Hyman, Richard. 1992. "Trade Unions and the Disaggregation of the Working Class." In *The Future of Labour Movements*, edited by Marino Regini, 150–168. London: Sage Publications.

——. 1996. "Changing Union Identities in Europe." In *The Challenges to Trade Unions in Europe*, edited by Peter Leisink, Jim Van Leemput, and Jacques Vilrokx, 53–73. Cheltenham: Edward Elgar.

——. 2001. *Understanding European Trade Unions: Between Market, Class and Society*. London: Sage Publications.

Hyman, Richard, and Rebecca Gumbrell-McCormick. 2010. "Trade Unions, Politics and Parties: Is a New Configuration Possible?" *Transfer: European Review of Labor and Research* 16 (3): 315–331.

IDI (Israel Democracy Institute). 2004. *Yahasei Avoda b'Idan shel Tmurot* [Industrial relations in an era of change]. Jerusalem: Israel Democracy Institute.

Ir Amim. 2010. *Absentees against Their Will: Property Expropriation in East Jerusalem under the Absentee Property Law*. Jerusalem: Ir Amim.

Ishay, Ram. 1986. *Shvitat Harofim* [A doctors' strike]. Tel Aviv: Zmora-Bitan.

Isin, Engin. 1999. "Citizenship, Class and the Global City." *Citizenship Studies* 3 (2): 267–283.

Isin, Engin, and Bryan Turner. 2007. "Investigating Citizenship: An Agenda for Citizenship Studies." *Citizenship Studies* 11 (1): 5–17.

James, Phil. 2004. "Trade Unions and Political Parties." In *Trade Unions and Democracy: Strategies and Perspectives*, edited by Mark Harcourt and Geoffrey Wood, 303–318. Manchester: Manchester University Press.

Kalb, Don. 2012. "Thinking about Neoliberalism as if the Crisis Was Actually Happening." *Social Anthropology* 20 (3): 318–330.

Kamat, Sangeeta. 2004. "The Privatization of Public Interest: Theorizing NGO Discourse in a Neoliberal Era." *Review of International Political Economy* 11 (1): 155–176.

Katz, Yitzhak, and Miri Bitton Zahori. 2002. "Privatization Policy: 50 Years of Low-Intensity Conflict." In *Public Policy in Israel: Perspectives and Practices*, edited by Dani Korn, 123–134. Oxford: Lexington Books.

Kav Laoved. 2012. *Employment of Palestinians in Israel and the Settlements: Restrictive Policies and Abuse of Rights*. Tel Aviv: Kav Laoved.

——. 2013. *Arab Citizens of Israel and Work: Trends of Workplace Discrimination and Violation of Labor Rights*. Tel Aviv: Kav Laoved.

Keating, Michael. 2009. "Social Citizenship, Solidarity and Welfare in Regionalized and Plurinational States." *Citizenship Studies* 13 (5): 501–513.

Keeley, Brian. 2015. *Income Inequality: The Gap between Rich and Poor*, OECD Insights. Paris: OECD Publishing.

Kemp, Adriana, and Rebecca Raijman. 2008. *Ovdim veZarim: Hakalkala Hapolitit shel Hagirat Avoda l'Israel* [Foreign workers: The political economy of migrant labor in Israel]. Jerusalem: Hakibbutz Hameuchad.

Kemp, Adriana, Rebeca Raijman, Julia Resnik, and Silvina Schammah Gesser. 2000. "Contesting the Limits of Political Participation: Latinos and Black African Migrant Workers in Israel." *Ethnic and Racial Studies* 23 (1): 94–119.

Keohane, Robert. 2002. "Commentary on the Democratic Accountability of Non-Governmental Organizations." *Chicago Journal of International Law* 3 (2): 477–479.

Klein, Menachem. 2008. "Jerusalem as an Israeli Problem—A Review of 40 Years of Israeli Rule over Arab Jerusalem." *Israel Studies* 13 (2): 54–72.

Klein, Zeev. 2013. "B'nigud l'Daat Lapid: Misrad Rosh Hamemshala Mekadem Hahok neged Shvitot" [Contrary to Lapid's opinion: PMO promoting law against strikes]. *Israel Hayom*, 7 June. Retrieved from http://www.israelhayom.co.il/article/92575.

Knoler, Yehudit. 2000. "Hashilush Hakadosh: Ovdim, Ma'avidim veHevrot Koach Adam o Kablanei Koach Adam" [The holy trinity: Workers, employers, and manpower agencies and subcontractors]. *Neto + 133*:113–114.

Korczynski, Marek. 2003. "Consumer Capitalism and Industrial Relations." In *Understanding Work and Employment: Industrial Relations in Transition*, edited by Peter Ackers and Adrian Wilkinson, 265–277. Oxford: Oxford University Press.

Koren, Dani. 1998. "The Decline of Parties and the Functioning of the Knesset." In *Ketz Hamiflagot: Hademokratia Ha'Israelit b'Metzuka* [*The Demise of Parties in Israel*], edited by Dani Koren, 251–262. Tel Aviv: Hakibbutz Hameuchad.

Koren, Ora. 2012. "Aharei 38 Shanim b'Israel: Intel Ma'adifa et Irland" [After 38 years in Israel: Intel prefers Ireland]. *TheMarker*, 1 June.

Korin-Liber, Stella. 2012a. "Anahnu Haba'alim shel Harakevet" [We're the railway owners]. *Globes*, 20–21 February.

———. 2012b. "Gdolim michdei Lipol" [Too big to fail]. *Globes*, 19–20 June.

———. 2014. "Hamemshala Mevakeshet Lehachriz al Hava'adim Hagdolim Kemonopol" [Government to declare big committees a monopoly]. *Globes*, 19–20 January.

Kristal, Tali. 2008. "Labor's Share of National Income and the Diversification in Sources of Income among Wage and Salary Workers." PhD diss., University of Tel Aviv.

———. 2013. "Slicing the Pie: State Policy, Class Organization, Class Integration and Labor's Share of Israeli National Income." *Social Problems* 60 (1): 100–127.

Kristal, Tali, and Yinon Cohen. 2007. "Decentralization of Collective Agreements and Rising Wage Inequality in Israel." *Industrial Relations* 46 (3): 613–635.

Kristal, Tali, Yinon Cohen, and Guy Mundlak. 2006. *Ha'igud Hamiktzo'i veGidul E-Hashevyon Hakalkali b'Israel 1970–2003* [The union and the rise in economic inequality in Israel, 1970–2003]. Jerusalem: Van Leer Institute.

Landau, Jacob. 1973. "The Arabs and the Histadrut." In *Labor and Society in Israel*, edited by Isaiah Avrech and Dan Giladi, 24–38. Tel Aviv: Tel Aviv University and Histadrut.

Lavie, Noa. 2006. "'Tofrim Leglobalizatzia': Globalizatzia, Hamedina veTa'asiyat Hatextil b'Israel" [Sewing to globalization: Globalization, the state and the textile industry in Israel]. *Te'oria uBikoret* 29:103–124.

Lehmbruch, Gerhard. 1977. "Liberal Corporatism and Party Government." *Comparative Political Studies* 10 (1): 91–126.

Leijnse, Frans. 1996. "The Role of the State in Shaping Trade Union Policies." In *The Challenges to Trade Unions in Europe*, edited by Peter Leisink, Jim Van Leemput, and Jacques Vilrokx, 239–252. Cheltenham: Edward Elgar.

Leisink, Peter, Jim Van Leemput, and Jacques Vilrokx, eds. 1996a. *The Challenges to Trade Unions in Europe*. Cheltenham: Edward Elgar.

———. 1996b. "Introduction." In *The Challenges to Trade Unions in Europe*, edited by Peter Leisink, Jim Van Leemput, and Jacques Vilrokx, 1–30. Cheltenham: Edward Elgar.

Levi-Faur, David. 1995. "Mediniyut Kalkalit Veleumit: Pituah Anaf Hatextil b'Israel Beshnot Hahamishim v'Hashishim" [Economic and national policy: Developing the textile branch in Israel in the 1950s and 1960s]. *Katedra* 77:139–160.

———. 2000. "Change and Continuity in the Israeli Political Economy: Multi-Level Analysis of the Telecommunications and Energy Sectors." In *The New Israel: Peacemaking and Liberalization*, edited by Gershon Shafir and Yoav Peled, 161–188. Boulder: Westview.

Levy, Gal. 2005. "From Subjects to Citizens: On Educational Reforms and the Demarcation of 'Israeli-Arabs.'" *Citizenship Studies* 9 (3): 271–291.

Lewin-Epstein, Noah, and Moshe Semyonov. 1993. *The Arab Minority in Israel's Economy*. Boulder: Westview.

Linder-Ganz, Ronny. 2011a. "Hadahat Roni Gamzu: Kach Ye'aseh l'Ish she'Hevich et Netanyahu" [Removal of Roni Gamzu: That's what will happen to anyone who embarrasses Netanyahu]. *TheMarker*, 20 November. Retrieved from https://www.themarker.com/consumer/health/1.1570335.

———. 2011b. "Hatochnit Hasodit shel Harof'im: Hachpashat Bchirim v'Haf'alat Itonayim" [The doctors' secret plan: Slander senior doctors and use reporters]. *TheMarker*, 7 November. Retrieved from https://www.themarker.com/consumer/health/1.1560583.

———. 2011c. "Netanyahu Bikesh m'Edelman: Hefsek et Shvitat Hara'av" [Netanyahu asks Edelman: Stop the hunger strike]. *TheMarker*, 2 August. Retrieved from https://www.themarker.com/consumer/health/1.677205.

——. 2011d. "Yor Hahistadrut Harefu'it lifnei Hodesh Vehetzi: 'Hasharap b'Rosh Seder Ha'adifuyot Shelanu'" [IMA chair a month and a half ago: "Sharap is our top priority"]. *TheMarker*, 11 April. Retrieved from https://www.themarker.com/news/1.623890.

Linder-Ganz, Ronny, and Nati Tucker. 2011. "Hamitmahim, Hayahtzanim ve'Hasi'im b'Shvitat Harof'im Shehistayima Etmol" [The medical residents, the PR people and the highs of the doctors' strike that ended yesterday]. *TheMarker*, 9 December. Retrieved from https://www.themarker.com/consumer/health/1.1587342.

Lissak, Moshe. 1998. "The Decline of the Political Parties and the Sectorial Blossoming." In *Ketz Hamiflagot: Hademokratia Ha'Israelit b'Metzuka* [*The Demise of Parties in Israel*], edited by Dani Koren, 129–140. Tel Aviv: Hakibbutz Hameuchad.

Litman, Tal. 2012. "Mevaker Hamedina: Misrad Hahakla'ut Yatzar Maslul 'Okef Hok' l'Matan Ma'anakim l'Hakla'im" [State comptroller: Agricultural Ministry created "law circumventing" track to give grants to farmers]. *Calcalist*, 1 May. Retrieved from https://www.calcalist.co.il/local/articles/0,7340,L-3569549,00.html.

Lockman, Zachary. 1996. *Comrades and Enemies: Arab and Jewish Workers in Palestine, 1906–1948*. Berkeley: University of California Press.

Loewenberg, Frank, ed. 1998. *Meeting the Challenges of a Changing Society: Fifty Years of Social Work in Israel*. Jerusalem: Magnes Press.

Lopes, Ana, and Timothy Hall. 2015. "Organizing Migrant Workers: The Living Wage Campaign at the University of East London." *Industrial Relations Journal* 46 (3): 208–221.

Lukes, Steven. 1974. *Power: A Radical View*. Houndmills: MacMillan Education.

Maanit, Chen. 2012. "Dafni Leef Letzad Gila Edra'i: La'atzor et Hafratat Harakevet" [Dafni Leef stands by Gila Edra'i: Stop the privatization of the railway]. *Globes*, 1 March. Retrieved from http://www.globes.co.il/news/article.aspx?did=1000729585.

Maanit, Chen, and Ela Levy-Weinrib. 2013. "Teva Kibla Hatavot Mas b'-12 Milliard Shekel" [Teva received tax benefits of 12 billion shekels]. *Globes*, 16 July. Retrieved from http://www.globes.co.il/news/article.aspx?did=1000862476.

MacKenzie, Robert. 2010. "Why Do Contingent Workers Join a Trade Union? Evidence from the Irish Telecommunications Sector." *European Journal of Industrial Relations* 16 (2): 153–168.

Mahoney, James, and Dietrich Rueschemeyer, eds. 2003. *Comparative Historical Analysis in the Social Sciences*. Cambridge: Cambridge University Press.

Maman, Daniel, and Zeev Rosenhek. 2007. "The Politics of Institutional Reform: The 'Declaration of Independence' of the Israeli Central Bank." *Review of International Political Economy* 14 (2): 251–275.

——. 2012. "The Institutional Dynamics of a Developmental State: Change and Continuity in State-Economy Relations in Israel." *Studies in Comparative International Development* 47 (3): 342–363.

——. Forthcoming. "'Financial Education Is about Everybody's Self-Regulation': Financial Literacy as a Moralizing Project." *Socio-Economic Review*.

Maor, Anat. 2012. "Israeli Governments as Leading Policy of Breaking Labour Organisations and Using Practices of Exploitative and Harmful Employment." In *Haasaka Poganit: Hadara veNitzul Shitati'im b'Shuk Ha'avoda* [Precarious employment: Systematic exclusion and exploitation in the labor market], edited by Daniel Mishori and Anat Maor, 45–60. Ramat Gan: Social-Economic Academy and Achva Press.

Maor, Anat, and Dorit Bar Nir. 2008. "Hashpa'at Hashimush Hagoref Bakli shel Hok Hahesderim b'Meshek Hamedina al Hape'arim Bashanim 2002–2005" [The effect of sweeping use of the arrangements law in the economy on disparities, 2002–2005]. *Bitachon Sotziali* 77:95–124.

Marshall, Thomas. 1963. *Sociology at the Crossroads and Other Essays*. London: Heinemann.

Martin, Andrew, and George Ross. 1999. *The Brave New World of European Labor.* New York: Berghahn Books.

Martin, Ross. 1983. "Pluralism and the New Corporatism." *Political Studies* 31 (1): 86–102.

Mautner, Menachem. 1993. *Yeridat Haformalizm Ve'Aliyat Ha'arkhim Bamishpat Ha'Israeli* [The decline of formalism and the rise of values in Israeli law]. Tel Aviv: Maagalei Daat Publishing.

——, ed. 2000. *Tzedek Halukati b'Israel* [Distributive justice in Israel]. Tel Aviv: Ramot.

Milkman, Ruth. 2000. *Organizing Immigrants: The Challenge for Unions in Contemporary California.* Ithaca, NY: ILR Press.

Ministry of Foreign Affairs. 2011. "President Peres Launches Initiative to Integrate Israeli Arabs into Hi-Tech Workforce." 9 February. Jerusalem. Retrieved from http://mfa.gov.il/MFA/InnovativeIsrael/Economy/Pages/President_Peres_initiative_integrate_Israeli_Arabs_hi-tech_workforce_9-Feb-2011.aspx.

Ministry of Industry, Trade and Labor, Justice Ministry, and Finance Ministry. 2004. "Doch Hatzevet Haben-Misradi Banoseh Tichnun Shitat Ha'asakat Ovdim Zarim b'Israel v'Tna'im l'Matan Rishyonot (Doch Endorn)" [Report of the interministerial team on modes of employing migrant workers and conditions for issuing licenses (the Endorn report)]. Jerusalem.

Mishori, Daniel, and Anat Maor, eds. 2012. *Haasaka Poganit: Hadara veNitzul Shitati'im b'Shuk Ha'avoda* [Precarious employment: Systematic exclusion and exploitation in the labor market]. Ramat Gan: Social-Economic Academy and Achva Press.

Modan, Baruch. 1985. *Refu'a b'Matzor: Shvitat Harofim—Mashber Ma'arekhet Habriyut* [Medicine under siege]. Tel Aviv: Adam Publishing.

Molina, Oscar, and Martin Rhodes. 2002. "Corporatism: The Past, Present and Future of a Concept." *Annual Review of Political Science* 5:305–331.

Morris, Benny. 1987. *The Birth of the Palestinian Refugee Problem, 1947–1949.* Cambridge: Cambridge University Press.

Mundlak, Guy. 1997. "Yahasim ben Irgunei Ovdim: Al Bizur Maarechet Yahasei Ha'avoda b'Israel" [Relations between workers organizations: On the decentralization of the labor relations system in Israel]. *Labor Law Yearbook* 6:219–285.

——. 1998. "The New Labor Law as a Social Text: Reflections on Social Values in Flux." *Israel Studies* 3 (2): 119–158.

——. 2007. *Fading Corporatism: Israel's Labor Law and Industrial Relations in Transition.* Ithaca, NY: ILR Press.

——. 2009. "Addressing the Legitimacy Gap in the Israeli Corporatist Revival." *British Journal of Industrial Relations* 47 (4): 765–787.

——. 2012. "Human Rights and Labour Rights: Why the Tracks Don't Meet." *Comparative Labor Law and Policy Journal* 34 (1): 217–243.

Mundlak, Guy, and Itzhak Harpaz. 2002. "Determinants of Israeli Judicial Discretion in Issuing Injunctions against Strikers." *British Journal of Industrial Relations* 40 (4): 753–777.

Mundlak, Guy, Ishak Saporta, Yitchak Haberfeld, and Yinon Cohen. 2013. "Union Density in Israel, 1995–2010: The Hybridization of Industrial Relations." *Industrial Relations* 52 (1): 78–101.

Nadiv, Ronit. 2005. *Kablanei Koach Adam b'Israel Hapoalim b'Rishayon* [Licensed manpower agencies in Israel]. Jerusalem: Ministry of Industry, Trade and Labor.

Navot, Doron, and Yoav Peled. 2009. "Towards a Constitutional Counter-Revolution in Israel?" *Constellations* 16 (3): 430–444.

Nisim, Sarit, and Orly Benjamin. 2008. "Power and Size of Firms as Reflected in Cleaning Subcontractors' Practices of Social Responsibility." *Journal of Business Ethics* 83:673–683.

——. 2010. "The Speech of Services Procurement: The Negotiated Order of Commodification and Dehumanization of Cleaning Employees." *Human Organization* 69 (3): 221–232.

Nissan, Yossi. 2012. "Rak Lo Lehitaged: Mankal Pelephone Mavtiah Hatavot Laovdim" [Anything but unionization: Pelephone CEO promises benefits to workers]. *Globes*, 23–24 September.

Nissan, Yossi, and Shay Niv. 2012. "Le'ahar Reva Sha'a – Hitpotzetza Hapgisha ben Katz l'Eini al Harakevet; Eini: 'Katz Yatzar Mashber velo Enahel Mum Kach'" [After quarter of an hour – meeting broke down between Katz and Eini about the Railway; Eini: "Katz created a crisis and I won't negotiate like this"]. *Globes*, 16 February. Retrieved from http://www.globes.co.il/news/article.aspx?did=1000725524.

Nissan, Yossi, Amiram Barkat, and Shay Niv. 2012. "Katz: 'Gila Edra'i Rotza Lishlot b'Sha'ilter – He Mitnaheget K'ilu Harakevet Shayach La; Lo Meanyenim ota Haovdim'" [Katz: "Gila Edra'i wants to control the switch – she behaves as if the railway belongs to her; the workers don't interest her"]. *Globes*, 5 March. Retrieved from http://www.globes.co.il/news/article.aspx?did=1000730517.

Nitzan, Jonathan, and Shimshon Bichler. 1996. "From War Profits to Peace Dividends: The New Political Economy of Israel." *Capital and Class* 20 (3): 61–94.

Niv, Shay. 2009. "Ha'alternativa l'Ofer Eini: 'Koach Laovdim' Kovesh et Hashetah" [The alternative to Ofer Eini: "Koach Laovdim" is conquering the territory]. *Globes*, 26 September. Retrieved from http://www.globes.co.il/news/article.aspx?did=1000500233.

——. 2010. "Itay Swirsky Meshane et Pnei Hahevra Ha'Israelit" [Itay Swirsky is changing the face of Israeli society]. *Globes*, 24 November. Retrieved from http://www.globes.co.il/news/article.aspx?did=1000603328.

——. 2011a. "Eini Noten Od Chance: Mamtin Im Hashvita B'Inyan Ovdei Kablan" [Eini grants another chance: Postpones strike on issue of contract workers]. *Globes*, 31 October. Retrieved from http://www.globes.co.il/news/article.aspx?did=1000693602.

——. 2011b. "Hahistadrut Me'ayemet: Shibushim Kashim b'Tnu'at Harakevot Me'hashavu'a Haba" [The Histadrut threatens: Serious disruptions to train movement from next week]. *Globes*, 29 December. Retrieved from http://www.globes.co.il/news/article.aspx?did=1000711123.

——. 2011c. "Mashber Harof'im Likrat Pitaron: Borer Ba'emtza Hatkufa" [Doctor crisis approaching solution: Arbitrator in middle of period]. *Globes*, 4 December. Retrieved from http://www.globes.co.il/news/article.aspx?did=1000703374.

——. 2011d. "Meltzer Lamitmahim u'La'Otzar: Nahelu Hidabrut Intensivit shel Shvu'ayim" [Meltzer to junior doctors and to Finance Ministry: Hold intensive talks for a fortnight]. *Globes*, 27 October. Retrieved from http://www.globes.co.il/news/article.aspx?did=1000692782.

——. 2012a. "Clal Bituah Shalha l'Beit Yor Hava'ad Zimun l'Shimu'a – b'21:00" [Clal Insurance sent summons for hearing to home of committee chair – at 21:00]. *Globes*, 10 June. Retrieved http://www.globes.co.il/news/article.aspx?did=1000755913.

——. 2012b. "Eini Daha Hatza'at Gishur; Doresh Hachra'a Hayom al Hazchut Lishvot" [Eini rejects mediation; demands decision today on right to strike]. *Globes*, 9 January. Retrieved from http://www.globes.co.il/news/article.aspx?did=1000713868.

——. 2012c. "Ha'atar Neged Hahitagdut b'Pelephone: shel Adler-Chomsky" [The website against the unionizing in Pelephone: From Adler-Chomsky]. *Globes*, 24 October. Retrieved from http://www.globes.co.il/news/article.aspx?did=1000792574.

——. 2012d. "Hahistadrut Doreshet me'Hava'adim Lid'og Le'ovdei Kablan" [The Histadrut asks the Committees to take care of contract workers]. *Globes*, 30 October. Retrieved from http://www.globes.co.il/news/article.aspx?did=1000794335.

——. 2012e. "'Hahistadrut Hayevet Lehagiv Hasaq Yoter b'Inyan Clal Bituah'" ["The Histadrut must respond more strongly on the Clal Insurance issue"]. *Globes*, 11 June. Retrieved from http://www.globes.co.il/news/article.aspx?did=1000756205.

——. 2012f. "Hahistadrut: Ovdim Nosafim Hitztarfu Lashvita b'Pelephone" [The Histadrut: Additional workers joined the strike at Pelephone]. *Globes*, 18–19 December.

——. 2012g. "Hahistadrut: Pelephone Adayin Mesakelet Hitagdut v'Mevaza et Beit Hadin" [The Histadrut: Pelephone is still preventing unionizing and is in contempt of court]. *Globes*, 12 September. Retrieved from http://www.globes.co.il/news/article. aspx?did=1000784852.

——. 2012h. "Hashvita b'Pelephone: Haovdim Heshvitu gam et Hamerkaz Halogisti" [The strike at Pelephone: The workers struck at the logistics center too]. *Globes*, 12 December. Retrieved from http://www.globes.co.il/news/article.aspx?did=1000805742.

——. 2012i. "Mankal Clal Bituah Mazhir m'Hakamat Va'ad Ovdim" [Clal Insurance CEO warns against establishing workers' committee]. *Globes*, 6–7 June.

——. 2013a. "59% Me'hascharim halo Me'ugadim: Lo Me'unyanim b'Va'ad Ovdim" [59% of non-unionized workers are not interested in a workers' committee]. *Globes*, 13 November. Retrieved from https://www.globes.co.il/news/article.aspx?did= 1000893744&fid=2.

——. 2013b. "Bachir Bahistadrut: 'Kvar Shalosh Shanim Ani Koreh l'Hafratat Hanamalim ve'Hamedina Mitnagedet. Ze Hazui'" [Senior Histadrut figure: "I've been calling for privatizing the ports for three years and the state opposes. It's crazy"]. *Globes*, 26 November. Retrieved from http://www.globes.co.il/news/article.aspx?did=1000897018.

——. 2013c. "Bchirim Leshe'avar b'Otzar Tokfim et Hayozma Levatel et Beit Hadin l'Avoda: 'Nisayon lo Legitimi'" [Former Finance Ministry officials attack initiative to cancel labor court: "Attempt is not legitimate"]. *Globes*, 30 January. Retrieved from http://www.globes.co.il/news/article.aspx?did=1000818372.

——. 2013d. "Habdiha Halo Mutzlahat shel Naftali Bennett: E Efshar Yoter im Hanamalim. Hezmanti Madbir" [Naftali Bennett's unsuccessful joke: We can't go on with these ports. We've called in pest control]. *Globes*, 23–24 May.

——. 2013e. "Hahistadrut Mesakemet Shana: 26 Elef Ovdim Hitagdu Bamea Mekomot Avoda" [The Histadrut sums up year: 26,000 workers unionized in 100 workplaces]. *Globes*, 25–26 December.

——. 2013f. "Hama'asikim neged Beit Hadin l'Avoda" [The employers against the labor court]. *Globes*, 5–6 February.

——. 2013g. "Hamismach Shehochiah she'Hahistadrut Heskima l'Namal Prati" [The document that proves the Histadrut agreed to a private port]. *Globes*, 25 July. Retrieved from http://www.globes.co.il/news/article.aspx?did=1000865603.

——. 2013h. "Lynn Doresh: Shnatayim Ma'asar l'Ovdim she'Yishvatu ekev Shinuim Mivni'im" [Lynn demands: Two years behind bars for workers who strike because of structural changes]. *Globes*, 16–17 July.

——. 2013i. "Lynn Megabesh Hakika l'Hagbalat Beit Hadin Ha'artzi l'Avoda" [Lynn formulating law to limit National Labor Court]. *Globes*, 21–22 January.

——. 2013j. "Ma'asikim Prati'im lo Yehuyavu Leha'asik Ovdei Nikayon B'ofen Yashir" [Private employers will not be compelled to employ cleaners directly]. *Globes*, 4 June. Retrieved from http://www.globes.co.il/news/article.aspx?did=1000849680.

——. 2013k. "Mikur Hutz Nosah HOT" [HOT version of outsourcing]. *Globes*, 14–15 August.

——. 2013l. "Mitos Hanamal Haprati" [The myth of the private port]. *Globes*, 22–23 May.

——. 2013m. "Pelephone Heviya Aleynu et Psak Hadin – Asta Kol Ta'ut Efsharit" [Pelephone brought this ruling upon us – it made every mistake possible]. *Globes*, 3 January. Retrieved from http://www.globes.co.il/news/article.aspx?did=1000811653.

——. 2014a. "Eliyahu Me'olam lo Hekir Bahem" [Eliyahu never recognized them]. *Globes*, 24–25 February.

——. 2014b. "Ke-2,000 Bahafgana mul Beit Eliyahu; 'Ose Ma'ase Pesha'" [Some 2,000 in demonstration in front of Beit Eliyahu; "He is doing a criminal act"]. *Globes*, 15 January. Retrieved from http://www.globes.co.il/news/article.aspx?did=1000909868.

——. 2014c. "Migdal v'Eliahu Yekansu b'-200 Elef Shekel im Yamshichu Lehafer et Tzav Beit Hadin" [Migdal and Eliyahu will be fined 200,000 shekels if they continue to violate labor court order]. *Globes*, 21 January. Retrieved from http://www.globes.co.il/news/article.aspx?did=1000910988.

——. 2017. "Nihsaf b-'Globes': Hevrat Knesset Yachimovich Titmoded Babhirot Lahistadrut" [*Globes* reveals: Knesset member Yachimovich to content in Histadrut elections]. *Globes*, 5 February.

Niv, Shay, and Yuval Yoaz. 2013. "Hashofetet Nili Arad: 'Israelim Ovdim Kashe v'Ohavim La'avod'" [Judge Nili Arad: "Israelis work hard and like working"]. *Globes*, 13 December. Retrieved from http://www.globes.co.il/news/article.aspx?did=1000901316.

NRG. 2013. "Lapid: B'Israel Lo Tehiyeh Hafrada ben Hadat Lamedina" [Lapid: In Israel there will be no separation between religion and state]. 29 October. Retrieved from http://www.nrg.co.il/online/1/ART2/517/840.html?hp=1&cat.

OECD (Organisation for Economic Cooperation and Development). 2010. *OECD Reviews of Labor Market and Social Policies—Israel*. Paris: OECD Publishing.

Offe, Claus. 1981. "The Attribution of Public Status to Interest Groups: Observations on the West German Case." In *Organizing Interests in Western Europe: Pluralism, Corporatism and the Transformation of Politics*, edited by Suzanne Berger, 123–158. Cambridge: Cambridge University Press.

——. 1985. *Disorganized Capitalism*. Cambridge, MA: MIT Press.

Ornan, Uzzi. 2013. "Denying 'Israeli Nationality' only Perpetuates Discrimination." +972 *Blog*, 9 November. Retrieved from http://972mag.com/denying-israeli-nationality-only-perpetuates-discrimination/81597/.

Osherov, Eli. 2011. "Haovdim Hafalestinim b'Mahtzevet Sla'it Osim Historia" [Palestinian workers at Salit quarries make history]. Retrieved from http://www.nrg.co.il/online/54/ART2/253/868.html.

Ozaki, Muneto, ed. 1999. *Negotiating Flexibility: The Role of the Social Partners and the State*. Geneva: International Labor Organization.

Palgi, Michal, and Shulamit Reinharz, eds. 2014. *One Hundred Years of Kibbutz Life: A Century of Crises and Reinvention*. New Brunswick: Transaction Publishers.

Parry, Geraint, and Michael Moran. 1994. "Introduction: Problems of Democracy and Democratization." In *Democracy and Democratization*, edited by Geraint Parry and Michael Moran, 1–20. London: Routledge.

Peck, Jamie, and Nik Theodore. 2012. "Reanimating Neoliberalism: Process Geographies of Neoliberalisation." *Social Anthropology* 20 (2): 177–185.

Peretz, Efrat. 2014. "Ushar Hesder Hahov b'Zim: 'Tisporet' shel ke-1.5 Milliard Dollar" [Zim debt restructuring approved: "Haircut" of about 1.5 billion dollars]. *Globes*, 26 June. Retrieved from http://www.globes.co.il/news/article.aspx?did=1000949612.

Peretz, Gad. 2012. "Mankal Pelephone: Ma'avak Haovdim Pag'a b'Totza'ot Hacaspiot shelanu" [Pelephone CEO: Workers' struggle hurt our financial results]. *Globes*, 14 October. Retrieved from http://www.globes.co.il/news/article.aspx?did=1000789624.

Peretz, Sami. 2012. "Hatragedia shel Shuk Ha'avoda b'Israel" [The tragedy of the labor market in Israel]. *MarkerWeek*, 20 April.

——. 2013. "Hadashot Tovot v'Ra'ot l'Ovdim Shemitagdim" [Good and bad news for unionizing workers]. *MarkerWeek*, 7 June. Retrieved from https://www.themarker.com/markerweek/1.2040401.

Peters, John. 2011. "The Rise of Finance and the Decline of Organized Labor in the Advanced Capitalist Countries." *New Political Economy* 16 (1): 73–99.

——. 2012. "Neoliberal Convergence in North America and Western Europe: Fiscal Austerity, Privatization and Public Sector Reform." *Review of International Political Economy* 19 (2): 208–235.

Peters, Michael. 2001. "Education, Enterprise Culture and the Entrepreneurial Self: A Foucauldian Perspective." *Journal of Educational Enquiry* 2 (2): 58–71.

Phelan, Craig, ed. 2007. *Trade Union Revitalization: Trends and Prospects in 34 Countries.* Bern: Peter Lang.

Piven, Frances Fox. 1991. "The Decline of Labor Parties: An Overview." In *Labor Parties in Postindustrial Societies*, edited by Frances Fox Piven, 1–19. Cambridge: Polity Press.

Portugali, Juval. 1993. *Implicate Relations: Society and Space in the Israeli-Palestinian Conflict.* Dordrecht: Kluwer Academic Publishers.

Preminger, Jonathan. 2013. "Activists Face Bureaucrats: The Failure of the Israeli Social Workers' Campaign." *Industrial Relations Journal* 44 (5–6): 462–478.

——. 2016. "The Contradictory Effects of Neoliberalization on Labor Relations: The Health and Social Work Sectors." *Economic and Industrial Democracy* 37 (4): 644–664.

——. 2017. "Effective Citizenship in the Cracks of Neocorporatism." *Citizenship Studies* 21 (1): 85–99.

Public Committee Inquiring into the Structure and Functioning of the Medical Association of Israel. 2013. "Doch Hava'ada Hatziburit Lebhinat Mivne u'Peilut Hahistadrut Harefu'it b'Israel (Va'adat Dorner)" [Report of the Public Committee Inquiring into the Structure and Functioning of the Medical Association of Israel (the Dorner Committee)]. Jerusalem.

Raday, Frances. 1994. "'Hafratat Zkhuyot Ha'adam' Vehashimush l'Ra'a b'Koach" [The "privatization of human rights" and the abuse of power]. *Mishpatim* 23:21–53.

——. 1995. "Herut Hashvita, Tvi'ot Tzad Gimel Veborerut Hova" [Freedom to strike, third party claims and compulsory arbitration]. *Labor Law Yearly* 5:143–152.

——. 2002. "E-Tzedek Hevrati: Hareforma b'Ha'asakat Ovdei Kablanei Koach Adam Vehanisyonot Lehakhshilo" [Social injustice: The employment of manpower agency workers and attempts to quash reform]. *Kaveret* 4:69.

Ram, Uri. 2000. "'The Promised Land of Business Opportunities': Liberal Post-Zionism in the Glocal Age." In *The New Israel: Peacemaking and Liberalization*, edited by Gershon Shafir and Yoav Peled, 217–240. Boulder: Westview.

——. 2008. *The Globalization of Israel: McWorld in Tel Aviv, Jihad in Jerusalem.* New York: Routledge.

Ram, Uri, and Nitza Berkowitz, eds. 2006. *E/Shivyon* [In/equality]. Beer Sheva: Ben-Gurion University Press.

Ram, Uri, and Dani Filc. 2013. "Ha-14 b'Yuli shel Daphni Leef: Alyata v'Nefilata shel Hameha'a Hahevratit" [Daphni Leef's 14 July: The rise and fall of the social protest movement]. *Te'oria uBikoret* 41:17–43.

Ravid, Barak, and *Haaretz*. 2011. "Netanyahu: Israel's Medical Residents Should Leave Patients Out of Struggle." *Haaretz*, 20 November. Retrieved from http://www.haaretz.com/israel-news/netanyahu-israel-s-medical-residents-should-leave-patients-out-of-struggle-1.396617.

Rosen, Bruce, and Hadar Samuel. 2009. "Israel: Health System in Review." *Health Systems in Transition* 2 (2).

Rosenfeld, Henry, and Shulamit Carmi. 1976. "The Privatization of Public Means, the State-Made Middle Class and the Realization of Family Value in Israel." In *Kinship and Modernization in Mediterranean Society*, edited by John Peristiany, 131–159. Rome: Center for Mediterranean Studies.

Rosenhek, Zeev. 2002a. "Globalizatzia, Politika Mekomit Veshinuim l'Medinat Harevaha: Tokhnit Bituah Ha'avtala b'Israel" [Globalization, local politics and changes to the welfare state: The unemployment program in Israel]. *Labor, Society and Law* 9:74–155.

———. 2002b. "Social Policy and Nationbuilding: The Dynamics of the Israeli Welfare State." *Journal of Societal and Social Policy* 1 (1): 15–31.

———. 2003. "The Political Dynamics of a Segmented Labour Market." *Acta Sociologica* 46 (3): 231–249.

———. 2006. "The Welfare State in Israel." In *E/Shivyon* [In/equality], edited by Uri Ram and Nitza Berkowitz, 234–241. Beer Sheva: Ben-Gurion University Press.

———. 2007. "Challenging Exclusionary Migration Regimes: Labor Migration in Israel in Comparative Perspective." In *Transnational Migration to Israel in Global Comparative Context*, edited by Sarah Willen, 217–232. Plymouth: Lexington Books.

Rosenhek, Zeev, and Michael Shalev. 2013. "Hakalkala Hapolitit shel Meha'at 2011: Nituah Dori-Ma'amadi" [The political economy of the 2011 protest: A generational-class analysis]. *Te'oria uBikoret* 41:45–68.

Sadeh, Shuki. 2012. "Shnei Va'adim, Hahramat Mechoniyot Vehafganot: Hamilhama b'Pelephone Ola Madrega" [Two committees, car confiscation and demonstrations: The war at Pelephone goes up a notch]. *TheMarker*, 15 December. Retrieved from https://www.themarker.com/markerweek/1.1885915.

Sa'di, Ahmad, and Noah Lewin-Epstein. 2001. "Minority Labour Force Participation in the Post-Fordist Era: The Case of the Arabs in Israel." *Work, Employment and Society* 15 (4): 781–802.

Saporta, Yitzhak. 1988. "Hevrot l'Avoda Zmanit b'Israel: Ti'ur Pe'ilutan v'Hekefa, v'Ma'amadan Hamishpati" [Temping agencies in Israel: Extent of their activities and legal status]. Master's diss., Tel Aviv University.

Sassen, Saskia. 2002. "Towards Post-National and Denationalized Citizenship." In *Handbook of Citizenship Studies*, edited by Engin Isin and Bryan Turner, 277–292. London: Sage Publications.

Sasson, Talia, Oshrat Maimon, and Tamar Luster. 2012. *Permanent Residency: A Temporary Status Set in Stone*. Jerusalem: Ir Amim.

Saward, Michael. 2005. "Governance and the Transformation of Political Representation." In *Remaking Governance: Peoples, Politics and the Public Sphere*, edited by Janet Newman, 179–196. Bristol: Policy Press.

Schechter, Asher. 2012. "Mifal sheyesh lo Ir" [A factory with a town]. *MarkerWeek*, 1 June.

Schmidt, Vivien. 2009. "Putting the Political Back into Political Economy by Bringing the State Back In Yet Again." *World Politics* 61 (3): 516–46.

Schmitter, Philippe. 1974. "Still the Century of Corporatism?" *Review of Politics* 36 (1): 85–131.

Schulten, Thorsten, and Nils Böhlke. 2012. "Hospitals under Growing Pressure from Marketization and Privatization." In *Privatization of Public Services: Impacts for Employment, Working Conditions, and Service Quality in Europe*, edited by Christoph Hermann and Jörg Flecker, 89–108. New York: Routledge.

Schulten, Thorsten, Torsten Brandt, and Christoph Hermann. 2008. "Liberalization and Privatization of Public Services and Strategic Options for European Trade Unions." *Transfer: European Review of Labour and Research* 14 (2): 295–311.

Semyonov, Moshe, and Noah Lewin-Epstein. 1987. *Hewers of Wood and Drawers of Water: Noncitizen Arabs in the Israeli Labor Market*. Ithaca, NY: ILR Press.

Shafir, Gershon. 1989. *Land, Labor and the Origins of the Israeli–Palestinian Conflict, 1882–1914*. Cambridge: Cambridge University Press.

Shafir, Gershon, and Yoav Peled. 2000a. "The Globalization of Israeli Business and the Peace Process." In *The New Israel: Peacemaking and Liberalization*, edited by Gershon Shafir and Yoav Peled, 243–264. Boulder: Westview.

——, eds. 2000b. *The New Israel: Peacemaking and Liberalization*. Boulder: Westview.

——. 2002. *Being Israeli: The Dynamics of Multiple Citizenship*. Cambridge: Cambridge University Press.

Shaked, Michal. 2002. "Hofesh Hahit'argenut Hamiktzo'it b'Israel: Ha'ovdim v'Hahistadrut b'Mishpat Ha'avoda" [Freedom of association in Israel: Workers and the Histadrut in Israeli law]." PhD diss., Tel Aviv University.

Shalev, Michael. 1989. "Jewish Organized Labor and the Palestinians: A Study of State/ Society Relations in Israel." In *The Israeli State and Society: Boundaries and Frontiers*, edited by Baruch Kimmerling, 93–133. Albany: State University of New York Press.

——. 1992. *Labor and the Political Economy in Israel*. Oxford: Oxford University Press.

——. 2000. "Liberalization and the Transformation of the Political Economy." In *The New Israel: Peacemaking and Liberalization*, edited by Gershon Shafir and Yoav Peled, 129–160. Boulder: Westview.

——. 2006. "Political Economy." In *E/Shivyon* [In/equality], edited by Uri Ram and Nitza Berkowitz, 204–211. Beer Sheva: Ben-Gurion University Press.

Shalev, Michael, and Lev Grinberg. 1989. *Histadrut–Government Relations and the Transition from a Likud to a National Unity Government: Continuity and Change in Israel's Economic Crises*. Tel Aviv: Pinhas Sapir Center for Development, Tel Aviv University.

Shamir, Hila. 2016. "Labor Organizing and the Law: Unionizing Subcontracted Labor." *Theoretical Inquiries in Law* 17 (1): 229–255.

Shapiro, Jonathan. 1976. *The Formative Years of the Israeli Labour Party: The Organization of Power, 1919–1930*. London: Sage Publications.

——. 1984. *Ilit Lelo Mamshikhim: Dorot Manhigim Bahevra Ha'Israelit* [An elite without successors: A generation of leaders in Israel]. Tel Aviv: Sifrut Poalim.

Sharone, Ofer. 2007. "Constructing Unemployed Job Seekers as Professional Workers: The Depoliticizing Work-Game of Job Searching." *Qualitative Sociology* 30 (4): 403–416.

Shenhav, Yehuda. 2013. "Hakarneval: Meha'a b'Hevra Lelo Opozitzia" [Carnival: Protest in a society without opposition]. *Te'oria uBikoret* 41:121–145.

Shlosberg, Inbal. 2012. "Bitui'im shel Igud Masorti v'Igud Mithadesh b'Ma'avak Sakhar: Mikre Shvitat Igud Haovdim Hasotziali'im b'Israel 2010–2011" [Elements of trade union revitalization in a wage struggle: The case of the social workers' union strike in Israel, 2010–2011]. MA diss., Ben-Gurion University of the Negev.

Shmil, Daniel. 2012. "Hashibushim Barakevet Yamshichu gam Mahar; Hahanhala Tifne l'Beit Hamishpat" [Disruption in the railway to continue tomorrow; management to turn to courts]. *TheMarker*, 8 January. Retrieved from https://www.themarker.com/dynamo/cars/1.1611869.

Shmil, Daniel, and Avi Bar-Eli. 2013. "Netanyahu: Idan Hamonopolim Nigmar, Af Ahad lo Yachol Limnoa Mibe'adenu Liftoah et Hanamalim Letaharut" [Netanyahu: The age of monopolies is over, nobody can prevent us from opening the ports to competition]. *TheMarker*, 4 July.

Shporer, Sharon. 2013. "Kulam Yad'u Veshatku" [Everyone knew and kept quiet]. *MarkerWeek*, 21 June.

Silver, Beverly. 2003. *Forces of Labor: Workers' Movements and Globalization since 1870*. New York: Cambridge University Press.

Skocpol, Theda. 1984. "Emerging Agendas and Recurrent Strategies in Historical Sociology." In *Vision and Method in Historical Sociology*, edited by Theda Skocpol, 356–391. Cambridge: Cambridge University Press.

Smith, Dennis. 1991. *The Rise of Historical Sociology*. Cambridge: Polity Press.

Sovich, Nina. 2000. "Palestinian Trade Unions." *Journal of Palestine Studies* 29 (4): 66–79.

Standing, Guy. 2009. *Work after Globalization: Building Occupational Citizenship*. Cheltenham: Edward Elgar.

——. 2011. *The Precariat: The New Dangerous Class.* London: Bloomsbury.

Stessman, Jochanan, and Leah Achdut. 2000. *Employment through Temporary Work Agencies and Social Security Provisions: The Israeli Case.* Helsinki: International Research Conference on Social Security.

Strauss, Anselm. 1978. *Negotiations, Varieties, Processes, Contexts and Social Order.* San Francisco: Jossey-Bass.

Streeck, Wolfgang. 2006. "The Study of Organized Interests: Before 'The Century' and After." In *The Diversity of Democracy: Corporatism, Social Order and Political Conflict,* edited by Colin Crouch and Wolfgang Streeck, 3–45. Cheltenham: Edward Elgar.

Sullivan, Richard. 2010. "Labor Market or Labor Movement? The Union Density Bias as Barrier to Labor Renewal." *Work, Employment and Society* 24 (1): 145–156.

Swirsky, Shlomo. 2013. *No Paradigm Change in Sight: The Economic Policies of the Second Netanyahu Government (2009–2012).* Tel Aviv: The Adva Center. Retrieved from http://adva.org/wp-content/uploads/2015/01/miracle21.pdf.

Tager, Michal. 2006. "La'avod bli Kavod: Zkhuyot Ovdim v'Hafaratan" [Work without dignity: Workers' rights violations]. Tel Aviv: Association for Civil Rights in Israel. Retrieved from http://www.acri.org.il/pdf/workersrights.pdf.

Tamari, Salim. 1992. "Shopkeepers, Vendors and Urban Resistance in the Intifada." In *Ha'Intifada—Mabat Mi'Bifnim* [The intifada—An inside view], edited by Shlomo Swirsky and Ilan Pappe, 87–103. Tel Aviv: Mifras.

Tarrow, Sidney. 1994. *Power in Movement: Social Movements, Collective Action and Politics.* Cambridge: Cambridge University Press.

Tovias, Alfred, and Hilary Wolpert. 1987. *Cooperation between the Textiles and Clothing Industries of Egypt and Israel.* Tel Aviv: Armand Hammer Fund, Tel Aviv University.

Tsipori, Tali. 2013. "Mishehu Helshin al Teva? Shilma Mas shel 0.3% Bilvad b'-2012" [Did someone snitch on Teva? It paid tax of just 0.3% in 2012]. *Globes,* 13 February.

Turner, Lowell. 2005. "From Transformation to Revitalization: A New Research Agenda for a Contested Global Economy." *Work and Occupations* 32 (4): 383–399.

Tzipori, Eli. 2013a. "Teva Kibla Hatavot Mas shel 3 Milliard Shekel b'-2011" [Teva received tax benefits of 3 billion shekels in 2011]. *Globes,* 11–12 March.

——. 2013b. "Teva lo Enoshi" [Inhuman nature]. *Globes,* 13 October. Retrieved from http://www.globes.co.il/news/article.aspx?did=1000885198.

Upchurch, Martin, Graham Taylor, and Andrew Mathers. 2009. *The Crisis of Social Democratic Trade Unionism in Western Europe: The Search for Alternatives.* Farnham: Ashgate.

Vosko, Leah, Mark Thomas, Angela Hick, and Jennifer Chun. 2013. "Organizing Precariously-Employed Workers in Canada." Unpublished working paper. Retrieved from http://www.irle.ucla.edu/research/documents/Canada.docx.

Voss, Kim, and Rachel Sherman. 2000. "Breaking the Iron Law of Oligarchy: Union Revitalization in the American Labor Movement." *American Journal of Sociology* 106 (2): 303–349.

WAC (Workers Advice Center). 2012. "Reshut Ha'atikot Mantziha Nitzul Ovdei Kablan b'Hafirot" [Antiquities authority perpetuates exploitation of contractor workers in excavations]. Retrieved from http://heb.wac-maan.org.il/?p=317.

——. 2014. "Zarfati Garage Flings False Accusations against Workers' Committee Chairperson." Retrieved from http://eng.wac-maan.org.il/?p=1051 and http://eng.wac maan.org.il/?p=1113.

——. 2017. "WAC-MAAN Signs a Groundbreaking Collective Agreement for Palestinians at Mishor Adumim's Zarfati Garage." 19 February. Retrieved from http://eng.wac maan.org.il/?p=1822.

Wacquant, Loïs. 2012. "Three Steps to a Historical Anthropology of Actually Existing Neoliberalism." *Social Anthropology* 20 (1): 66–79.

Walsh, Jane. 2012. "A 'New' Social Movement: US Labor and the Trends of Social Movement Unionism." *Sociology Compass* 6 (2): 192–204.

Webb, Sidney, and Beatrice Webb. 1897. *Industrial Democracy*. New York: A. M. Kelly.

Weinblum, Shay. 2010. "A Work in Progress: Union Revitalization in the Israeli 'New General Federation of Labor.'" MA diss., Global Labor University.

Weissberg, Hila. 2013. "Ad 2059: Haharedim veha'Aravim Yehiyu 50% meha'Ochlusia" [By 2059: Haredim and Arabs will be 50 percent of the population]. *TheMarker*, 31 October. Retrieved from https://www.themarker.com/career/1.2153691.

Weissberg, Hila, Haim Bior, and Lior Dattel. 2011. "Aserot Alfei Ovdei Kablan Mu'asakim b'Gufim Sheheshvitu et Hameshek" [Tens of thousands of agency workers employed in organizations that went on strike]. *TheMarker*, 8 November.

Weissberg, Hila, Haim Bior, and Tali Heruti-Sover. 2013. "Zinuk shel 60% b'Mispar Haovdim Shehitagdu b'Israel me'Thilat Hashana" [Rise of 60% in number of workers who have unionized in Israel since start of year]. *TheMarker*, 5 June. Retrieved from https://www.themarker.com/career/1.2038433.

White, Gordon. 2004. "Civil Society, Democratization and Development: Clearing the Analytical Ground." In *Civil Society in Democratization*, edited by Peter Burnell and Peter Calvert, 6–21. London: Frank Cass.

Who Profits. 2013. "Palestinian Workers in Settlements: Who Profits' Position Paper." Who Profits and Coalition of Women for Peace. Retrieved from http://whoprofits.org/sites/default/files/palestinian_workers_in_settlements_wp_position_paper.pdf.

Wolkinson, Benjamin. 1999. *Arab Employment in Israel: The Quest for Equal Employment Opportunity*. Westport: Greenwood Press.

Wood, Geoffrey. 2004. "Introduction—Trade Unions and Democracy: Possibilities and Contradictions." In *Trade Unions and Democracy: Strategies and Perspectives*, edited by Mark Harcourt and Geoffrey Wood, 1–18. Manchester: Manchester University Press.

Wright, Chris. 2013. "The Response of Unions to the Rise of Precarious Work in Britain." *Economic and Labor Relations Review* 24 (3): 279–296.

Wright, Erik Olin. 1994. *Interrogating Inequality: Essays on Class Analysis, Socialism and Marxism*. London: Verso.

——. 1997. *Class Counts: Comparative Studies in Class Analysis*. Cambridge: Cambridge University Press.

——. 2000. "Working-Class Power, Capitalist-Class Interests and Class Compromise." *American Journal of Sociology* 105 (4): 957–1002.

Yalkut. 1994. "Hashlakhot Ifshariyot shel Heskemei Hashalom al Anaf Hatextil v'Hahalbasha b'Israel" [Possible implications of the peace accords on the textile and clothing industry in Israel]. 135:1–8.

Yashiv, Eran, and Nitza Kasir. 2013. *Shuk Ha'avoda shel Araviyei Israel* [The labor market of Arab Israelis]. Tel Aviv: Tel Aviv University.

Ynet. 2007. "Sherut Hata'asuka Matzia: Israelim bimkom Ovdim Zarim" [Employment services propose: Israelis instead of foreign workers]. 15 February. Retrieved from http://www.ynet.co.il/articles/0,7340,L-3365559,00.html.

Zarhia, Zvi. 2012. "'Hahanhala Horata lo Lehotzi Rakevet kidei Lehasit neged Haovdim'" ["The management ordered train not to be taken out so as to incite the public against the workers"]. *TheMarker*, 15 February. Retrieved from https://www.themarker.com/dynamo/1.1642355.

Zarhia, Zvi, and Ora Coren. 2012. "Hok 'Harevahim Haklu'im' Ushar Sofit; Ha'avarat Kesef l'Hevra Bat Dina k'Meshichat Dividend" ["Trapped profits" law approved; transfer of money to subsidiary will be considered like drawing dividend]. *TheMarker*, 5 November. Retrieved from https://www.themarker.com/news/1.1857361.

Zohar, Hannah, and Shir Hever. 2010. *The Economy of the Occupation: A Socioeconomic Bulletin*. Tel Aviv: Kav Laoved and the Alternative Information Center.

Zonszein, Mairav. 2014. "African Asylum Seekers: We Will Continue to Strike until Demands are Met." *+972 Blog*, 7 January. Retrieved from https://972mag.com/african-asylum-seekers-we-will-continue-to-strike-until-demands-are-met/85188/.

Court documents

Collective Dispute 11241-08-13
Collective Dispute 13125-12-13
Collective Dispute 13381-07-12
Collective Dispute 15391-12-11
Collective Dispute 20420-05-11
Collective Dispute Appeal 25476-09-12
General Collective Dispute 722-09-11
General Collective Dispute 2376-10-11
High Court (HC) 7569/11
High Court (HC) 8382/11
High Court of Justice (HCJ) 5666/03
High Court of Justice (HCJ) 6076/12
Inter-Organizational Dispute 9685-07-12
Inter-Organizational Dispute 31575-02-13
Inter-Organizational Dispute 32690-10-10
Inter-Organizational Dispute 50718-07-10
Jerusalem Labor Court (JLC) 1307-09
Labor Dispute 664-07-12
Labor Dispute 30184-09-11
Labor Dispute Appeal 24/10
Request for Appeal 18551-12-12
Request for Appeal 50556-09-11
Tel Aviv Labor Court (TALC) 5630-12-10

Websites

+972 Magazine: http://972mag.com
Abraham Fund Initiatives: http://www.abrahamfund.org/
Ani Israeli: http://ani-israeli.org/site
Challenge/Etgar/al-Sabar: http://www.challenge-mag.com
Globes: http://www.globes.co.il
Haaretz: http://www.haaretz.co.il
Maan-Tech: http://maantech.org.il
NRG: http://www.nrg.co.il/
Sindyanna: http://www.sindyanna.com
TheMarker: http://www.themarker.com/
TheMarkerWeek: http://www.themarker.com/markerweek
WAC: http://www.wac-maan.org.il/he/home
Ynet: http://www.ynet.co.il

Index